THE FINANCIAL IMAGINARY

The Financial Imaginary

ECONOMIC MYSTIFICATION AND THE LIMITS OF REALIST FICTION

Alison Shonkwiler

University of Minnesota Press
Minneapolis
London

The University of Minnesota Press gratefully acknowledges the generous assistance provided for the publication of this book by Rhode Island College.

Portions of chapter 1 were published in an earlier version as "Towards a Late View of Capitalism: Dehistoricized Finance in *The Financier,*" *Studies in the Novel* 41, no. 1 (Spring 2009): 42–65; copyright 2009 The Johns Hopkins University Press and the University of North Texas; reprinted with permission of The Johns Hopkins University Press. Chapter 4 was originally published as "DeLillo's Financial Sublime," *Contemporary Literature* 52, no. 2 (2010): 246–82; reprinted courtesy of the University of Wisconsin Press.

Published by the University of Minnesota Press
111 Third Avenue South, Suite 290
Minneapolis, MN 55401-2520
http://www.upress.umn.edu

Printed in the United States of America on acid-free paper

The University of Minnesota is an equal-opportunity educator and employer.

23 22 21 20 19 18 17   10 9 8 7 6 5 4 3 2 1

Library of Congress Cataloging-in-Publication Data
Names: Shonkwiler, Alison, author.
Title: The financial imaginary : economic mystification and the limits of realist fiction /
    Alison Shonkwiler.
Description: Minneapolis : University of Minnesota Press, 2017. | Includes bibliographical references and index.
Identifiers: LCCN 2016022211| ISBN 978-1-5179-0151-6 (hc) | ISBN 978-1-5179-0152-3 (pb)
Subjects: LCSH: American fiction—20th century—History and criticism. | Money in literature. | Finance in literature. |
    Realism in literature. | Capitalism and literature—United States—History—20th century. | Economics and
    literature—United States—History—20th century.
Classification: LCC PS374.M54 S56 2017 | DDC 813.009/3553—dc23
LC record available at https://lccn.loc.gov/2016022211

CONTENTS

ACKNOWLEDGMENTS

This book was emotionally financed by A. K. Summers and Franklin Summers, who provided love, care, and free distracted singing. I am grateful for the ongoing intellectual support, friendship, mentoring, and expense sharing of Elizabeth Freeman. Peter Agree, Angela S. Allan, Kristie Allen, Maura Burnett, Hamilton Carroll, Hillary Chute, Samuel Cohen, Marianne DeKoven, Richard Dienst, James English, Molly Hite, Caren Irr, Zubeda Jalalzai, Lee Konstantinou, John McClure, Dan Moos, Jennifer Schnepf, Alexandra Socarides, Sunny Stalter, Karen Steigman, and Patricia Stulke read parts of the manuscript or provided encouragement at different stages in its conception. I value all of those conversations. Thanks to Danielle Kasprzak, Anne Carter, and the staff at the University of Minnesota Press for their patience and professionalism, and Sue Breckenridge for attentive editing. Finally, my thanks to the Penn Humanities Forum at the University of Pennsylvania for making it possible to substantially advance this project and to Rhode Island College for a series of course releases that enabled me to complete it.

Representing Financial Abstraction in Fiction

The argument of this book is that the growing abstraction of contemporary capitalism demands new imaginative conceptions of the real. The following chapters examine the ways that today's fiction is fully engaged in articulating economic abstraction as a problem of narrative realism. The more that a post-1970s finance-driven and neoliberally inflected capitalism has appeared to outpace familiar terms and strategies of representation, the more that questions about the control, mystification, and virtualization of capitalism have gained a new sense of political urgency. In his seminal 1996 essay "Culture and Finance Capital," Fredric Jameson argued for the need to formulate a new theoretical account of abstraction, one suited not only to the advancements of late capitalism (which he summarized as the "cybernetic revolution," the autonomization of capital, and the "liberation" of financial speculation) but also to its cultural and aesthetic features.[1] Literary writers of the 1990s and after can be read as translating this theoretical challenge into fictional-narrative terms. Their works, as much as the writings of theorists, critics, and journalists, locate anxieties over the meaning of "lateness" and the formal problems that are manifested in the contemporary novel's search for strategies to represent what Jameson summed up as "the closing of [capitalism's] productive moment."[2]

The "financial imaginary" is what I call the formal project, in this narrative context, of imaginatively grasping the historical and cultural processes by which the seeming realities of the economy are reconceived as phenomena of virtuality and representation. My purpose is not to question whether the processes of abstractification associated with financialization are "really" happening or not—the consensus that they exist is widespread, even if debates continue about the best paradigm for understanding them.

Nor is it to fall back on the comforting misconception that money is more "real" than other forms of value—though it may be one of the less risky forms of abstraction. Nor is it to condemn abstraction as such, despite the well-documented dangers in recent years of outlandishly creative and poorly understood financial instruments. Journalists writing about the 2008 financial crisis (and the tech and real-estate bubbles that preceded it) have criticized the evolution of complex financial devices such as risk tranches, credit-default swaps, mortgage-backed securities, and collateralized debt obligations.[3] Leftist critics, among others, have blamed a highly virtualized, tech-driven, globally mobile financial system for producing a charade of "fantasy valuations" and a tendency toward instability and crisis.[4] Abstraction, while not synonymous with finance or financialization, is nonetheless key to explaining how the rise of an abstract and speculative finance has generated "trillions of dollars of empirical evidence that do not fit any established analytical paradigms."[5]

Most importantly for this project, abstraction is the term that negotiates between economic and cultural forms. In using finance as an index to chart and analyze abstraction, I do not presume that finance is the only way to think about abstraction, but that finance effectively metonymizes the exceptionally fluid processes of rationalization and mystification, designed to the ends of value capture, that can be generalized beyond stock exchanges, hedge funds, and the circuits of global investment. I will discuss the problem of abstraction in more detail below. For the moment, what is meant by *finance*? And is the specter of widespread financialization simply synonymous with a leftist critique of the economy? In this book I associate finance with the movement of value, broadly conceived, from labor to money. Finance, at its most basic level, is the domain in which value is less likely to be *produced* than captured and/or extracted, typically by managing a degree of risk. Often it refers to specific instruments such as derivatives and securities. Often it is speculative and/or debt driven. But elsewhere it can simply be summed up by the privileging of the imperative to generate profit regardless of whether profit is accompanied by underlying or "real" growth.[6] In essence, under the rule of finance, risk replaces money as the most abstract form of value and works to produce value through a "compounding" of abstractions. An active financial market is one that tends to "translate risk from that against which one insures to that in which one invests."[7] One critic has suggested that a finance-oriented analysis of any economic situation can be as simple as asking "where are profits generated?" rather than "what is produced?"[8]

One might argue that the rise of speculative finance is not a new phenomenon, as histories of eighteenth-century credit systems and Dutch tulip bubbles attest.[9] But it is also generally conceded that the contemporary financial system is unique in its abilities to rival and exceed the power of the state, to jeopardize whole regions and economies, and to encompass ever more far-reaching asymmetries of time and space. Arjun Appadurai, who in 1990 included "financescapes" as one of his famous "disjunctures" of modernity, updated the description in 2006 as the "wanton urge of global capital to roam without license or limit." In 2016 he updated it again to describe a monetized present of "deep financialization."[10] David Harvey links finance to contemporary neoliberalism, stating that "neoliberalization has meant, in short, the financialization of everything."[11] Although the flourishing of speculative capital is hardly unique to the late twentieth century, what has been theorized, particularly since the publication of Harvey's *The Condition of Postmodernity* in 1991, is a distinctly new historical regime of accumulation based not on production but instead on the capturing or diverting of value from one part of the system to another.[12] Edward LiPuma and Benjamin Lee argue that the "decoupling" of finance capital from production is occurring in ways that are "more encompassing, more powerful, and also perhaps more permanent than anything that has gone before."[13] They describe the rise of contemporary circulation-based global capitalism as "the simultaneous advent and intervention of something entirely new." "The striving toward totality that has always characterized capitalism," they argue, today "has gone global in a way that is not imaginable from the perspectives of the imaginaries of the citizen-state and the national public sphere."[14] The financial imaginary has replaced a nation-based imaginary with something both more encompassing and less socially embedded.

Contemporary fiction writers do not stand apart from journalists, academics, and other writers in their critical efforts to assess the "reality" of a postindustrial, multinational capitalism dominated by information and services. In the following chapters I read contemporary writers such as Richard Powers, Don DeLillo, Jane Smiley, Teddy Wayne, and Mohsin Hamid as navigating the idea that abstraction, for better or worse, presently dominates not only the economic but also the historical, cultural, and aesthetic domains. The financial imaginary, as conceived here, is produced by the social uncertainties and precarities that result from the expansion of financialization over multiple domains of life. It invites critical attention to the problem of recognizing a system that is understood to be less and less tethered to the material, less directly connected to specific modes of production, and therefore less tangible, visible, or controllable.

Perhaps predictably, contemporary fiction often reveals the insufficiencies of both postmodern and realist strategies to penetrate late capitalism's abstractions or to forge an adequate representation of a postmodern and global context. Contemporary realist, neorealist, and hybrid realist-postmodern forms highlight the ways that twenty-first-century capitalism does not resemble the world of the industrial factory and cannot share in the assumptions of nineteenth-century social and material relations, even if the abstractions of financialization today appear to call as directly and urgently for demystification as the abstractions of the commodity did for the Victorians. In today's fictions, individuals are likely to confront systems and structures not only beyond their own capacity to evaluate but at times apparently beyond the novel's capacity as well. As I will discuss in the pages that follow, this imaginary exposes various formal consequences—in the representation of character, in description and scale, in temporality and narratorial authority, and in the use of language itself as a vehicle for new divisions of labor and calculations of value. These consequences reveal how an emerging imaginary of abstraction strains the dimensions and assumptions of our narrative models.

Joshua Clover argues that abstract capitalism is *the* problem for narrative in the twenty-first century.[15] While he questions the assertion, made most notably by Jameson, that capitalism is necessarily a problem *of* narrative (and while he indeed raises the possibility that capitalism's processes of structuration have subsumed narrative altogether), he argues that we need literary forms that can register narrative's ongoing displacement. Whereas Clover turns to poetry in consequence, I argue that the novel remains a particularly effective site to examine the breakdown of certainties that an older realism once took for granted. Remaining in the domain of narrative allows us to interrogate the novel's limits, both historically and formally, and to recognize the persistence of a realist narrative impulse toward *demystification* even when such an impulse seems to have little purchase on reality. Other scholars have argued for the centrality of narrative in understanding the temporal logic of finance capitalism, specifically its colonization of the future by way of the present. Mathias Nilges has called the "turn toward the pure flow of capital . . . an epistemological and narratological crisis."[16] The M–C–M^1 formula of accumulation articulated by Marx, which described the circulation of the money form through the mediation of the commodity, he writes, "no longer appears to describe the dominant logic of the economic structure, nor is it able to provide a logical basis for narrating reality." The desire to narrate "reality" already suggests a reason contemporary fiction has turned to various realisms, as if postmodernism, in its discursive and metafictional tendencies, is inadequate to reference a financial reality that seems perfectly capable of *realizing* itself on postmodern terms. (Clover elsewhere writes that postmodernism is not a tool to critique the representational fictions of finance but instead is the very "thought form" of financialization.)[17] In calling attention to the novel's realisms, however, my point is not that realism is the mode to "solve" this crisis of representation, let alone that it can secure a foundational epistemology of the real, but that the very familiarity of its formal categories help to reveal the changed contours of the capitalism with which the novel has developed in conjunction. Ultimately it is not that finance capital exposes the novel as outdated but that the novel's efforts to keep pace reveal their deeper, shared narrative logics. Even the contemporary novel's nostalgia can be productive, therefore, in thinking through literature's resources and tools of mediation for a financialized present.

I contend that one of the factors in the twentieth-century displacement of realism, in particular, is the disarticulation of class. This disarticulation is of course not limited to the novel but reflects the political weakness of anticapitalist critique more generally. In academic discourse, class analysis has been subsumed into cultural analysis. In mainstream discourse, the language of austerity tends not to generate critiques of neoliberal economics, despite increased popular awareness of the disparities between worker and CEO pay, or the inflation in college tuition, or the ways in which globalization displaces the environmental costs of consumption. The financial crashes of 2000 and 2008, while generating public outrage, certainly did not lead to discussion about potential alternatives to capitalism, even as the controversy over bank bailouts confirmed widespread suspicion on left and right alike about whose interests the financial system is designed to serve. The slogan of the 99 percent promoted by anti–Wall Street protesters in the early 2010s might seem a notable exception to this rule about popular class discourse. But even here, such class identification is made possible through an *expansion* of the category of class, such that it encompasses nearly everybody in an undifferentiated "middle" and narrows the object of critique—the elite 1 percent—to an outlying extreme harder to identify with. And while the rhetoric of the 99 percent is far more inclusive than, say, the categories of capitalist and worker classes, it also underscores the difficulty of defining "capitalist class" or "working class" in an age when retirement portfolios, mortgage and consumer debt, and other forms of financial investment give the vast majority of Americans as much reason to see themselves as the former rather than the latter.

Not coincidentally, in the past two decades references to a new Gilded Age have abounded in popular economic and cultural writings.[18] Such allusions to nineteenth-century class structures and inequality, I contend, should be seen as concerted efforts to raise a counterdiscourse against the abstractions of lateness. The 1990s form of this abstraction was the New Economy fantasy of limitless wealth and technological advancement that would break all previously known business rules. In his introduction to *The New Gilded Age*, a collection of *New Yorker* essays on the boom years of the 1990s, David Remnick reports that it appears that "a technological revolution has not merely accelerated growth but created an entirely new economy, a new world, one with its own rules and without economic or imaginative limits."[19] Yet this "utterly blithe and lucky time," Remnick argued, is also full of contradictions, with only a small percentage of the American population able to partake of the feast. The growing wealth disparities of the late 1990s, which saw the rise of overnight tech fortunes, a new culture of luxury consumption, and even the reemergence of a professional servant class to the super elite, might seem to make class analysis more relevant than ever.[20] Yet even as historical references to nineteenth-century plutocracy invoke a contrast of haves and have-nots, they express, more than not, the contemporary limitations of a class-based critique. Bruce Robbins notes that the media occasionally "rediscovers" class, as in the *New York Times* "Class Matters" series that appeared in eleven parts in 2005.[21] But the first-person model of journalism followed by many of the articles in the series, and in the subsequently published book of the same title, demonstrates precisely how anecdotes of individual experience tend to substitute for structural (and political) analyses of class. Even when basic notions of private property, labor exploitation, or the distribution of the social surplus seem to demand revisiting, then, mainstream critiques of capitalism with few exceptions tend not to get beyond the kind of neo-Keynesian critique that LiPuma and Lee observed in 2004 to be the limit of "acceptable" discourse about capitalism.

Abstraction offers a powerful way to understand this class displacement. Indeed, it is by *concealing* the social origins of wealth that abstraction arguably performs its most significant cultural-imaginative work.[22] By extracting capitalism from its embedding in social relations, abstraction makes it difficult to identify how and where value is created, how and where we as individuals are situated in a field of economic relations, where the agency of the system is located, and what change could possibly be effected. The elimination of visible production in the age of financialization enables the elimination of visible *relations* of production as well. For instance, search engines and social-networking sites capture content, relying on the free labor provided by users and commodifying the affects, desires, sociabilities, and browsing histories of these unpaid laborers to sell back to market researchers and advertisers. The result is a "Google model" of production in which there is no "product" other than the production of multiple and evanescent sets of relations.[23] Abstraction from social relations thus blurs definitions between producer and consumer, provider and user, information and content.

Moreover, the virtualization of capitalism makes it difficult to identify an object against which to protest. LiPuma and Lee ask, "How does one know about, or demonstrate against, an unlisted, virtual, offshore corporation that operates in an unregulated electronic space using a secret proprietary trading strategy to buy and sell arcane financial instruments?"[24] The sense that there is no there there beyond the shadowy interest of shareholders—among whose ranks we may in fact count ourselves—forestalls any effective figuration of agency, let alone of the structure of capitalist social relations more generally. This virtualization makes a material analysis of work, possession, and value more difficult to apply. It contributes to the overwriting of class by culture and by subject position.

The novel, I argue, is one of the primary sites for examination of the cultural and subjective relations arising from finance's "drive to structuration." Cultural critics of the "new" capitalism have discussed the ways that subjects are asked to negotiate a world structured by competition and exchange value. Sociologist Richard Sennett writes on the kinds of personal and character adaptations demanded by the late twentieth-century need to tolerate increased risk and creative disruption. The workplace now devalues "old" employee traits like loyalty and raises up "new" values such as innovation and flexibility.[25] Randy Martin describes a new domain of self-management "where risk management and credit are part of labor's burden in daily life." These subjective adaptations might be understood as the development of a new shareholder model of selfhood: "The investor becomes a model for the ideal kind of beings, who manage their affairs and take care of their own future."[26] But if representations of class have been replaced by representations of entrepreneurial selfhood in cultural discourses of all kinds, it does not mean categories of class have become irrelevant to the novel. Instead, it is possible to read these very displacements of the economic "real" as being reshaped and articulated as novelistic problems—even if sometimes received as novelistic failures. Jameson describes the function of nineteenth-century literary realism as the "demystification and cancellation of illusions." With the advent of twentieth-century modernism, he argues, this function gave way to a new mode of "defamiliarization and renewal of perception."[27] The contemporary novels I examine in this book arguably revive the premodernist interest in demystification. While they raise questions about realism's changed capacity for social and economic critique, they nonetheless demonstrate the contemporary persistence of the realist impulse to unmask the unreal.

LiPuma and Lee characterize the economic present as full of nostalgia for outdated "certainties" such as the "foundational logic that once seemed to bind work to wealth, virtue to value, and production to place."[28] It is perhaps no surprise that contemporary fiction turns for its representational needs to the supposedly "grounding" strategies of realism. The realist novel's accumulation of detail, its commitment to social description, and its narrative authority would seem a logical form to examine capitalist unreality. In positive and negative ways, realism, a mode that historically has also had a privileged relationship to capitalism, offers the promise (however illusory) of a materialist critique. The character-in-the-world realism represented in the nineteenth-century European novel would seem an obvious model for interrogating the social categories of class, agency, and possession that structure the bourgeois world. Classic realism's investment in psychological interiority together with its exterior narrative control is designed to address mismatches between perception and reality. The recourse to realism today to examine limitations of understanding in a world more complex than it appears may or may not be nostalgic, but it nonetheless invites a more reflective assessment of its present historical functioning.

Contemporary writers would not necessarily describe their fictions as "returning" to nineteenth-century realism, nor do I suggest they do so in any naïve sense. Yet even as they represent the subject's participation in a commodified postmodern culture, the novels under consideration here resist the collapse of the real into consumer signifiers.[29] They ask formal questions about how to understand economic relations when these do not appear clearly guided by real money and real work. They examine the influence of abstraction on categories of virtue, agency, and subjectivity. They highlight the ways that late capitalism asks us to negotiate new market subjectivities while suspending familiar understandings of capital, property, and labor. They in many ways find traditional narrative realism inadequate to examine the present, as the "economic virtue" of nineteenth-century fiction ceases to map the economic landscape. Most significantly, they investigate the ways subjects are asked to negotiate capitalism as agents but no longer as producers.

In consequence, we see realist narrative strategies used in ambivalent and selective ways. Narrative omniscience competes with narrative constraint. Realist totalities appear necessary yet unreliable. Narratives oscillate around structural tensions between synchronic and diachronic, global and local, subject and object. Description reveals possibilities for dereification, revitalization, and new ways of resisting the stasis of the status quo. While character offers a repository of the remaining claims of the subjective, guaranteeing a history of memory, sensation, and affect, the novel's "investment" in character also appears as a formal habit that may block desirable avenues of political critique and even let structural analyses off the hook. First-person, second-person, and third-person points of view redivide and redistribute their formal responsibilities, replicating the global asymmetries of capitalist self-reproduction. Genre forms such as the epic, the Bildungsroman, or the self-help manual interact with extranarrative archives of data and information. Time is a site of virtual manipulation but also of real history in which the value of change and accumulated difference can be measured temporally. Even if there is no return to an empirical, foundational, or unmediated real behind postmodern representation, there are nonetheless *processes* of realization—for which financialization is the paradigm—that create, circulate, and redistribute values in ways that have fully concrete, material consequences.

Moreover, even as contemporary fiction reveals the ways that traditional realist categories of class, agency, and economic virtue offer no demystification of capitalist relations, they lead to the obvious question of whether such categories ever did or could. If the distinction between real and unreal capitalism seems unstable today, it already felt crisis-prone in the late nineteenth and early twentieth centuries, with the perception of what historian Steve Fraser calls the rise of a "second, phantom economy."[30] Today's novelists are not the first to question the explanatory power of class in a strange New Economy or to probe the capacities of fiction to represent the cultural and subjective effects of capitalist unreality. A key first step of my argument, then, is to examine the formal problems confronted in an earlier period of American economic realism. Writers such as William Dean Howells, Henry James, Theodore Dreiser, and Frank Norris grappled with a similarly disorienting sense of economic change and crisis as they conceived of turn-of-the-century capitalism as widening beyond the scope of individual agency and responsibility. Their fictions chart the ways in which an emerging imaginary of abstraction already strains the dimensions and possibilities of the social novel. Though they do not engage the same discourses of globalization and neoliberalism, their efforts to define the real against the ephemerality of capitalism, to articulate new forms of "economic selfhood" to inhabit, and to find a basis for value in something other than recognized forms of hard work, reveal an original mismatch between the experience of abstraction and the vocabularies of realism.

The representation of the rentier in Henry James's "The Jolly Corner," for instance, shows how unearned income complicates the literary terms of economic Bildung. It is a conveniently literal example since the main character lives on the rents of a New York City apartment building. As I discuss in the first chapter, the contradiction in this text between aristocratic values and modern American commercial interests can only be resolved ironically through a kind of playacting at labor. The "virtue" of ownership is rewritten as a convenient opportunity for aesthetic self-realization. Already, then, James's 1908 text touches on the ways that economic activity that cannot be tied to "honest" labor is ultimately displaced into a kind of negative agency. Here and in other texts of the period we see labor threatened with the dominations of abstract labor time, by financial temporality, and by an emergent aestheticization of the M–M¹ moment—Marx's representation of pure money accumulation—from which the material threatens to drop out of sight.

In the contemporary novel too, rentierism explains the ways that hard work appears as a residual value in an economy propelled more by assets than labor. In some cases rent-seeking activity is obvious, as in the seizure of private ownership rights over a communal resource (water) in *How to Get Filthy Rich in Rising Asia*, or the intellectual-property dispute in *Kapitoil* between employer and employee over a financial program the employee has created. But rent seeking can be more broadly conceived than as about controlling material or intellectual property rights, although those are the original basis of the concept.[31] It can be understood as a default *orientation* toward financialization through the maximization of ownership value. Rent seeking, in the "plainest and broadest sense," according to economist Joseph Stiglitz, is all the activities that involve "getting income not as a reward to creating wealth but by grabbing a larger share of the wealth that would otherwise have been produced without their effort."[32] Regressive taxation could also be included since it produces inequality, increases poverty, and contributes to the hollowing out of the middle class. Indeed, for some leftist economists and critics, rent is in effect a present-day synonym for "profit," and rent seeking is necessary to explain the whole of capital's global expansion, including the turn from spatial avenues of growth to temporal ones.[33] If globalization is the externalization, rentierism is the internalization and "deepening" of value capture. Postwar history has thereby led exactly in the opposite direction from Keynes's prediction when in 1936 he called for the "euthanasia of the rentier."[34] The rentier, like the speculator, was once lambasted as a parasite upon the "real" economy. But under financialization, rent profit becomes the ideal paradigm of production rather than a contradiction of it. Accumulation no longer depends on production; it is transformed *into* a mode of production.

Though today's rentierism may no longer connect to a feudal system of accumulation or to aristocratic privilege, the devaluation of work relative to ownership has broad cultural implications. Capital's tendency toward rentierism is one of the ways that wealth takes on the "disproportionate importance" cited by Thomas Piketty in his monumental analysis of the return of nineteenth-century levels of wealth inequality.[35] The advantages conferred on existing capital over labor income are certainly central to any structural analysis of economic inequality. The ways finance works to "preserve, augment, and disguise inherited wealth," in Bruce Robbins's words, contribute to the persistent racial disparities in the United States measurable by the difference between income and inheritance.[36] But aside from deepening existing economic inequalities, capital's tendency to organize itself around rent profit also performs the cultural "sorting" function Randy Martin describes when he argues that today "finance divides the world between those able to avail themselves of wealth opportunities through risk taking and those who are considered "at risk."[37] Martin's influential analysis of the "financialization of everyday life" demonstrates the specific impact of risk and volatility on the middle-class subject: "The perverse effect of financialization in daily life is to exchange security for volatility, to recast the recently revered ideals of middle-class stability in terms of risk."[38] Middle-class stability tends to depend on consumer finance: mortgages, retirement investments, health and life insurance, student and credit card debt. Neoliberal privatization, state withdrawal, and market volatility threaten these identity markers, bringing middle-class precarity and middle-class entitlement into uncomfortable proximity. In other words, financialization becomes most culturally visible when it is the middle class that is exposed to it. Or to think about it differently, "middle" may be a decreasingly operative class distinction today than the distinction between those who work for money and those whose money works for them.

That the main characters of Smiley's *Good Faith* and Powers's *Gain* are both real-estate agents underscores the ways that that "production" has been displaced into an asset-based economy. The rising value of ownership and consequent devaluation of work corresponds to the shift in the United States and the U.K. since the 1970s toward a middle-class security based on financial assets. Economist Jan Toporowski argues that rising property values and a rising stock market are the basis of a middle-class "welfare state."[39] Inflated real-estate and financial asset markets have helped the middle class to acquiesce to wage stagnation and to accommodate itself to the more general shift from an income-based to a property-based model of wealth. Regressive property taxes amplify the advantages of ownership and penalize nonownership, which is often the only option for the poor. (I discuss the impact of 1980s tax resistance on national politics in chapter 2.)

"In an era of finance," Toporowski writes, "the mass of the middle class is sedated and deprived of the need to think by escalating property values." The result is a middle class increasingly divided between the "balance-sheet rich" and the "balance-sheet poor."[40] In a balance-sheet economy, rent seeking is one of the forms of financial abstraction that asks subjects to navigate capitalism as agents but not as producers. It is but a short step to the argument that the "consumer-defined middle class" has been "divided into the self-managed and the unmanageable."[41]

Toporowski argues that the "final decades of the twentieth century have seen the emergence of an era of finance that is the greatest since the 1890s and 1900s and, in terms of the values turned over in securities markets, the greatest era of finance in history."[42] The growth of global financial markets at the twentieth century's end, the return to Gilded Age–levels of inequality, and the emergence of new technologies have made the logic of late capitalism clearer. They are evident in the ascent of shareholder value, the return of rentierism, the "pursuit of a market in almost everything,"[43] the extension of the logic of risk into private and subjective realms, the market's underwriting of violence, imperialism, and war, and the circulation of consumer affects and desires as new forms of "production." The structural pressures of abstraction, we might conclude, that were emergent in the nineteenth century are now fully articulated in the twenty-first. Taking these two specific moments together—the end of the nineteenth century and the end of the twentieth century and beyond—is not meant to elide differences between these historical moments but to articulate a problem of representation shared between them.

Alex Woloch, in his study of the nineteenth-century English and French novel, identifies the constitutive tension of the realist-fictional genre to be its division of attention between the demands of the historical/particular as against those of the structural/typological. Such tensions can be located in all of the contemporary texts I examine. In Jane Smiley's *Good Faith*, for instance, a habit of character reading operates in conflict with a structural narrative of Reaganomics. In Richard Powers's *Gain,* the multinational corporation embodies the aspiration to an "epic" unity that will resolve the split between global capital and individual experience. In Don DeLillo's *Cosmopolis*, the reduction of all material relations to exchangeable units of value manifests itself in a formal pressure toward third-person narration. Hamid's *How to Get Filthy Rich* and Wayne's *Kapitoil* rewrite the Bildungsroman to accommodate asymmetrical global perspectives. The entrepreneur, the financier, and the corporation all engage in turn with abstract structures. The resulting formal tensions concern the extent to which the structural is already preemptively controlled by capital or whether the logic of abstract value and equivalence can be coopted for less violent and antisocial ends. Ultimately, I hardly suggest that problems of agency and the displacements of labor have been resolved or are resolvable. But as contemporary writers revisit the impossibility of "securing" an economic reality, their fiction makes more fully visible how this formal challenge has been historically recycled. I do not propose that contemporary writers offer better aesthetic resolutions. Instead they help to elaborate the problem, demonstrating to what extent, deep in the "autumn" stage of the American century, we continue to read through the familiar social and formal lenses of the realist novel.

Abstraction and Representation

Abstract and *abstraction* are among the most common terms in both theoretical and mainstream discussions of capitalism. Jameson situates *abstraction* as the key to developing a cultural account of finance, arguing that, "as [Giovanni] Arrighi teaches us, nothing is quite so abstract as the finance capital which underpins and sustains postmodernity as such."[44] Arrighi's account of capitalism as a world-historical system has been enormously influential for arguments that the period since the 1970s has seen not simply a rise in speculative activity per se but a shift of *all* capital toward more speculative and liquid forms. Capitalism's maturation into financial capitalism represents its "autumn" stage (Arrighi borrows the terminology of historian Fernand Braudel), or "highest" or "end" stage of development. In this mature or even "terminal" stage, capital is freed to operate abstractly in the sense of without reference to its origins in production. Jameson was among the first of the cultural theorists to draw on Arrighi's powerful historical and structural model of capitalism to begin to develop a cultural account of abstraction. As Jameson writes: "So it is that in any specific region of production, as Arrighi shows us, there comes a moment in which the logic of capitalism—faced with the saturation of local and even foreign markets—determines an abandonment of that kind of specific production, along with its factories and trained workforce, and, leaving them behind in ruins, takes its flight to other more profitable ventures."[45] The "flight" to speculative and transitory forms thus narrates capital's global expansion both as a historical moment and as a structurally immanent movement. It is a structural movement that repeats itself in different historical moments with, of course, different historical consequences and symptoms. The result of this double-sided quality is that we see accounts of neoliberal globalization describe capital's abstraction as both determined and determinative, as both cause and effect. For theorists seeking to develop *cultural* accounts of financialization, then, abstraction provides a conceptually powerful tool to register the circulations between economic and cultural forms. Coronil, for instance, argues that wealth is being "transformed through a process of growing homogenization and abstraction" and capitalism is defined by the "ever more abstract commodification of its elements across time and space."[46]

Abstraction is used differently in mainstream discourses of finance, where it has been accused of having a straightforward function of ideological mystification. Sophisticated mathematical and technical-economic models all too neatly idealize the economy and contribute to the illusion of what Doug Henwood disparages as the "theoretical utopia of perfect markets." Henwood quotes a former president of the American Economic Association as saying, in a presidential address, that "the field has been 'helped by greater abstraction.'" The "science" of economics is thus served by the deliberate obfuscation of the real. Criticizing Wall Street for its sleight-of-hand practices, Henwood points out that there is always a strong incentive to invent new financial products, since profits are higher on these products until competitors figure them out and imitate them. In the case of derivatives, for example, abstraction appears primarily to conceal the fact that such speculative instruments have no socially redeeming purpose whatsoever. Derivatives simply shift risk around to different people, Henwood argues, and in consequence their existence may leave society worse off than it would otherwise be ("The irony of these individualized approaches to risk management is that they seem to increase systemic risk even as they lower individual risk, at least for the smarter or luckier or more practiced users").[47]

Relatedly, Leigh Claire La Berge argues that words such as *complex*, *fictitious*, and *abstract*, when they appear in contemporary journalism, tend to construct finance as too difficult for the layperson to understand. The language of abstraction, she argues, works to "call forth an immediately knowable and representable world of institutional financial transactions and then to suspend knowledge and description of that world by claiming its mechanisms are beyond our collective cognitive, linguistic, and epistemological reach." The abstract is thus employed specifically because it "organizes and structures" even while it "eludes definition and representation." With scholars, too, often vague about what *abstraction* designates, La Berge argues for developing more critical specificity in using the term:

> It could be that one ideological requirement of finance is that its
> subjects understand it as an abstraction. Or it could be that *abstraction*

is itself a metonym for something undefined in this emerging field of critical studies of finance. Or it could be that finance is abstract, in which case the onus falls on us scholars to attend to its specifications. Or it could be that finance constitutes yet another kind of abstraction, what Marx called a "rational abstraction," or simply a conceptual shortcut. Any of these may be true with proper citation and consideration.[48]

While Marxism has studied the abstractions of *capital*, La Berge argues, it has not considered the specific abstractions of *finance* capital. Studies of finance must take up the structuring relations between abstract and concrete that are already understood to be at the heart of the money and commodity forms.

In other words, the seemingly greater intangibility of finance only aids and abets the familiar misrepresentation of the (very real) tension Marx locates between labor and abstract labor in the first instance. Abstraction, in short, expresses the problem of its own relationship to value. The abstract/concrete relationship poses the same conceptual difficulty that Marx's M–M^1 formula of pure money accumulation poses, which is to elide the question of where profits come from. Value has to come from somewhere. If not labor, then from somewhere else—risk, temporality, circulation, and so forth. The "violence" of abstraction, according to one critic, is produced by its separation from the concrete. Its "universal pretensions"[49] are enabled whenever the concrete drops out of sight. Abstractification segregated from concretization mystifies whether new value is being generated or existing value redistributed. Abstraction isolated helps to keep unexamined the possibility that financial instruments such as derivatives do not enlarge the pie of value but merely compete for a bigger slice of the existing pie. Richard Godden, drawing from Moishe Postone's work on the "serial abstractions through which labor power passes en route to the marketplace," argues that capitalist value must be understood as having "a dual and contradictory character . . . at once labor *and* value, concrete *and* abstract."[50] Godden's insistence that the form of value under finance "remains structurally duplicitous" thus offers an important corrective and counterbalance to Jameson's account of financial capital as appearing on its surface to be a "radically new form of abstraction," without contradicting Jameson's key point about the importance of analyzing the cultural effects produced by abstraction's fetishized appearances.[51]

Despite these appearances, then, finance must be understood a *process* of abstractification and concretization. Finance continuously seeks the path of the shortest, fastest, and highest return. It works by running the possibilities, comparing hypotheticals and actuals, and trading on the difference, thereby *realizing* that which had been hypothetical or unreal. "Financialization actually produces a new concreteness," critics have claimed.[52] Or as Godden argues, financialization "stands as the structural core of the real."[53] It is always possible that the direction will be reversed too; in a financial crisis, for example, the concrete can quite suddenly be made abstract—even unreal.[54] But this is not an unreality that denies the material. It is a process of realization that can be highly unstable and highly profitable at the same time.

Thus it is important to forestall the conclusion that *more abstract* means *less real*. Henwood's statement that "less than 1 percent of annual trading end up being consummated in possession-taking" seems to invoke a clear distinction between the fictitious and the real. It suggests that underlying the whole superstructure of paper trading is a "real" commodity (the 1 percent) that can be possessed. But is possession of a paper contract less real than possession of a commodity? Is money not also paper? Money may be more abstract than a bushel of wheat or a barrel of oil, but for most buyers and sellers it would be no less real. Or perhaps "possession taking" should be understood to refer to a moment of productive potential (let us call this possession with intent) rather than a continuation of exchange. But the moment of consumption, such as it is, can only be determined in hindsight. We can't know in advance when future trading has been foreclosed. The bushel of wheat and the barrel of oil can always end up back on the market. The assertion of the "real" can always be deferred. Even if the bushel and barrel re-enter the market in different forms—such as bread or electricity—these too are commodities defined by exchange value. The idea of the real, we might say, requires attachment to the idea that the moment of use value rules definitively over the flux of exchange value.

Even if one accepts that abstraction is inherent in all value forms, and that the difference in level of abstraction between commodity, money, or derivative is simply a matter of degree (i.e., that the second-order abstractions of finance are built upon the first-order abstractions of money), the result is potentially to equate everything with the fictitious. For some leftist critics the self-evident problem with this argument is that it disables any serious political critique of the economy. If there is really no difference between speculative capitalism and any other kind—an argument that can certainly (if inconveniently for some) be made based on Marx's own account of fictitious capital—then this neutralizes the possibility of political resistance to the rise of speculative capital, to global divisions of production, and to the social violence that financialization perpetrates.

Nonetheless, abstraction, like virtuality, is not unreal. When LiPuma and Lee describe a capitalism made up of "transnational nuclei of concentrated financial political power crystallized in spaces so virtual and electronic that their only addresses are encrypted web pages,"[55] "virtual" doesn't mean illusory or powerless. Quite the reverse, it is the reality of abstraction that allows finance capitalism to achieve its extensive reach and concrete effects. Global structures of inequality, the politics of immigration, the outsourcing of work, the dismantling of social protections, the "realism" of austerity politics, and all kinds of social, political, and environmental violence are very real. Financialization specializes in putting distance between these concrete effects and the structural violence of an abstract value that is measured by nothing but the stock market.

The financial imaginary, in my use of the term, is where the relations between abstract and concrete tend to be elided. It is therefore also where we should look to find an active contest of representation. For instance, it is the site of capitalism's effort to control its own representation coming and going. Capital becomes abstract and concrete, real and fictitious. It is allowed to assume agency while deflecting responsibility. LiPuma and Lee observe, for instance, that "the market" can "*act, indicate, warn, hesitate, climb,* and *fall* but is usually not able to take second-order verbs such as *reflect, assume guilt,* or *take responsibility* in the ways that a national people might."[56] In effect, capital gets to negotiate favorable terms for its own autonomization: "Abstraction produces the appearance of capital's becoming 'subject': If productive labor once constituted the 'reality' of the economy, in the age of finance and speculative capital it seems that instead of the economy driving the markets, the markets are driving the economy."[57] Within the financial imaginary, then, capital gets to have it both ways. It forms part of the social contract and does not form part of it (as exemplified in recent bank bailouts that, as critics complained, privatized financial profits and socialized losses). It chooses when to cash in and become concrete. It is the site of endless deferral of the "real" in favor of a *process* of realization that can always select the most advantageous moments to pause and demand account.

We can regard the contemporary novel as in *argument* with finance over the deployment of representational forms. The financial imaginary is not without its own forms (temporal, narrative, metonymic). But its "logic" is a narrow one, ultimately directed toward one end, that of producing particular terms of value. The novel recapitulates the representational logic of this imaginary but adds friction, slows it down, expands it, subjectivizes it, adds data and history. The novel aims to resituate finance's logic within its own formal terms. But because it shares many of the same narrative and temporal strategies, its engagement with the terms of "realism" may ultimately offer capitalism another kind of alibi. My interest in the following pages is not to examine the narrative and temporal strategies of finance itself but instead the novel's effort to engage, critique, and disrupt them, and to develop a standpoint from which to do so. Such a standpoint may be impossible, in fact, if we see fiction as a full participant in the "financial print culture" that Leigh Clare La Berge describes, a multimodal circulation of genres that mutually narrativize and periodize finance's formal operation.[58] But that theoretical impossibility has not stopped writers and critics from attempts to discover a wedge for critique, even through narrative forms that share the same representational and temporal logics of finance. This book focuses on these attempts, arguing that even if the contemporary novel is as complicit in affirming the validity of the capitalist status quo as the bourgeois realist novel ever was, it is nonetheless a *site* at which social and aesthetic imaginaries continue to be constructed—and thus, in theory, can be unconstructed.

Even though I use *finance* and *financialization* in relatively broad terms in the following chapters, therefore—at times as a direct object of analysis and at others as a figure for a more general process of abstraction and/or virtualization—it is a more specific term for my study of the novel than *late capitalism*, or *neoliberalism*, since it invites a way to think about *both* periodization and formalization at once. Let me address each of these in turn. I have mentioned Arrighi's model of history as offering a compelling way to think about periodization. To reiterate, Arrighi conceives the 1970s and capital's response in the Reagan era as moments within a longer historical process that also included the late nineteenth century (specifically the depression of 1873–96) and the periods of world war (1914–45). Arrighi thus conceives of all three moments as belonging to the single "cycle" of accumulation of the long twentieth century. In short, Arrighi uses M–C–M[1] as a template for an entire historical process, not just as a formula of accumulation in the sense Marx used it.[59] But Arrighi's model of financial expansion is not the only one to produce this periodization. Other recent economic accounts also link the structural transformations of the last forty years to the previous turn-of-century. Thomas Piketty's historical characterization of 1870–1914 as the "'first globalization' of finance and trade" and the period since the 1970s as the "second globalization" has much in common with Arrighi's long twentieth century.[60] What Piketty refers to as capital's fall after 1914 corresponds to Arrighi's phase of material expansion in the M–C–M[1] historical movement. The difference is that one sees capital as politically restrained by the exigencies of war and depression and the other sees capital as temporarily directed through a "C"-based or material-based outlet. Either way, politics represents a check on capitalism's tendency, when unrestrained, to develop toward the abstractions that lead to wealth concentration and inequality.

Despite Piketty's insistence that he is not a Marxist—and his superficial critique of Marx—his conclusion that the basis for contemporary wealth inequality is *political* puts him squarely in line with the Marxist argument that neoliberalism functions as a project for the restoration of class power. Piketty's comparison of late nineteenth- and twenty-first-century wealth inequality is based on capital, not finance specifically. In other words, he is more interested in the opposition between income from capital (including all profits, dividends, interest, rents, etc.) and income from wages. However, although he does not limit his scope to profits generated exclusively through $M–M^1$ channels, his emphasis on the process of M^1 generation in ways that deemphasize production and devalue labor exactly parallels the way I use "financialization" in this book as a marker for the reorientation toward the nonproductive.[61] Piketty's capital-focused account and Arrighi's finance-focused one both add weight to the theory that the two turns-of-century are not just superficially similar moments in history but in fact necessarily connected through one and the same historical process.

Hence, even though the "capitalist imaginary" might have seemed a more appropriate title when it comes to talking about novels that are less obviously about finance, I insist on the usefulness of "finance" to specify the difference between the dematerializing tendencies at the two ends-of-century as opposed to the material expansion of the middle. In my argument the "middle" of the twentieth century—including, in the United States, the wartime mobilizations of the 1910s and 1940s, the economic boom of the 1920s, and the stable affluence of the postwar 1950s—all belong to a Fordist, production-based growth economy, where even the stock market volatility of the 1920s did not indicate a systemic slowing of production or an urgent need for capital to compensate by seeking abstract outlets externally or internally. Indeed, it appeared during the period of Keynesian consensus, at least until the 1970s, as if the basic contradictions of the system had been resolved and that the expansion of markets in the future was still unlimited.

This periodization also explains why the late-capitalist or neoliberal imaginary are not the main terms for this book; these refer to the theorization of a post-Fordist, flexible, and service-based economy and to the combination of political and economic ideologies that support a deregulated, privatized, free-market system. Late capitalism is obviously inseparable from financialization, as many critics have observed, and there is no question that the development of a neoliberal *subject* is integral to any analysis of what one might call late-capitalist realism.[62] But for the kind of historical comparison I make, these terms elide more than they illuminate. While I describe financial abstraction as emergent in the late nineteenth century, it would be difficult to use *late* or *neoliberal* capitalism to apply to this period without blurring the historical specificity of these terms. And even if nineteenth-century writers react against liberalist constructions in ways that resemble anti-neoliberalist reactions today, there are signal differences of historical context to consider. For instance, although personal responsibility might be a logical consequence of the kinds of financial individuality and agency that late nineteenth-century writers explored, the cultural resonances were simply not the same. The values attached to "private" were not yet in the context of "privatization." "Laissez-faire" was a defense against regulation not yet implemented rather than an argument for rolling it back. Social dependence, while anxiety producing, was not yet pathologized in the terms of a bureaucratic welfare state. The Horatio Alger model of robust self-reliance and entrepreneurial selfhood was seen as a path for selected, deserving individuals to rise, not as a requirement for a previously established middle class to avoid decline.

The second argument for using the term *financial* is a formalist one. It arises from the question whether financial representation and literary representation are fundamentally different. As critics have observed, fictionality is as necessary to finance as to the novel. Representation is a process of creating value: a speculative value has to be projected and believed (or at least not too greatly disbelieved) before it can be cashed out, that is, made real. An imagination of value—financial or fictional—can only be gauged successful or not by whether it *realizes* some suspension of disbelief, either on the part of the market or the reader.

Two recent critics, one writing about nineteenth-century realism and one about contemporary fiction, address the difference between capitalist and literary forms of representation. Anna Kornbluh, in her work on the Victorian novel, emphasizes the performative aspect of literary representation over the nonperformativeness of financial representation. Through literature's "counterfactual vitality" and "contemplative agency," she argues, realism mediates aesthetically rather than representing mimetically. In contrast to arguments that the function of realism in the nineteenth century is to document or record reality as faithfully as possible, Kornbluh emphasizes the novel's performative counterthinking. Through its fictional capacities, the novel is uniquely positioned to "think" the problem of fictitiousness in capitalism: "It is as fiction—the creation of excessive, aberrant, counterfactual realities—and not as documentary evidence—that realist literature is able to think the conditions of fictitious capital." Instead of working to induce belief that the fictional is (mimetically) real and thereby stabilize a capitalist reality, the novel destabilizes a "reified reality."[63]

Timothy Bewes applies a different set of terms to a similar question.[64] Whereas Kornbluh sets into opposition *instantiate* and *perform* ("Literary language—even in the high realist novel—works not instantiatively, but performatively"),[65] Bewes suggests that representation itself cannot be separated from instantiation. Instantiation does not take place in a moment of representation but is instead the logic of objecthood itself. Under capitalism, therefore, representation is in fact already instantiated at the outset. (The same argument would hold that "reified representation" is redundant.) But there exists the possibility that literature can challenge capitalist instantiation through its ability to call the scene of its representation into question. Literature's ability to offer both a representation and a model of representation—that is, to move between theory and example— potentially disrupts the logic of instantiation.

Both accounts suggest that literature, having different aesthetic resources than those of capitalism, can work against the inherent tendency of representation toward reification. Both suggest that the novel disrupts the logic of abstraction by modeling its formal reflexivity, and both locate literature's resistant capacities in its nonstatic performativeness. Yet even if the novel has the capacity to disrupt capitalist representation, it is difficult to insist upon the formal distinction that finance *represents* but unlike literature cannot *perform*. Even if literature indeed has deeper aesthetic resources and traditions, it does not have a monopoly on the formation of fictitiousness. The concept of literary performativity would thus seem expansive enough to help develop a financial account of relations between abstract and concrete. If the nineteenth-century novel can "think" capitalism, perhaps twenty-first-century capitalism thinks more like fiction— creating totalities, locating temporal and spatial discrepancies, imagining counterfactualities, and reflecting on its own processes of structuration. It may be the financial imaginary, in fact, that ultimately allows us to think through the limitations of the novel instead of the other way around.

My emphasis on the financial imaginary's *capacity of representation* differs from two other recent critical formulations of the idea. Haiven and Berland define the "financial imagination" as a "field of knowledge and action" that is delimited in the present by the politics of crisis and neoliberal austerity.[66] In a "world without guarantees," they argue, in which leverage, speculation, and risk are assertions of control, capital's "imagination" is concurrent with a dangerously utopian fantasy of abstraction, propounded by the logic of post-postindustrial capitalism, in which the systemic effects of neoliberal global capitalism are obscured and its multiple local realities overwritten. While the dystopian flavor of this account is not unjustified, its totalizing stance is not necessarily shared by the texts that negotiate the terrain of financial subjectivity and agency, and it is inadequate to the finer-grained explorations of the struggles between would-be subjects. Relatedly, Langenohl associates the financial imaginary with the "imaginary totality of 'speculative capitalism.'"[67] Again, however, if the imaginary is where capitalism seeks to project its "ideal" form, this is never a guaranteed outcome. To understand the imaginary as a domain of representational contest enables us to ask how the struggle between subject and object plays out. Particularly, it enables us to examine this contest in the novel, a form that offers not simply a confirmation of neoliberal limits but performatively models its conflicts. As the literary writers under examination here both engage and resist the financial imaginary, they grapple with the same contradictions of abstraction confronted by theorists and historians of capitalism. That their works do not always succeed in resolving these contradictions is all the more revealing of the structures of the financial imaginary in the first place.

If the novel has, at various times in its history, aimed to destabilize capitalist reality, its ambition today is perhaps more modest: to register the competing narrative pressures of the diachronic and synchronic, abstract and concrete, temporal and spatial. Even where the literary text successfully interferes with capital's representational process, questioning the financial logic that subjects everything to the same measures of value, such effort may remain at the level of a minor disruption. Contemporary economic realism, instead of being complicit with a bourgeois status quo or even nostalgically invoking empty past realisms, may consist of the negative space that the novel continues to hold open for the concrete, or for its remainders. I do not, therefore, conclude that any of the texts I discuss here finally achieves an aesthetic stability or realizes a coherent critique. But by recognizing how literary texts have repeatedly evoked and attempted to compensate for this inadequacy of representation, therefore, we can see how the "illegibility" of an increasingly abstract, intricate, and global capitalism has conditioned and limited the twentieth-century historical imagination.

The book begins with an examination of the "economic novel," a genre loosely (and often incoherently) consolidated around Howells and his contemporaries in the late nineteenth and early twentieth centuries. The economic tensions of the original Gilded Age continued well beyond the late 1860s and 1870s, the period to which Twain and Warner's 1873 novel gave its famous name.[68] This is not to suggest that finance in the decades around 1900 achieved the same dominance over other sections of the economy that it would a century later. But the period saw an incredibly rapid consolidation of the power of Wall Street and a marked shift in the sources of wealth. "By 1870," according to historian Steve Fraser, "a quarter of all the financial resources of the country were concentrated in New York."[69] Even after the official end of the freebooting, post-Reconstruction period, the contrasts between haves and have-nots continued to deepen. The Gilded Age thus set the stage for later reactions and developments in the 1880s and 1890s, such as populist revolts against the "money interests" of Wall Street, the battle over the gold standard, and the rise of corporations, trusts, and monopolies, in which "colossal corporate combinations" of wheat, steel, and railroad shipping were strong enough to control entire markets and to wield enormous political influence.[70] These conglomerates served as much to subdue labor as to control business competition. Their rivalries, market corners, and other sensational exploits of the period shared headlines with strikes and labor riots across the 1870s and 1880s. The Haymarket riot of 1886 disturbed Howells enough that he began to reconsider his political views in the years between the publication of *The Rise of Silas Lapham* in 1885 and the publication of *A Hazard of New Fortunes* in 1889–90, which portrayed the violent conflict between capitalism and socialism.

In many ways the story of late nineteenth-century capitalism is a story of increasing concentration of power and of top-down control. The rise of the corporation and turn-of-the-century merger mania certainly changed the landscape for small-scale entrepreneurialism. The corporation could be said to represent a stabilizing force—even if an oppressive and humanly uncontrollable one. In contrast, finance might appear to represent a destabilizing force: its interests are unpredictable and unaligned with anything productive. The financier, like Wall Street, was understood to benefit from a money economy "haunted by chaos and insecurity."[71] While not contesting that the corporation was *one* site for the reckoning of economic abstraction in the novel, I suggest that it is more often than not an individual who (sometimes bewildered, sometimes not) confronts this second-order sphere of abstraction beyond the "real." My argument thus builds from an initial claim that in the late nineteenth-century novel, financial agency tends to be worked out in character-based terms—even though the place of "character" is at times held by a corporation.

The first chapter, "Virtue Unrewarded," therefore examines the ways in which the individual confronts an emergent set of perceptions about capitalism as an abstract system, from the prelapsarian "economic virtue" of Silas Lapham, who exhibits almost no grasp of abstraction and no productive agency in navigating it, to the nonproductive "genius" represented by Dreiser. With the rise of new financial notions of value, social realists and the naturalistic writers who followed them revised the economic individualism of earlier American narratives of wealth and speculation in order to represent the displacement of agency into disembodied market forces. Although the results were sometimes ironic or contradictory, the Howellsian businessman, the Jamesian rentier, and the Dreiserian financier all articulate ambivalences about the loss of material and tangible forms of industrial capital and the rise of new forms of abstraction that might prove immune to social and moral restraints.

In the remaining four chapters I take up a series of contemporary novels that together reveal the structural tensions of a realist representation of unreal capitalism. The chapter "Reaganomic Realisms" explores a narrative reworking of Howellsian moral realism for the Reagan era. Jane Smiley's novel of 1980s real-estate speculation, *Good Faith*, contests the adequacy of narratives of economic character for end-of-century neoliberalism, even while it emphasizes a persistent, unresolved investment in character types and genres as sources of moral legibility. I examine the figure of the con man alongside the novel's representation of a rapidly transforming economic landscape, complete with references to deregulation, tax politics, and savings and loan (S&L) lending. Real estate, I argue, becomes a text through which interrelated cultural, structural, demographic, and moral shifts are given the most concrete account. The concurrent use of the con man exposes the misalignment between this account of structural change and narratives of individual virtue. I draw upon analyses of the representation of character by Deidre Lynch, Alex Woloch, and others to argue that character is revealed in Smiley's text as a site of abstract typification onto which, paradoxically, moral and social regulatory functions become ever more persistently displaced.

"Epic Compensations" considers the narrative attempt to mobilize a contemporary epic form adequate to the demands of a capitalist totality. I read Richard Powers's *Gain* (1998) as using multiple narrative structures to examine the aesthetic dissonances that such an epic scale produces. The corporate epic can be seen as a response to the perceived limitations and responsibilities of traditional genres of realism. While Frank Norris's famous monster corporation in *The Octopus* appears to come in conflict with the novel's realist ambitions, Powers's self-proclaimed "crackpot realism" challenges any straightforward reading of *Gain*'s politics as anticorporate and thus very differently interrogates the novel's mediations of capitalist reification and totalization.

The fourth chapter, "Financial Sublime," considers Don DeLillo's novel *Cosmopolis* (2003) as engaging the problem of representing the autonomous subject at a historical moment when capitalism can be imagined as no longer dependent on persons to propel itself forward. Drawing on the language of the so-called New Economy, the novel produces an experiment in subjectivity that reflects neither character nor social class. As capitalism becomes one of the large systems beyond human grasp invoked across DeLillo's fiction (explored in related terms in *White Noise*, *Libra*, and *Underworld*), *Cosmopolis* signals its own inability to reach into the realism of actual material relations. The sublime relationship between technology and capital is used to expose the representational limits of the contemporary novel. Ultimately, the novel can be read as an experiment in form—even as a theorization of its own failure—to find ways of seeing virtual capitalisms that are perceived to elude the power of narrative representation. *Cosmopolis*'s controversial, largely negative reception shows how this experiment disrupts readers' expectations—and demonstrates how strongly the representation of capitalism continues to be associated with the familiar moral and social lenses of the economic novel.

Finally, "Liquid Realisms" discusses two recent novels centered on the financialized global commodities of oil and water. Teddy Wayne's *Kapitoil* (2010) and Mohsin Hamid's *How to Get Filthy Rich in Rising Asia* (2013) complicate common critical distinctions between the "postmodern" and the "political" novel. I argue that these texts' embrace of and resistance to the logic of abstraction can be analyzed through their unusual narratological features—in one, a narrator with limited understanding of idiomatic English; in the other, a self-help book narrated in the second person. With these asymmetries of perspective that echo and recapitulate the asymmetries of global inequality, these texts refer to realisms while not using them in any uncomplicated sense. I read both novels as experimenting with literary language as a revitalizable site of value and valuation—a metaphor for both processes of accumulation and, crucially, a way to resist financial extractions of value.

CHAPTER ONE

Virtue Unrewarded

Financial Character in the Economic Novel

The writers I discuss in this chapter—William Dean Howells, Henry James, and Theodore Dreiser—were among those once called "economic" novelists by literary critics in the 1930s. Leftist critics, eager to identify an American literary tradition critical of capitalism, used the category to describe the late nineteenth-century fascination with industrialization, urbanization, and the drama of the wage laborer against increasingly consolidated forces.[1] To distinguish turn-of-the-century fiction from the then-emergent critical category of modernism, these critics emphasized the realist novel's representations of wealth disparity and class conflict, and its critique of poverty and the rise of "money interests" on Wall Street.

The generic and historical confusion of such a category, however, is made immediately evident by the two most exhaustive efforts to survey it, Claude Reherd Flory's *Economic Criticism in American Fiction* (1937) and Walter Fuller Taylor's *The Economic Novel in America* (1942).[2] Neither of these texts resolves the problem of defining the genre formally or historically. My own purpose in this chapter is not to try to salvage a coherent definition of the "economic novel" but to isolate one of the primary assumptions that underlay the critics' classifying effort: namely, that the goals of literary realism are synonymous with the delineation of social difference. Taylor called the preoccupations of class representation and of realism "class truth" and "realist truth." Even in the study of American literary realism today, the intertwining of these categories is often treated as self-evident, however much the terms *class* and *realism* have been critically destabilized.

This chapter resists the presupposition that realism and class representation go hand in hand. I thus make use of the term *economic novel* only to identify a point of departure. In readings of Howells's novel *The Rise of Silas Lapham*, James's short story "The Jolly Corner," and Dreiser's novel

The Financier, I argue that class is demonstrated to be inadequate as a heuristic for understanding the changes from a predominantly industrial economy to an increasingly financial one. As these texts seek out modes of representing abstract forms of capitalism, they background more familiar critiques of social and class inequality and instead foreground the capitalist as a problem of character representation. As financial activity destabilizes to some degree the boundaries and agency by which personhood is defined, the result is a formal tension over how character is constituted: what should be understood as internal or external, as belonging to it or not. These texts' explorations of "financial individuality" and provisional definitions of "financial character" demonstrate how the work of character and characterization bear the formal pressure in the novel of new modes of capitalism that are increasingly difficult to personify.

Economic virtue is a particularly useful term for measuring the ways in which these writers adapted moral models of personhood for newly financialized conditions in which morality appeared beside the point. This phrase comes from critical analyses of the many eighteenth- and early nineteenth-century American fictions that decried speculation. As applied by critics to this earlier context, *economic virtue* refers to the ability to maintain the integrity of the self in the face of gambling temptations.[3] I borrow the phrase for its implication of the possibility of drawing a clear distinction between morally sanctionable and unsanctionable economic activity. The point is not to claim that a moral compass was lost somewhere in the nineteenth century (though some literary writers certainly believed that it was) but that literary fictions around the end of the century often reveal the uneven ways in which it persists—in modified, ironized, or artificially preserved form. My argument could be said to begin with Walter Benn Michaels's statement that character represents for Howells "a kind of still point, a repository of values, that resisted the fluctuations and inequalities of industrial capitalism."[4] This chapter builds on Michaels's observation by analyzing the ways "character" was used to conceptualize a finance capitalism that appeared both increasingly impersonal *and* personality driven. Silas Lapham famously complains of a "shrinkage of values" affecting the market for his paint. What becomes apparent in these fictions is an effort to respond to this shrinkage of values—and the equal threat of inflation—with new measurements of selfhood. *Financial individuality* and *economic virtue* reveal to what extent character is used as device to engage with the very conditions of economic instability that would appear to superannuate it.

This approach contrasts with the widespread critical focus on the corporation as a figure for turn-of-the-century capitalism. Alan Trachtenberg's influential *The Incorporation of America* used the term *incorporation* not only to describe the literal transfer of governing power to monied corporations during this period but also to metaphorically encompass a wholesale reorganization and nationalization of cultural perceptions. Trachtenberg writes that new economic conditions in the three decades following the Civil War "marked a radical discontinuity with the past difficult for many Americans to grasp. The new breed of business leaders were often skilled in finance, in market manipulation, in corporate organization: entrepreneurial skills on a scale unimaginable to most manufacturers before the war."[5] Other historians have similarly focused on the cultural effects of the amalgamations and "consolidations" of the era. Wilfred McClay describes an anxiety of agency emerging from economic centralization.[6] Jeffrey Sklansky argues that as the corporation increasingly took over the legal definition of sovereignty, social theorists faced the challenge of reconceiving the relationship of the individual to the social and economic order.[7] The "corporate" model of the self that emerges by the late nineteenth century in Sklansky's account displaces an earlier "sovereign" selfhood of eighteenth-century moral philosophy and political economy.

The story that emerges from these accounts is of the corporate "taming" of the economy. Regional and wildcat economies were actively consolidated and organized into a national unified body. The lawless individualism of the robber-baron era gave way to a "post-entrepreneurial" stage of American capitalism that saw the ascendance of a class of respectable, corporate professionals and bureaucrats. Trachtenberg describes the shift from "self-employed proprietors to large corporations run by salaried managers," in which capitalism was reconceived along the lines of "an emergent form of ownership in which power is distributed inwardly along hierarchical lines and outwardly in new social configurations and cultural perspectives."[8] Such a description would seem to correspond with arguments that "social" selfhood was being newly defined in terms of socialization, cooperation, and self-expression rather than in the classic terms of individualism and self-possession.

But the novels I examine tell a somewhat different story. In the three economic fictions discussed in this chapter, the corporation either is a marginal player or does not appear at all. A main character confronts a "new" form of finance-related capitalism and conceives (or rejects) some form of financial agency. What historicizing critical readings focused on the corporation tend to overwrite, I suggest, are the ways that abstraction appears to be changing the rules of engagement at capitalism's individual level. The individual becomes the "ground" of the encounter with unreal finance. If the corporation represents the "facelessness" (or headlessness, in the famous case of Norris's *The Octopus*, a text I introduce later in chapter 3) of a disembodied turn-of-the-century capitalism, finance represents its complete dematerialization. Whereas anxieties about the deflection of personal responsibility within these corporate systems are but one form of encounter with abstraction, what I am identifying is more closely approximated by discourse about the "money interests" and the notion of a "second, phantom economy."[9] "Money interests" was already a close synonym with "Wall Street," which by the 1880s and 1890s had risen to metonymize the entire American banking system in the way it does today. But "money interests," especially when used as an epithet by populists and by free-silver advocates, was still routinely associable with particular names such as Morgan, Rockefeller, Gould, Drew, or Carnegie. The "phantom economy," in contrast, was far less attachable to specific agents. I suggest that the rise of a virtual economy, and the problems of value that it raised, was linked to a perception of abstraction that marked the loss of agency and legibility, as well as the rise of seemingly more "determinative" economic systems.

Wai Chee Dimock has argued that the "networking" of the world in the late nineteenth century demanded a new "cognitive style." She writes, "Nineteenth-century Americans, in short, had to adapt not only to an expanded geographical universe but also, even more crucially, to an expanded causal universe, in which human agency, social relations, and moral responsibility all had to be redefined."[10] There is little doubt that the newly connective bands of the railroads, the linking of local markets to Wall Street, and the consolidations of monopolies, trusts, and financial markets all contributed to the developing perception of a "symptomatic network" of causes and effects. The market offered a powerful figure for the displacement of causality from the level of individuals to the level of systems. Yet in the novel, these "systems" tend to become visible only at the moment of individual conflict—when a character discovers himself trapped, thwarted, ruined, or simply confronting a dilemma of economic action. Thus, what is formally problematic or contradictory in each text appears most strongly at moments in which financial agency, intention, or responsibility is being articulated in personified terms. Fraser makes an argument about the outsized relevance of character at this moment in American history that is a useful corollary for the literary argument I make in the following pages. The "morganization" of the economy (Fraser's word) means the transition from an image of swashbucklers of speculation to conservative, white-shoe financial management. But as the phrase suggests, despite a historical shift from the terms of colorful but immoral *character* to controlled and rationalized *systems*, the imagination of financial character persisted as a kind of cultural hangover. Morgan's lionization, around the time of the panic of 1907, represented "Napoleonic fantasizing" as compensation for the loss of individualism.[11]. Claiming that much of the public discourse of capitalism in the 1900s borrowed its language from the agrarian era, Fraser makes in effect the same point that Trachtenberg attributes to Henry Adams, writing about the Gilded Age thirty to forty years earlier: "Corporate life, as Adams observed, was still too new for Americans to recognize except in the familiar but already outmoded language of individualism."[12]

Literary accounts of fictions of speculation and Wall Street have similarly narrated a decline of colorful individuals, as nineteenth-century hucksters such as Twain's comic Colonel Sellers and Melville's confidence man gave way to the "realist" turn-of-the-century businessman, later to become Sinclair's George Babbitt and, still later, Wilson's man in a gray flannel suit. But even in the case of Howells, a writer whose work would presumably represent a definitive point in this transition, a reverse account proposes itself, in which character appears to provide ballast *against* the perceived inscrutability and ephemerality of financialization. Even those writers who question the representational possibilities of character, in other words, can be seen, in complex ways, to grip them more tightly than ever. The persistence of focus on personhood, even as novels demonstrate the very conditions that make such a focus outdated, make apparent the formal problems in developing the truly "coherent and incisive critique" of capitalism that critics such as Walter Fuller Taylor sought to locate in the economic novel.

If incorporation appears to represent the abstract taming of the economy, finance represents its untaming. It does not stabilize questions about the value of money or where wealth comes from. In generating a sense that there is no *there* there in capitalism, finance threatens to disconnect social, political, and class-based modes of legibility. Howard Horwitz, in discussing Frank Norris's *The Pit*, argues that the novelistic representation of finance demonstrates the way in which a "sense of the destabilization of value finds its way into the literary imagination." Horwitz here characterizes finance in terms similar to my own, as a "new" form of capital represented by an independent "fund of money values" that "bears only a remote and fluctuating relation" to actual production.[13] As mentioned in the introduction, there are multiple ways to specify finance's relationship to the destabilization of value (for instance, the formation of fictitious capital, the structures of debt and credit, or the creation of new exchanges of investment and trade such as futures markets). But for my purposes in this chapter, the key site of finance's destabilization of value is its relationship to labor. What "financial individuality" allows us to gauge is how work represents the anxieties about the perceived separation between a "base" of real productive activity and a superstructure of value that might bear no relationship to it. (I say "anxiety" even though at least one of the characters discussed, Dreiser's Cowperwood, manifests no apparent anxiety at the prospect of this separation at all.) Unproductive accumulation changes the cultural meanings of work, the value realizable through work, and the terrifying and/or exalting possibility that a direct correspondence between the two might not be maintained.

Lapham's Economic Innocence

Toward the end of *The Rise of Silas Lapham* (1885), the mineral paint king of Boston confesses to his wife that he has been dabbling in stocks in an attempt save his failing business: "I give you my word of honor, Persis, that I never was in it at all till that scoundrel began to load me up with those wild-cat securities of his. . . . To make a long story short, I began to buy and sell on a margin—just what I told you I would never do."[14] A few pages later, in a late burst of hope, Lapham arranges to meet with a group of West Virginia paint manufacturers whom he suspects are poised to push him out of the market:

> He found the West Virginians full of zeal and hope, but in ten minutes he knew that they had not yet tested their strength in the money market, and had not ascertained how much or how little capital they could command. Lapham himself, if he had had so much, would not have hesitated to put a million dollars into their business. He saw, as they did not see, that they had the game in their own hands, and that if they could raise the money to extend their business, they could ruin him. (317)

Together Lapham's confession and his action reveal some of the formal challenges Howells negotiates to keep his businessman honest. After the novel chronicles Lapham's decline and bankruptcy in Boston, the concluding chapters weigh what actions he may and may not take in order to retreat with honor to his family farm in Vermont. Within the ethical framework of the novel, it is unimaginable for Lapham to save himself through paper speculation, which is morally equated with gambling ("It's like betting on the turn of a card" [298]). Lapham's brief, desperate turn to buying and selling on margin is thus eventually repented by this character who prides himself on having earned every dollar and ultimately repudiated by a novel that endorses his bootstrap self-sufficiency as his most redeeming—although his most socially awkward—personal characteristic.

Lapham nonetheless demonstrates crucial market acumen when he quickly sizes up his competitors' advantage before they even recognize it for themselves. The paint king's "practical" sense reasserts itself in a scene over the confusion and misjudgment that have clouded his affairs. "When it really came to business," the text insists, "his practical instincts, alert and wary, came to his aid against the passions that lay in wait to betray after they ceased to dominate him" (317). The "passions" that earlier led him astray now checked, Lapham sees clearly that the West Virginians have a natural geographic efficiency in their new mine that will enable their paint to undersell his no matter how well he runs his business. His "practical instincts" inform him on the spot of the advantage of their position and the likely ramifications on the entire paint market. His wish that he had a million dollars to put into their business is not a speculative passion but the disinterested recognition of a (literally) well-grounded investment.

To the modern reader of the text the distinction between speculation and investment—the right and wrong kind of financial activity—is likely to appear unsustainable. In Howells's novel the distinction is perhaps most usefully understood as a moment of wishful idealization for a world in which the wrong kind of economic action could be more sharply defined. The novel has already acknowledged elsewhere that the difference between immaterial speculation and material investment, or risky paper and secure paper, is difficult to discern. For instance, the mills in Ohio that Lapham has been holding as collateral for a loan turn out to be worth much less than he thought. After accepting the collateral from a former business partner, Rogers, and making him the loan, Lapham visits the mills and learns that a large conglomerate has recently bought the local railroad, a fact that he immediately suspects Rogers to have known and suppressed. In light of its purchase, the railroad has consolidated a local monopoly and will be able to buy the mills at whatever low price it demands. Thus, Lapham's understanding of the railroad's *likely* interest turns his solid note overnight into worthless paper. Or at least this is Howells's ethical staging of the situation. For Lapham to view this outcome as a probability rather than a possibility is already to indicate a limitation in his choices: the *probable* is seen as a fait accompli rather than as a possibility that continues to compete with other possibilities until action is taken and the alternatives foreclosed. Once Lapham considers the railroad's interest to be inevitable, he cannot in good conscience pass off the soon-to-be-devalued mills to an ignorant buyer as they have been passed off to him. The "realism" of Howells's approach here lies not in the calculation of economic outcomes but of ethical choices.

Moreover, since the market consequences of the railroad's interest are a given, Lapham's failure lies only in his judgment of moral character, not of the market. Although Lapham exhibits lapses of judgment (stemming from guilt toward a former partner, whom he ill-advisedly tries to support), and although he certainly gets in over his head (his wife and elder daughter sit up at night to help him tally his accounts), his failure ultimately is not due to financial short-sightedness or miscalculation but to his principled resistance to an action that he considers a breach of conduct—even at a moment when this action would save his family from ruin. Ironically, he does the gentlemanly thing in allowing this ruin. In returning poor but principled to the family farm in Vermont, he becomes symbolically closer to the code of class behavior to which he has aspired—as represented by the aristocratically mannered but financially straitened Corey family—than he ever could have attained as a successful capitalist in Boston.

Such tests of character exemplify the formal tension between the ethics of individual action and the depiction of market forces. We might note that Lapham does not start with a presumption of economic innocence but *attains* it through various tests of experience. While "character," in both the literary and moral sense, is ostensibly given full realist complexity in *Silas Lapham*, the circumstances within which character is defined are formally restricted. For all his vigor and activity, Lapham exists in a relatively passive relationship to the market. Choices are thrust upon him. A businessman as much by chance as by aptitude, he is shielded by the narrative against a full examination of the meaning and operation of his self-interest. The novel thereby also shields itself against the implications of its own moral engagement with capitalism. In the highly staged encounter between the moral decision Lapham makes and the economic opportunities and choices that he actually confronts, Lapham models a kind of nostalgic innocence at a historical moment when, for Howells, the possibility of ethical self-definition outside the terms of the market appeared to be diminishing.

One way Lapham is protected from the full pressure of self-interest is to have so little complicity in the system of production. Though a self-made man, his success is also accidental; his wealth is drawn out of a hole in the ground: a mineral paint mine discovered by his father at the Lapham family farm. At its origins, therefore, Lapham's capital is an agrarian ideal as well as a gift of fortune. Even in its raw state the paint proves to be a valuable commodity with an already existing market. The task of selling it involves little more than packaging and distribution. And although Lapham has worked throughout his career to increase sales (his sincerity about his product is further demonstrated once he realizes and resigns himself to the knowledge that the newer West Virginia paint is superior), the honest man has essentially risen to wealth on a "natural" business selling a found commodity for which there is limited competition, and that is driven in the market by existing demand rather than artificial supply. He never aims to expand demand and, in fact, is initially reluctant to take on the young Tom Corey as a foreign sales representative because the paint seems to be adequately selling itself. Even his advertisements are presented as much as a quaint gesture of pride in his product rather than as a forward-thinking commercial strategy. His billboards are not seen in a positive light for their commercial payoff but only as a negative social liability, as when the Coreys refer slightingly to the landscape covered with the Lapham name. His name is so closely associated with his product that Lapham's pride in his paint is, ironically, even more socially indelicate than if the billboard advertisements were *just* business.

Therefore, even if we question the distinction between fulfilling demand and creating it, Lapham's wealth accumulation is a remarkably passive operation. He is lucky to have been handed a valuable paint and unlucky in turn when a better paint appears elsewhere. The triumph of the West Virginia operation is assured, in Lapham's view, since capital will objectively recognize the advantages of his rivals and fall behind them. Lapham abandons the idea of competing against the West Virginians on a large scale. The ethical decision, as Howells presents it, is also the efficient decision: recognizing and aligning oneself with the natural distribution of assets rather than struggling to artificially increase, inflate, or reorganize them. Back on the Vermont farm, Lapham limits himself to developing the premium "Persis" paints for the luxury market, a refined grade that his rivals "confessed that they could not produce" and therefore "willingly left" to him (353). Thus does a potential rivalry sort itself out according to principles of natural efficiency.

Lapham is "honest" in the sense that he has followed the fortunes of his product rather than actively trying to shape the market in his own interests. The difference is important, for it underscores how the possibility of his character's moral innocence has been preserved even as his material fortunes have risen to the most gilded levels. Market circumstances may change—as when wartime boosts Lapham's sales or a recessionary moment dries them up—but these instabilities do not alter his understanding and recognition of opportunities as *given* rather than developed. In this sense, Lapham is not a character who demonstrates the process of recognizing new economic opportunities that had not been recognizable before. Instead, the opportunities around him are presented as objectively fixed. It is an instance of Lapham's virtue that he proposes a partnership to the West Virginians in what Howells describes as a "fair and open" way:

> He frankly proposed a union of their interests. . . . Lapham made them
> three propositions, each of which was fair and open: to sell out to them
> altogether; to buy them out altogether; to join facilities and forces with
> them, and go on in an invulnerable alliance. Let them name a figure at
> which they would buy, a figure at which they would sell, a figure at
> which they would combine,—or, in other words, the amount of capital
> they needed. (317)

By laying out the range of options in full, Lapham essentially presents a
collective view of the market that includes every party's interests rather
than a narrowly partial or self-interested one. In this way the novel pro-
pounds the ideal of a complete transparency of interests visible against a
set of common and acknowledged market expectations—or at least, we
might say, as much of a transparency and objectivity as realistically possible. Lapham recognizes the same rules of interest whether they happen
to work for or against him. The result is mixed: he succeeds in getting
the West Virginians to agree to a partnership, but the figure they name
is too high for him to meet. Nonetheless, this exchange is a high point of
Lapham's "practical sense," in which his fairness and openness are an
acknowledgment of the market's rationality.

One of the ironies of the novel is that although Lapham may be too
nouveau to succeed in social terms, he is not nouveau enough to succeed
in capitalist terms. The novel's strict association between the value of
character and the value of business explains both his social failure and his
financial failure. In his hour of need, Lapham attempts to raise cash on the
basis of his solid reputation and discovers that creditors want firmer collateral: "He found that people of whom he hoped to get [the money] were
in the conspiracy which had been formed to drive him to the wall. Somehow there seemed a sense of his embarrassments abroad" (319). Dogged
by rumor, Lapham is unable to *become* the financier he needs in order to
save his business. His pride wounded by the earlier friendly advice of a
Corey family connection who had "subjected his figures to an analysis
which . . . proved he was not so rich and not so wise as he had seemed,"
Lapham refuses to turn to him for help. Unable to find "capitalists on the
scale he required," he reflects on the lack of loyalty by people who have
refused to lend, or who want to take time to look into the state of the business first, even though, we are told, "he knew the state of the business
would not bear looking into" (319). Although Lapham laments having
no "capitalist" to turn to, therefore, the problem is that he finds *only*
capitalists around him. People who place their self-interest above his fail
to honor what Lapham appears to regard as a social responsibility to

"befriend" those in need. Yet it is clear from Lapham's own account that anyone who lent him money would be generous to the point of foolish. Among outsiders, it is not at all unreasonable for financial suspicion to be circulating around him. (Rogers mentions that he has heard around town that Lapham has been trying to borrow money.) The text hardly condemns those who refuse to help Lapham; their calculation of interest seems only likely and prudent, and Lapham's expectation of friendly assistance weak and naïve. The fault is at least partly his own: he would not need a capitalist if he could have acted like one—that is, recognized limits on his moral responsibility. But, hampered by his inability to act on the narrowest terms of self-interest—a stance Howells both applauds and appears to recognize as realistically untenable—Lapham cannot transform himself from an older model of businessman whose "fair and open" dealings are accessible to social scrutiny into a modern one who deals exclusively in abstract values.

Critics have commented on Lapham's peculiar passivity in the climactic scenes of the novel, in which his former partner, Rogers, offers to buy back the devalued mills at the original price and absolve Lapham of all responsibility for them. These scenes mark the famous "turn" of the text in which Lapham conclusively sets himself on the moral high ground and thereby fulfills the spiritual "rise" of the book's title. They certainly demonstrate Lapham's unwillingness to risk any shadow of a potentially unethical action. At Rogers's insistence, Lapham first meets a group of Englishmen who claim to represent a third party that is interested in the property. Suspecting Rogers of having deceived the buyers about the property's value, he arrives at the meeting prepared to denounce Rogers on the spot. He finds the buyers strangely uninterested in the matter, however ("When he became plain with them in his anger, and told them why he would not sell, they seemed to have been prepared for this as a stroke of business, and were ready to meet it" [323]). Explaining that they represent an "association of rich and charitable people" in England seeking a spot on which to develop a planned community, they say they have inspected the site and found it suitable for their unusual purposes. They insist that Lapham name his price, adding that "the loss, if there is to be any, will fall upon people who are able to bear it. . . . But we're quite satisfied there will be no loss" (325). Lapham is not reassured. Dimly sensing that he is in a "deeper game," he cannot identify the right principle of action. Since he "could not tell the Englishmen that he believed them a pair of scoundrels and should have nothing to do with them," while at the same time he could "no longer treat them as innocent dupes," Lapham abruptly quits the room declaring he will not give an answer until the morning.

Returning home, he finds Rogers waiting to urge Lapham to sell the mills back to him instead. "I don't say what I'm going to do with the property," he announces, "and you will not have an iota of responsibility, whatever happens" (329). Reflecting on this, Lapham cannot find any hole in Rogers's logic: "It was perfectly true. Any lawyer would have told him the same. He could not help admiring Rogers for his ingenuity, and every selfish interest of his nature joined with many obvious duties to urge him to consent. He did not see why he should refuse. There was no longer a reason. He was standing out alone for nothing, any one else would say" (330). Still, Lapham hesitates and tells Rogers he will not make a decision until the next day. In the morning a letter arrives from the railroad with its offer for the mills, a development that makes it impossible under any circumstances to negotiate further, "even with victims so pliant and willing as those Englishmen" (331). Lapham and Rogers are ruined. Decision is reached through indecision. Just as the accidental burning of Lapham's new house earlier in the novel acted out Lapham's reluctance to sell the property that represented all his social aspirations, the problem of the mill is taken out of his hands.

It is not even clear that Lapham has made the most ethically defensible choice. At least one critic argues that there is little justification for him to refuse to sell since any understanding of "customary business practices, defensible legal opinions, and acceptable moral principles" all would support the decision to sell.[15] Lapham essentially fails to accept the principle of limited responsibility. We might say, then, that his fear of selfish interest conflicts with the more *realistic* need for a business to limit liability. Realism and ethical self-interest diverge. Unable to make a clear judgment about the right course of action, he makes no judgment at all, avoiding even the accidental possibility of causing a future wrong. This avoidance demonstrates how the novel requires Lapham's almost complete suspension of agency in order to register the full moral weight of the situation. Lapham represents an economic innocence that can only make judgments when the basis for them is open and transparent. But as such judgments are less reliable or stable, in the face of complex, contradictory, and illegible financial interests, such a model of full disclosure has become outdated. Inadequate to the moral ambiguities and contextual demands of the market's expanding compass, Lapham is left, in his words, "standing out alone for nothing."

In the final paragraph of the novel, the Reverend Sewell asks Lapham if he has any regrets. "About what I done? Well, it don't always seem as if I done it," Lapham replies. "Seems sometimes as if it was a hole opened for me, and I crept out of it." The hole can be understood to refer not only to the source of his paint but to the contradiction of his economic self-definition. Lapham can accept the choices he is given or not—just as he can draw the paint from the ground or not—but he cannot define the terms of those choices. The hole is Howells's ideal economy. It preexists any form of exploitation or ethical complexity. Under such circumstances, how do we know what is *earned* by the capitalist? How can earned income and found income be distinguished? The difference is not confronted on the page; in fact, the entire question of ethical production versus unethical production is ultimately left in the hole. Indeed, the impossibility of Howells's ideal economy that would defer to "natural" principles of efficiency in the use and distribution of resources demonstrates the very conditions that make a critique of capitalism through "economic virtue" incoherent.

James's Rentier Aesthetic

Like *Silas Lapham*, Henry James's 1909 short story "The Jolly Corner" presents a problem of defining self-interest at a moment when older forms of economic selfhood appear superannuated.[16] However, "The Jolly Corner" gives the notion of economic innocence a mischievous twist. Although the text similarly focuses on responsible personhood, it does so through the terms of productive and nonproductive work—rather than ethical and unethical action—that the definition of self-interest becomes even more sharply and ironically drawn.

Returning to the United States after a thirty-three-year absence in Europe, Spencer Brydon is fascinated and appalled by the "newnesses," "queernesses," and "bignessess" of his native New York City, a place in which it seems "proportions and values were upside down" (436). Commercial activity in the city is the source of all that is "terrible," "modern," "monstrous," and "sordid" (436–37). The streets themselves have become a figure of economic excess, their "dreadful multiplied numbering which seemed to him to reduce the whole place to some vast ledger-page, overgrown, fantastic, of ruled and criss-crossed lines and figures" (439). The "lively stir" of commercial activity is, for Brydon, entirely dissociated from the matter that has brought him to New York. Quotation marks and narrative circumlocutions in the text signal Brydon's success at distancing himself from his proprietary relations: "He has come—putting the thing pompously—to look at his 'property,' which he had thus for a third of a century not been within four thousand miles of; or, expressing it less sordidly, he had yielded to the humour of seeing again his house on the jolly corner, as he usually, and quite fondly, described it" (437). Deborah Esch describes James's frequent use of quotation marks as a way of calling attention to the figurative status of the word or expression in a character's discourse.[17] One might go a step further and say that this self-reflexivity at the outset of "The Jolly Corner" not only marks the movement of the narrator's perception between literal and figurative, as Esch says, but signals an ironic relationship to possession. Ownership is expressed as a cognitive *process* rather than a static actuality. Brydon raises the question internally whether the house on the jolly corner is or is not a "property"—and to what extent "property" can be understood in a literal sense, as something that can in fact be possessed. After a description of the house, followed by a description of another, commercial rental property that Brydon also owns, the text circles back to this sentiment by revising it and re-presenting it without quotation marks—"These were items of property indeed" (437)—suggesting that Brydon has intellectually resolved his ability to assert ownership without recourse to the figurative. This process of sentimental recuperation allows "properties" external to become incorporated as "properties" internal.

Brydon's visit to New York is apparently motivated by a recent change of status at each property, which has set his possession of them on new footing. The old house on the jolly corner has lately come "wholly into his hands," and the building on the other, commercial property has collapsed outright—"the mere number in its long row, having within a twelvemonth fallen in." This second property, although "not quite so 'good'," has, together with a lease on the first, allowed Brydon to "live in 'Europe,' as he had been in the habit of living on these flourishing New York leases." (The quotation marks around "Europe" summon up the Jamesian idealization of an entire European lifestyle of leisure that the American commercial economy underwrites.) In fact, the rebuilding of second property offers the prospect of Brydon's being able to live "all the better" in the future since "renovation at a high advance had proved *beautifully possible*" (437, emphasis mine). The reason for the building's collapse is not mentioned, nor the fate of the tenants paying the leases, and though rents had "never been depressingly low" in the first place, negligence on the landlord's part surely cannot be ruled out. If the distinguished house on the jolly corner confronts Brydon with the "sordid" nature of property ownership, we might expect the site of the building that actually generates his income (the interchangeable currency of "the mere number in its long row") to present an even greater sense of unease for his aristocratic values. But the now "beautifully possible" notion of reconstruction and improvement offers a redeeming affective consolation.

Mark McGurl has discussed James's conjoining of the "beautiful" with the "impossible" as a means of using romance as a mode of resistance to unpleasant reality.[18] In this way, he argues, the romance of what is affectively pleasing yet unattainable operates for James as a formal vehicle to criticize realism's harsh truths. Though McGurl's discussion focuses on *The Golden Bowl*, the "beautifully possible" serves the same double-edged function in "The Jolly Corner" to simultaneously affirm and deny Brydon's self-interest. Even his descriptions of his properties emphasize Brydon's view that financial responsibilities have been thrust upon him. In language that is tactfully stripped of purpose, the house on the jolly corner comes "into his hands." To come to "look" at his "property" is "pompous," but to have "yielded to the humour of seeing" it again is less "sordid," as if this syntactical subordination of purpose could offset the indelicacy of ownership.

But the "beautifully possible" is more than a form of aesthetic resistance to reality, I argue: it signals a displacement in the arena of production that allows the aesthetic and sentimental to be cast as "real" work. In a scene in which Brydon visits the construction site, for example, aesthetic refinement itself is staged as a form of labor: "He looked about his 'work' undeterred—secretly agitated; not in the least 'minding' that the whole proposition as they said, was vulgar and sordid, and ready to climb ladders, to walk the plank, to handle materials and look wise about them, to ask questions, in fine, and challenge explanations and really 'go into' figures" (438). Brydon discovers his practical talents with amused irony, his actions appearing in quotation marks that cancel out the meaning of the action and that reinforce his self-perception of being innocent of all relations of production (It "had been not the least of his astonishments to find himself able, on the spot . . . to participate with a certain intelligence, almost with a certain authority"). Brydon's imitation of labor ironically confirms his identity as a member of the nonlaboring class. But the charade also makes it possible for Brydon to take proprietary possession of his property in terms acceptable to a self-identifying member of the leisure class.

The paradox of the rentier, then, is that he is simultaneously productive and unproductive of value. His is not a *disguising* of production but a *mimesis* of production that is, in effect, parasitical upon less pleasing and more "sordid" forms of labor. Brydon's economic "work" is aesthetic, and the aesthetic staging of production and nonproduction both become sources of value—precisely in creating distance from the sordidly "real." Brydon enthusiastically insists on his "decent feelings" for the house on the jolly corner. "The beauty of it, I mean of my perversity, of my refusal to agree to a 'deal'—is just in the total absence of a reason. Don't you see that if I had a reason about the matter one way or the other, it would inevitably be a reason of dollars?" (446). Again, Brydon's "perversity" is to find beautiful whatever *appears* to resist the demands of the market. Developing property becomes an opportunity for the further cultivation of a different kind of narcissistic self-interest in apparitions (namely, ghosts). Aesthetic imagination becomes a form of productive labor in which Brydon attempts to "'cultivate' his whole perception" (459) and in which to see the "strange apparition" of the ghost is to be "projecting into it always a refinement of beauty" (466).

From this point of view, Brydon's "morbid obsession" with knowing what he might have been, or would have been, had he only stayed in New York and gone into business as his father desired, is more than a failure of self-recognition. The obsession with his ghostly alter ego is a mode of self-production that extends and builds upon the self-interest established from the first line ("'Every one asks me what I "think" of everything,' said Spencer Brydon; 'and I make answer as I can—begging or dodging the question, putting them off with any nonsense'" [435]). In his obsessive self-regard he resembles John Marcher in James's earlier "The Beast in the Jungle," whose preoccupation with his unknown fate prevents him from recognizing it. When Brydon reveals to his companion, Alice Staverton, his habit of stalking his alter ego, he "confess[es] for the first time the intensity within him of this absurd speculation—which but proved also, no doubt, the habit of too selfishly thinking" and thereby "affirm[s] the impotence there of any other source of interest" (448). Brydon declares himself, in other words, too *self-interested* for a productive mode of life. Having lived according to the "abysmal conceit" of his "own preference" (449) and leading, "these thirty years, a selfish frivolous scandalous life" (450), he laments that his narcissistic immunity to any other "source of interest" besides himself affirms him to be not cut out for the market.

The irony of the contradiction is not lost on Alice Staverton, who remarks, "In short you're to make so good a thing of your sky-scraper that, living in luxury on *those* ill-gotten gains, you can afford for a while to be sentimental here!" (444). If the house on the jolly corner cannot be separated in economic terms from the property under construction two blocks west, together making possible his rentier life in Europe, then the "not so 'good'" property is precisely where Brydon can indulge in the comforting sentiment that he is *not* a real businessman. Thus, although the "great gaunt shell" on the jolly corner, because of its vacancy and its remove from the "lively stir" of commerce, soon becomes the symbolic center of Brydon's fantastic imaginings of ghosts, it is the building under construction that suggests an even more primary fantasy governing the narrative: namely, that James's character has no active part in the "gross generalisation of wealth and force and success" (439) that he finds so alien and alienating.

Working from McGurl's argument that the romance mode allows aristocratic values to "continue to be possessed"—though as a "function of consciousness," or an "intellectual property"—we might read Spencer Brydon as nostalgic for the days of a possessor class that by the date of James's story was no longer secure of its possessorship.[19] But Brydon's rentier lifestyle is hardly a backwards or *pre*modern one but is generated, ironically, by a newly financializing economy in which rising commercial property values happen to also benefit inherited wealth and aristocratic landownership. Brydon's sentimentality about the property on the jolly corner disavows his implication in one of the most modern sites of financial accumulation—urban real estate development. He imagines himself to be an aristocratic anachronism, although his wealth is generated by the leading edge of the city's expansion. As new modes of financial accumulation are made possible by the "lively stir" of capitalism and the "multiplied numbering" of streets, so too the rise of property values is fueled by a cycle of gentrification and rising rents to which Brydon's own project of "renovation at a high advance" contributes.

Nicola Nixon has read the drama of Brydon and his rival in historical terms as drawing upon the "mysterious illegibility" of corporate entities and corporate figureheads in the turn-of-the-century popular imagination.[20] The vacant house at the center of "The Jolly Corner," Nixon writes, "resonates with the ambiguity of an establishment neither quite commercial nor quite domestic, a non-place characterized by the hugely suggestive absence that James found so remarkable about the United States."[21] In this reading Brydon's search for the specter that haunts the empty house becomes an "act of incorporation," an attempt to consume and integrate an alter ego in a way that ultimately fully implicates the self more fully in new "corporate" forms of personhood. The strength of this argument is its insistence on the insufficiency of approaching the text exclusively as a Jamesian drama of consciousness. Nixon's tracing of the narrative's commercial and financial context emphasizes the specific historical interval of time between these two central figures:

> The alter ego is . . . very much the businessman Brydon might have
> been, had he stayed in the United States and remained statically placed
> in a reconstruction economy, or the scarred businessman that
> Christopher Newman presumably would have been, had he not backed
> away from the ferocity of the U.S. market and gone to Europe. James's
> insistence on the semantics of Brydon's fantasy of the "might have

been" accentuates, in its conditionality, not just the hypothetical but the historically distant hypothetical of thirty-three years prior to Brydon's return.[22]

The "ravaged" specter encountered in the climactic scene, with its maimed hand and horrifying visage, suggests a nostalgic projection of an economy of "transparent legibility." Embodying the wounds of the market, the specter *appears* to be at one with his activities, in what might be called, following Walter Benn Michaels, a gold standard of selfhood. Ironically, therefore, when Brydon renounces his alternative self, what he truly reveals is the outdatedness of his fantasy of what his business self would look like. His is a backwards, anachronistic imagination of the businessman's body as physically marked, as opposed to the reality of the modern businessman's "mysterious illegibility." Reading the "fictional dissolution and disincorporation of the individual" as a testament to Brydon's commercial contemporaneity" dramatizes the making of modern corporate personhood, in which the visible scars of capital have been replaced by an abstract figuration of circulation or exchange.[23]

This reading of the "spectral" figure of corporate-hood valuably highlights the story's perceived discrepancy between old and new economies. It less adequately accounts for the irony of the story's conclusion. Critics have disagreed about whether the discordant introduction of sentimentality in the final scene is happy, sinister, or something else entirely.[24] Nixon compares the scene of Brydon's sentimental "recuperation" by Alice to similar "lachrymose scenes" in *Silas Lapham,* Frank Norris's *The Pit*, and Dreiser's *The Financier*, in which the "bruised capitalist hero is comforted, unmanned, and reborn into domestic harmony promised by the sympathy and love of his wife or lover." But, she argues, Brydon is not "simply . . . another Lapham, Jadwin, or Cowperwood, tearfully cushioned in a feminine lap" because he has not actually been vanquished. He has won against his rival by coming to embody the corporeality of the new economy, successfully performing modern corporatism's dispossession of self and "dissolution" of individuality. Brydon's "destabilization" of coherent selfhood, Nixon argues, is evidence of his immunity to the restorative power of such sympathy.[25]

But returning to a reading of the text as drama of consciousness reveals the extent to which this sentimentality—or in McGurl's terms, romance—constitutes a final, triumphant displacement of productivity into performative terms. Nixon is right to identify the last scene as self-consciously generic. In my reading, however, there is an asymmetry of insight and of language between the characters that disturbs the sentimental surface of the scene. If Alice appears to represent the power of a female-identified sympathy that could potentially rehabilitate the male hero, it is because Brydon projects *his* sentimental vision onto her. In fact, Brydon's insistence on reading them together as characters in a nineteenth-century romance who triumph over market values makes it only more plausible that he misinterprets Alice's meaning throughout, failing to grasp that his devoted companion—like John Marcher's companion in *Beast in the Jungle*—has a startlingly realistic view of his limitations.

In fact, Alice may belong to a different—and more realist—genre of fiction altogether. As she cradles Brydon's head in her lap, she remarks that she knew, and had known all along, that he would finally see his alternate self.

> "Ah but I didn't!" cried Brydon with his long wail. "There's somebody—an awful beast; whom I brought, too horribly, to bay. But it's not me."
>
> At this she bent over him again, and her eyes were in his eyes. "No—it's not you." And it was as if, while her face hovered, he might have made out in it, hadn't it been so near, some particular meaning blurred by a smile. "No, thank heaven," she repeated—"it's not you! Of course it wasn't to have been."
>
> "Ah but it *was*," he gently insisted. And he stared before him now as he had been staring for so many weeks. "I was to have known myself."
>
> "You couldn't!" she returned consolingly. (482)

The conditional tense of what he "might have made out" in her face suggests a comfortable misreading that is commensurate with the equally conditional failure of "what might have been" in his life. Though Brydon takes quick consolation from Alice's response, she has not actually denied his relation to the beast. All that she has affirmed with "it wasn't to have been" and "You couldn't!" is Brydon's failure of self-recognition. And even while reassuring him of the incommensurability of his two selves, Alice demonstrates a clearer-sighted ability to confront the strange on its own terms:

> "And when this morning I again saw [him] I knew it would be because you had. . . . *He* seemed to tell me of that. So why," she strangely smiled, "shouldn't I like him?"
>
> It brought Spencer Brydon to his feet. "You 'like' that horror—?"
>
> "I *could* have liked him. And to me," she said, "he was no horror. I had accepted him."
>
> "'Accepted'—?" Brydon oddly sounded.

"Before, for the interest of his difference—yes. And as *I* didn't
disown him, as *I* knew him—which you at last, confronted with him in
his difference, so cruelly didn't, my dear—well, he must have been, you
see, less dreadful to me." (484)

Shocked that Alice does not reject the ghostly alter ego, Brydon does not
entertain the possibility that the living ego she holds in her arms is an even
worse "horror." Alice conceivably accepts Brydon's assertion of difference
from his rival as a necessary self-deception. Reading Alice as having a
more "realist" point of view means that Brydon's horrified rejection of his
alter ego as "not me" no longer looks like the turning point in the narrative that critics have conventionally interpreted it to be, but instead as the
confirmation and intensification of his willful mystification of economic
selfhood. His expressions ("thanks to you, dearest") mark his confidence
in the power of nineteenth-century sentimental convention to "save" him
from the twentieth-century market. But there is no reason to think Alice,
who in this conversation "kept the clearness that was like the breath of
infallibility," shares the illusion. Her use of the term "interest" ("for the
interest of his difference"), in contrast to his language of the beautiful (she
"beautifully" smiled) suggests that she does not artificially separate the
market from sentimental spheres but instead accepts their necessary interdependence. If she has "saved" him, as he believes, it may be by preserving
the necessary fiction of his noneconomic selfhood.

Perhaps, then, this is where the text's real turn to the grotesque is
located: in Brydon's continuing to identify as a sentimental actor rather
than an economic one. His sense of himself as thirty-three years behind the
times is a consoling fiction that conceals his membership in an emergent
financial class. Yet it is exactly this nostalgic anachronicity that defines the
modern rentier consciousness, in which self-interest is sentimentally incorporated as a component of modern ownership and displaces the "reality"
of wage-labor and of laboring bodies.

This reading of production as a movement into the realm of consciousness might seem to confirm the claim to modernism for James's work. Yet
it is a modernism that depends on a repression of economic relations—
a distorted economic innocence—that is ironically made possible by new
modes of financial circulation. The option to retreat to agrarian landownership like Lapham is presumably diminished. However, Brydon's self-
distancing from *relations* of production (his "return" to himself at the end
of the story) is, in its way, forwardly oriented. He does not withdraw;
instead, in a perhaps even more historically illuminating twist, he finds
a way to both have his property and rent it too. It is this destabilization

of the value hierarchy of productive and nonproductive work where, we might say, that modern proportions and values are truly upside down.

Dreiser's Financial Naturalism

Like Silas Lapham, *The Financier*'s Frank Cowperwood quits speculating in the stock market because it is too much like "gambling."[26] This is not a withdrawal from the sphere of finance, however, but the beginning of a deeper engagement. Cowperwood buys up municipal streetcar stocks and "pyramids" them into a set of local monopolies. In cooperation with an inept city treasurer, he also manages the investment of a city loan fund, where he manipulates the fluctuations of value and timing of payments to make a handsome personal profit. Cowperwood's downfall comes in the panic of 1871. When nervous creditors call in their loans, he is unable to service his empire of debts and is left at the mercy of jealous rivals. His former patron, enraged that Cowperwood is unrepentant about having a secret affair with the patron's daughter, ensures he is tried and harshly sentenced. Soon after his release from prison, Cowperwood takes advantage of another panic to recoup his lost fortune, and the novel ends as he and his mistress prepare to leave Philadelphia and start over in Chicago—the setting of the sequel, *The Titan*.

Cowperwood disdains speculation, but this means only those market actions that cannot be completely predicted or controlled. To the extent that Cowperwood is "subtle" enough (Dreiser's word) to artificially manipulate the market, he is right to claim that he is no mere gambler. To be against speculation, in this context, is to redefine speculation as normal business. Whereas Lapham unsuccessfully tries to draw a clear distinction between the speculative and the nonspeculative, and Brydon blurs the distinction between productive and unproductive, the only principle operative for Cowperwood is his predictive judgment about the market. Finance becomes purely a matter of reading the market regardless of its "real" basis of value.

To expand credit and to manipulate market fluctuations might seem to represent a more vigorous form of economic individualism than to discover paint in the ground, or to recognize one's property interests in aesthetic or sentimental terms. Yet the passivity that strategically protects Lapham and Brydon from their own financial interests plays a role here too. "Mastery," a word frequently associated with Cowperwood, is used alternately as subject and object: Cowperwood is "masterful" and "finance was his master" (216). His "financial individuality" is marked by a powerful self-interest, a "subtle" personality, and a disinterested ability to reject conventional codes of behavior. Early critics of the novel used these traits to explain the financier in sociobiological and evolutionary terms—positing either his dominance of will or, alternately, his ability to "give up" free will in order to align himself with the forces of natural law.[27] Later critics have read the financier's sexual desires as a heuristic for his capitalist desires, and vice versa, as a method for exposing the text's systems of value and representation.[28] As I read it here, however, Cowperwood's "financial individuality" refers to his situatedness between capitalist and historical temporalities. To be a genius of finance—as Cowperwood is referred to many times—is to embrace a contradiction in which self-interest is most free when it subordinates itself to structural and historical logics.

Gustavus Stadler has characterized a popular nineteenth-century conception of genius as being in "possession by alterity," or an imagination of the individual in question as definitively "other," possessed by "temporalities and histories unassimilable to the dominant 'common sense' of the present."[29] In *The Financier*, genius is allied to the temporalities of finance, which exist in asynchronous relationship to history. Transcending the temporality of the present, genius leads to knowledge that is not new but undiscovered. For instance, the debt instruments Cowperwood thinks up are presented as if timeless:

> Already he had conceived in his own mind the theory of the "endless chain," or "agreeable formula," as it was later termed, of buying a certain property on a long-time payment and issuing stocks or bonds sufficient not only to pay your seller, but to reimburse you for your trouble, to say nothing of giving you a margin wherewith to invest in other things—allied properties, for instance, against which more bonds could be issued, and so on, ad infinitum. It became an old story later but it was new at the time, and he kept the thought closely to himself. (102)

Such a passage suggests that the cutting edge of financial strategies in the late 1860s is not new at all—or that it can be new many times over. Cowperwood does not invent the "endless chain" but reanimates it. In the multilayered temporality of the passage—from the first "already" to the "old story later"—the same idea becomes repeatedly discoverable under different circumstances. Genius is how the financier *realizes* capital in historical time.

Though Dreiser was hardly alone among naturalist writers in conceiving of the market in terms of natural "forces," *The Financier* is perhaps the most ambitious representation of "financial individuality" in American literature. The novel uses the financier as a formal vehicle for the realization of the dynamics between abstract and concrete. It is no coincidence,

therefore, that there is an unusually charged relationship between naturalism and historicism in the text: a complex accommodation of order and
disorder, progression and disruption, accident and determination. Like the
narrator, the financier sees from an unusually broad temporal perspective.
With his intuition of the "boundless commercial possibilities which existed
potentially in so vast a realm" as the American continent (77), Cowperwood is identified early in the novel with an expansive historical vision.
Dreiser explains, "His was not the order of speculative financial enthusiasm which, in the type known as the 'promoter,' sees endless possibilities
for gain in every unexplored rivulet and prairie reach; but the very vast-
ness of the country suggested possibilities which he hoped might remain
undisturbed" (77). Cowperwood sees beyond the immediate profitability
of the present to an altogether more comprehensive and systemic imagination of development. Likewise, his economic farsightedness is linked
to moral indifference, as in his startlingly disinterested assessment of the
threat of secession and the coming war between the states as "bad for
business."

While on the one hand the text narrates a kind of historical teleology
of finance capitalism in the United States, on the other hand it is deeply
preoccupied with finance's technical details. In its attention to these minu-
tiae, this long and unwieldy novel is perhaps unequalled in American literary realism. The technical descriptions become the formal register of a
naturalism that cannot be reduced to or conflated with its more conventional and recognizable modes, such as the laws of physical attraction or
competitive survival. In my reading, this attention to financial structures
begins to constitute a formal narrative claim that they exist beyond any
realization of them in actual time:

> He knew instinctively what could be done with a given sum of money—
> how as cash it could be deposited in one place, and yet as credit and the
> basis of moving checks, used in not one but many other places at the
> same time. When properly watched and followed this manipulation gave
> him the constructive and purchasing power of ten and a dozen times as
> much as his original sum might have represented. He knew instinctively
> the principles of "pyramiding" and "kiting." He could see exactly not
> only how he could raise and lower the value of these certificates of loan,
> day after day and year after year—if he were so fortunate as to retain his
> hold on the city treasurer—but also how this would give him a credit
> with the banks hitherto beyond his wildest dreams. (99)

Cowperwood's instincts lead him to recognize a set of abstract possibilities
that, in the narrative's view, already have some prior, ahistorical realization.

His "intuitions, the 'hunches' to act," that Dreiser insists "could not be so easily explained" (241), realize the financial movement between abstract and concrete.

Historically, then, the text narrates the era's financial lawlessness—scant regulation, haphazard enforcement, the public "interest" largely unarticulated—while at the same time focusing on the market as an abstract sphere of order, with laws of probability, cause and effect, action and reaction. If not a closed system, the laissez-faire market is nonetheless a delicately calibrated one, where each action reverberates on other parts of the system. And since the laws of interest cannot be subverted, the plot turns on the way that they are underestimated or misjudged, or that actions or intentions are misinterpreted, usually because of someone's limited perception of the totality of interests at stake.

The frequent use of the conditional tense to posit alternative outcomes confirms that Dreiser's history is a narrative of missed opportunities. Cowperwood gains advantages over his rivals for no reason other than that certain possibilities do not occur to them in time: "If they had thought at all on the matter, they would have decided that they did not want any outsider to interfere. As a matter of fact the street-railway business in Philadelphia was not sufficiently developed at this time to suggest to any one the grand scheme of union which came later" (101). Cowperwood's rivals fail to preempt him because they do not think. But thought itself is passive (the business was "not sufficiently developed . . . to suggest"), and the path of development is only to be *re*-cognized, not cognized in an original sense. Indeed, it is at moments when characters seem most actively in command of their own thought processes that Dreiser undermines them by resorting to the conditional tense: what someone *would have* decided under the circumstances, what *would have* happened if a different element had been introduced. Dreiser's conditionals do not frame persons or events as formations of habit, as Bill Brown argues that Frank Norris's do in *McTeague*, for instance, in which he describes the overall movement of the narrative toward repetition, reiteration, and predictability as signaling an effect of "everydayness."[30] In contrast to the "wouldness" of style of *McTeague*, where Brown describes characters as predictably constituted through their iterative patterns of thought and action ("McTeague would walk out to the end of the Union Street car line . . ."; "Very often . . . Trina would pause in her work . . ."),[31] Dreiser's "woulds" do not fuse description and narration in a truly iterative mode. Instead they alert us to the possibility of alternative outcomes: the infinite contingencies of cause and effect. The many "If . . . then" sentence constructions open the text to speculation on other historical outcomes and probabilities.

One way to understand the tension between naturalism and historicism in Dreiser's novel is to align these terms with Georg Lukács's "description" and "narration." In "Narrate or Describe?" Lukács posits description as antithetical to true historicality in the novel.[32] The more documentation-minded a text is, for Lukács, the further removed it is from a meaningful and unalienated relationship to history. Lukács acknowledges that in practice the difference between narration and description is hardly clear-cut, and neither truly exists without the other. Nonetheless, as Jennifer Fleissner observes, naturalist fiction is for Lukács a "profoundly ahistorical" genre.[33] It succumbs to the inevitably "contemporizing" effect of excessive description, failing to achieve the totalizing "proportions" of historical relations to be found in the great realist novels. Critics attending to the formal deficiencies of *The Financier* have noted its awkwardly alternating plot structure, the "transcriptive" quality of its financial descriptions, and its heavy-handed historical framing (at least one critic calls the historical narrative the novel's most "forced" aspect).[34] I suggest the problem of integration of the text's different narrative modes can be most clearly seen through its formal conflation of the historical and the ahistorical. The text seeks to *narrate* finance as opposed to describing it. Dreiser, in fact, often admits the inadequacy of description, pausing to acknowledge that readers might not understand what they are reading: "The plan Cowperwood developed after a few days' meditation will be plain enough to any one who knows anything of commercial transactions and financial manipulations, but a dark secret to those who do not" (93).

This is not then simply ahistoricism in Lukács's sense. Finance becomes a way of organizing history, its abstractions imposing a narrative structure on reality. It is only *in relation* to the historical that these structural pressures of capitalism can be perceived in the first place. The form of the novel as a whole expresses the contradiction of Dreiser's project: to historicize an account of capitalism that he conceives of as only partially historically accountable. In fact, we might say that just as the text seeks to *narrate* finance, it also attempts to *describe* history, as seen in the narrative's synchronic survey perspective: "Many of the things that we and [Cowperwood] knew later were not then in existence—the telegraph, telephone, express company, ocean steamer, city delivery of mail. There were no postage-stamps or registered letters. The street car had not arrived. In its place were hosts of omnibuses, and for longer travel the slowly developing railroad system still largely connected by canals" (5). To summarize: Dreiser's descriptions refer us to framing events, yet the framing narrative, in its tendency toward historical conditionality and circularity, ultimately functions as another, more elaborate form of description.

The text registers the constant pressures of other, probable outcomes and eventualities, reflecting its inescapability from the descriptive. Invoking endless possibilities of interaction, the text appears to construct, and aspire toward, a Lukácsian horizon of totality, while underscoring its own double movement.

Synchronic and diachronic temporalities are brought to crisis in scenes of financial panic. Cowperwood is ruined in 1871 when a great fire in Chicago precipitates business failures overnight in New York, which spreads panic to Philadelphia and causes creditors of all kinds to recall their loans. A long, circular series of scenes—Larzer Ziff describes them as "epitomiz[ing] the glacial power" of Dreiser's prose—shows Cowperwood struggling against the competitors who would force him to sell his streetcar shares at bargain prices and expose him to prosecution for his manipulation of city funds.[35] David A. Zimmerman has argued that the scenes of panic demonstrate the limits of narratability. Like the technical passages about finance, the panic "frustrates any attempt to bring the future into line, to plot it, to see it prospectively." This reading of the frustration of narrative would seem to confirm a diagnosis of ahistoricism in the Lukácsian sense. Zimmerman argues that *The Financier*'s "will-to-account" represents the "apotheosized abstraction" of the text; it "precedes human subjects, constituting them, shaping their ambitions, providing both the instrument and language in which individuals, acting out the mandates of nature, understand and carry out their plots."[36] However, even as the descriptive passages lead toward the abstract, as Zimmerman observes, the text as a whole does not abandon the historical for the structural. The abstract details, despite their "seeming marginality," always threaten to burst into historical time: they are secrets that *will become known*.

Thus, the circular telling and retelling of events during the panic does not foreclose narratability but instead underscores the conflict of temporalities. The conditions of the panic make temporarily visible a tight network of causes and effects. Having taken the reader through the ins and outs of Cowperwood's financial schemes, the narrative radically slows down to accommodate his race against the clock. The formal structure of Dreiser's narrative at this point, as Leigh Claire La Berge reads it, reflects the "temporal unevenness" of financial accumulation, its formal ability to "produce time by arranging it."[37] As Cowperwood says to his creditors, "It's time I want" and "Time is the only significant factor in this situation" (218). Putting it another way, history *stops* financial time at an instant when Cowperwood has a gap on his books that cannot be accounted for under the unexpected scrutiny of fixed time. Calculations of the future and accounts of the present are forcibly collapsed together. The historical actuality of the moment at least briefly overtakes the deferred, future temporality of capital and—for a few catastrophic days—holds the expansive temporality of capital hostage to the present. In other words, a capital conceived as formal is made suddenly, violently historical.

The recurring panics thus contribute to the sense of contingency that June Howard, in *Form and History*, calls intrinsic to the genre of naturalism—the sense that history might have turned out differently.[38] But to call the market a place where accidents will happen, as Walter Benn Michaels does—where cunning in Philadelphia cannot outwit bad luck in Chicago— is to register only its chanciness.[39] Bruce Robbins also addresses the contingency of the market in arguing that Cowperwood models a "no fault" attitude.[40] (Cowperwood declares that he should not be blamed by his creditors: "I did not create this panic. I did not set Chicago on fire" [233].) But to focus only on accident neglects the other side of the equation. Since finance is, in the naturalist imagination, always already systemic, "chance" is an ultimately makeshift explanation for causalities too subtle for observation and "accident" a weak way of naming unidentified forces. The accident is by definition an instance in which historical narrative is reduced to the descriptive.

In fact, we might see Dreiser's revision of the novel in 1927 as a recommitment to the basic conflict between description and narration. Following the successful publication of *An American Tragedy* in 1925, Dreiser rewrote *The Financier* in a way that eliminated about a third of the original text. The revised version—the only one in print today—effectively replaced the 1912 version in Dreiser's oeuvre. At least one critic feels that the revised novel softened the financier, making Cowperwood more "subtle," his egocentrism less insistent, his moral standing more legible to an audience that had recently encountered George Babbitt (in 1922) and Jay Gatsby (in 1925).[41] More to the point, in my view, Dreiser significantly reduced the philosophical framing but not the amount of financial description (even though his publisher had already tried unsuccessfully in 1912 to convince him that the lengthy descriptive and historical passages were peripheral to the novel). As a result, the 1927 text downplays the language of social competitiveness. Going beyond the resources of social-Darwinist discourse, it more insistently situates its naturalism in the struggle between synchronicity and diachronicity. In a scene in the 1912 edition, a speculator facing ruin begs Cowperwood's employer to cancel his most recent trades. The employer, acting on "hard logic, sad and cruel," refuses. In the 1927 edition this scene is reduced to a brief description without spoken dialogue, deemphasizing individual suffering in favor of the general panorama of chaos. Financial crisis becomes a descriptive disruption that clarifies the movement of history. The panic of 1873 is characterized as "one of those peculiar things which spring naturally out of the optimism of the American people and the irrepressible progress of the country" (435). According to the "equational law" of Dreiser's naturalism, by which actions in one part of the system produce equal and opposite reactions in another, the panic appears as the painful but necessary "correction" occasionally called forth by the teleology of history.[42]

That the financier achieves his greatest strength at a moment of widespread ruin might suggest that the text shares the ambivalence of the age about finance, reflecting Americans' fascination with and mistrust of Wall Street. The text is clear-eyed about the historical consequences of financial concentration and of business's ease in outpacing the law. But the sweeping descriptions of historical events tend to read less as social critique than as paeans to the New Economy of the late nineteenth century and to the titans who realize its possibilities. The text is less about the loss of autonomy or control on the part of the individual than about the scramble to "align" oneself with market opportunities. As the genius of this moment, the financier emerges to negotiate between competing models of history. Positioned to exploit gaps and inconsistencies between progressivist and naturalist temporalities, the financier represents the formal conflation of the historical and antihistorical in Dreiser's narrative.

Like Howells and James, Dreiser similarly uses character as a device for controlling the representation of abstraction. But in the naturalist novel, where capitalism is increasingly conceived as a "determinative" system, the consequences are different. The financier does not evoke resistance against the financial imaginary but becomes a catalyzing figure for it. And, paradoxically, a naturalized, abstract system of finance does not mitigate the demands of economic individualism. If anything, it raises the stakes — but in the terms of exceptionality (genius) rather than production. Again, the difference is evident across the three texts. In a Howellsian realism stabilized by labor, the value of production is emptied out: Lapham is left "standing out alone for nothing." In the Jamesian ironization of modern financial consciousness, the rentier seeks nostalgic refuge in aesthetic nonproductivity. And in Dreiser's naturalization of finance as a rational system rather than an irrational force, the financier's genius replaces production altogether. Cowperwood resembles Lapham and Brydon in becoming a curiously passive figure at important moments of financial action. But his strategic passivity — his apparent indifference to productive agency — does not reflect the same anxieties about the waning of an economy on which the legibility of ethical relations and class relations had depended. Nor does the text aim to reassert a stable or possessive value over the dangers of immaterial, speculative, and abstract value. Instead, the formal incorporation of financial abstraction as the "logic" of the text marks the historical end of one kind of capitalist realism, where market value is grounded in character, and the beginning of another kind of capitalist realism, where character and history are both grounded in the market.

The chapter that follows—on a novel of 1980s real estate—continues the focus on character, arguing that *Good Faith* carries forward the theme of "economic virtue" to the late twentieth century. However, the subsequent chapters do not. Instead, I expand the discussion of the financial imaginary beyond the issues of agency, class, and labor to encompass other formal dimensions such as those of "epic" narrative aesthetics, systemic relations of subject and object, and the accumulative aesthetics of the global. With the exception of Frank Norris's *The Octopus*, which I take up in chapter 3, my objective is not to propose a strict correlation between the late nineteenth-century texts already discussed and the contemporary texts to follow. Instead it is to shift the representation of capitalist abstraction into contemporary terms and to compare what these newer systems of the financial imaginary reveal about the formal and historical persistence of the novel's attachments to "realist truth."

CHAPTER TWO

Reaganomic Realisms

Real Estate, Character, and Crisis in
Jane Smiley's *Good Faith*

Realist Attentions

In 1991 a *New York Review of Books* reviewer asserted that all recent
books about the S&L crisis had been published prematurely. In light of
the large volume of journalistic writing about the crisis—the review covered seven books representing a combined 2,200 pages—Michael Thomas
argued that "it is still too early to get the picture whole, in a way that will
raise and broaden public awareness of very large, unpleasant, and unignorable questions about what kind of a country we have turned out to be and
what we may expect . . . from the future." Even after the passage of time
it will still be "an extremely difficult story to tell in a fashion that would
provoke the kind of outrage it deserves. Very probably, it needs a novelist
to get it right in its larger dimensions."[1]

Jane Smiley's novel *Good Faith* takes up just such "large, unpleasant,
and unignorable" moral questions about America in the 1980s.[2] Instead
of modeling the novel's ability to meet the demand for outrage, however,
it even more powerfully underscores the misalignment between narratives
of virtue and narratives of crisis discovered by Thomas in the journalistic
accounts. Examination of this narrative misalignment in Smiley's novel
offers evidence that the shift toward financial modes of accumulation,
away from a "real" capitalism based on production of goods and services,
doesn't reduce the pressure on moral character as a basis for predicting,
evaluating, and understanding market behavior. In fact, just the reverse:
financial abstraction presses notions of character into greater service. Even
as character becomes a less stable or reliable index to economic legibility,
therefore, the interpretive demands made upon economic virtue have persisted and even strengthened.

The reading that follows takes two paths. The first is to analyze a narrative redistribution of realist attention. As the terrain of social legibility moves from the individual and the person-based to the topography of real estate in the novel, it is houses that become reading matter, landscapes that become a primary text of historical and cultural shifts. The second path is to examine how this displacement of character reading and movement toward a structural canvas ends up recentered on character. The paradox of Reaganomic realism is that it is more about character than ever. Even where the contemporary economic novel appears to seek a landscape-oriented mode of reading rather than a portrait one, it exposes how powerfully attached to portrait modes we remain. In what follows I argue not that we should shift our mode of reading *from* the characterological to the structural but to examine how the structural is inevitably thrown back into the personified terms of economic virtue, agency, intentionality, and choice. Together these two paths of analysis demonstrate some of the contradictory terms of contemporary economic realism.

Real estate is *Good Faith*'s primary site for examining the historical and economic transformations of the 1980s. The novel can be read as proposing housing as the most fundamental "text" of late twentieth-century financial topographies. Without attention to the landscape, it seems, Reaganomics cannot be understood all the way down. To represent this landscape, a full interpenetration of economic, moral, and aesthetic realisms is required. "Taste is not a moral issue," protests the narrator at one point, as he expostulates with an aesthetically principled subcontractor who rejects a customer's request for a particular fence style. But the narrator is wrong; taste *is* a moral issue. The problem goes deeper than the fence-builder's personal objection to postmodern aesthetic incoherence. The real-estate landscape in *Good Faith* represents with powerful specificity how questions of social distribution and economic privilege have been increasingly channeled into narrower and privatized terms, such as those of consumer preferences and styles. Changing real-estate tastes become symptoms of the deeper economic restructurings of the period, as well as other cultural and subjective transformations in which they play a part.

There can be no doubt about the novel's investment in economic realism. "This would be '82," begins its retrospective first-person narrator. References abound to economic and business indicators of the early 1980s, including high inflation and interest rates, S&L deregulation, changes in the mortgage industry, and scattered mentions of tax restructuring, junk bonds, T-bill futures, capital gains, and gold markets. At the same time, the transformations of the 1980s are not just business. Changing attitudes, values, and class markers also produce the neoliberal shift to new modes of accumulation. Economic realisms are required for a moral and ethical analysis of Reaganomics, according to the novel, and any moral and ethical analysis leads back to the economy. Marcus Burns, a would-be real-estate developer and the novel's cheerleader for financial risk taking, often refers to "what's happening in Washington" and the "recent election" to support his theory of a coming business revolution. "Experience doesn't count anymore," he argues. "It's just a drag on you, because if you make decisions according to your experience, you will have no idea what is happening in this country" (76). Ironically, all of this promoter's predictions about the 1980s come true. People *will* buy drinking water if it is carbonated and bottled in small greenish bottles. S&Ls *will* be allowed to invest in anything. One *can* avoid paying debts simply by taking out bigger loans.

For readers who fault the novel for lack of suspense—as at least one reviewer complained—Marcus's heartiness is one of the cues that make his status as the villain of the story predictable. It is warning enough that Marcus is the sort of person who, in 1982, is eager to see the savings and loan industry become high-risk. His melodramatic laugh clinches it. Here he and the narrator discuss a local banker:

> [Marcus] "So he started out as a teller when he was twenty-two,
> putting money in a drawer and taking it out, and he's been thinking
> small for fifteen years. The S and L business has hardly been high-risk."
> "God forbid," I said.
> Marcus laughed, a loud, hearty laugh. Then he said, "Look, why
> don't you stay away from Crosbie? I'll do the talking." (110–11)

If the shadiness of Marcus's character is never in doubt, it is not because of a failure of character development but because of the fact that a typological abstraction—the con man—has been substituted for the particularization of personality and motivation that are associated with moral realism. To the reader with even the sketchiest knowledge of the S&L collapse to come within a few years, the plot of the novel will feel overdetermined. From this perspective, the hearty laugh is not a cue to the movement toward realist interiority but instead a signal that the text will resist "developed" realism in favor of genre flattening. The laugh suggests that the suspense in this contemporary realism is not about the revelation of an interior psychology but the ambiguity of a character's formal *status*. Within an otherwise highly realist framework, I argue, the novel features its own struggle to resolve the status of "character" for contemporary economic fiction. *Good Faith* adapts a Howellsian realism of character-based economic virtue to an analysis of the de-realization of the 1980s economy through real estate.

S&L Financescapes

To Marcus it is obvious where the gold rush of the 1980s will happen. "I'm telling you, house owning isn't like it ever was before in the history of the world. Inflation killed the old world, and the population explosion is remaking it!" (78). When a timid, small-town zoning board is daunted by the size of his proposed new housing development, he dazzles the board into consent by simply making the project bigger:

> Two hundred houses there, four hundred houses here, the little shopping center—I think Jim Crosbie is going to go for it in a big way, especially when he realizes that with this deregulation of the S and Ls that Congress just passed, he can get a branch of his savings-and-loan out here before anyone else thinks about it. And they're going to let S and Ls develop properties now. It looks to me like they're going to let them do just about anything they want. . . . A savings-and-loan branch and a few tasteful and convenient stores and some office space would brighten the area up, is what I think. And with six hundred houses, there would have to be a school. That's always a lucrative project. (177)

The S&L references here link the financial restructuring of the post-1970s with its specific impact on the local landscape. The springing up of branch offices at shopping intersections metonymize the ramping up of otherwise hard-to-figure forms of financialization and "disembedding" of capital that marked the beginning of "late" capital accumulation—even before full deregulation of the savings and loan industry in 1982 made the S&Ls an ideal speculative tool.

Without reviewing the widely available history of S&L deregulation, it is worth focusing briefly on one aspect of the change: the industry's delocalization. Before the Garn–St. Germain Act of 1982—which an S&L spokesman publicly called the "Emancipation Proclamation for America's savings institutions"[3]—savings and loan operations had been limited to fifty-mile regions.[4] Afterward, they could not only nearly "do anything" as Marcus gleefully predicts above but could do it anywhere. The act granted S&Ls the freedom to invest in nearly any kind of business, not just mortgages, and to compete for deposits everywhere, not just from local depositors.[5] In 1985 *Business Week* boldly declared: "Start an S&L. Offer a premium interest rate and watch the deposits roll in. Your depositors are insured by Uncle Sam, so they don't care what you do with their money. And in states like California, you can do almost anything you want with it. Add enormous leverage—you can pile $100 of assets on every $3 of capital—and you've built a speculator's dream machine."[6] Domestic and locally based

mortgage lending could suddenly operate more like other kinds of globally fluid investment. The contemporaneous arrival of computer technology made it possible to transfer funds quickly, and the "thrifts" were able
to draw on geographically unlimited capital to underwrite far-flung ventures. By amalgamating local funds and funneling them upward and outward, the thrifts began a process of emancipation from local economies in
a way that parallels accounts of capital's material and territorial "disembedding" following the end of the financial contractions of the 1970s.

Smiley's S&L references call attention to the ways in which 1980s financial restructuring is both *delocalizing* and *relocalizing*. The small town, as
portrayed in the novel, is being reorganized by the same fluid investment
capital as the urban centers around which the processes of gentrification,
redevelopment, and renewal have been so extensively theorized. Local
economies are being resituated within a national division of financial spe-
cialization. (Marcus at one point offhandedly mentions that most of the
big national real-estate-development companies are in North Carolina.)
A total history of the ways that post-1970s investment dollars began to
compete across greater distances would have to address how the consequent fluctuations of value (in rent and commercial real-estate prices)
reshaped speculative markets at a national level, produced new geographic
divisions of labor across the country, and produced new sortings of the
population according to work, housing, and immigration opportunities.
These work and population shifts in turn reshaped the map of developable
and marketable areas of the United States. In other words, even a small
Rust Belt town that "was missed when the railroad went southeast of here
in the early part of the century" (91) suddenly becomes visible to develop-
ers from the high-speed political and economic corridors running between
Washington and California. Indeed, the undeveloped small town looks increasingly attractive, its aesthetic of "localness" marketable as an alternative to suburban sprawl. Second homes, Marcus muses. People from the
city. ("You heard of a time-share?" [78].)

In this context, middle-class homeownership makes available a densely
layered cross-section for the structural analysis of Reaganomics at the
most local level. The novel's references to S&Ls link local business development to a post-1970s narrative of inflationary crisis, overaccumulation,
and real estate as an investment haven for national and global capital.
Indeed, Marcus predicts the coming flood of investment capital that can
reshape the country:

> It's all changing! I'm telling you, this time last year I was reading
> income tax returns. It's like reading the book of the future, to read

income tax returns all day. There's money everywhere. Money money
money! You know what they say at the IRS? Reported income is like
cockroaches. For every dollar you see, there are a hundred more in
hiding. And it's looking for a home! Don't you understand how things
work? There's a lot more money than there are good investments, or
even investments at all, even bad investments. . . . Money these days is
like water. It can't stop looking for a place to go. It's filled up all the
places it usually goes, and now it's lapping at the shore and seeking out
other nooks and crannies. (178–79)

He is right: the rules *have* changed. With the deflationary crises of the late
1970s in the rearview mirror and deregulation in full swing, the search is
on for new opportunities for risk as well as for places to "park" capital
that are protected against global market volatility. Marcus's analysis
aligns perfectly with critical accounts of the international speculation in
the 1980s as investment dollars seeking high-return markets found their
way to real estate.[7] The explosive growth of real-estate markets in major
financial centers New York and Boston, and corresponding urban redevelopment and gentrification, was significantly driven by international investment. In the United States, domestic anxieties about American economic
competitiveness would become most famously articulated around the sale
of Rockefeller Center to Japanese investors in 1989.

But the story of real estate in this period is not just the urban and suburban development of the postwar era; it is a story of finance becoming
"local." In an increasingly global economy, the financial processes of delocalization are combined with the cultural re-valuing of authentic, small-
town "localness" to produce a 1980s version of the frontier narrative. It
is the "lesson of the history of American settlement," Marcus declares,
that "you should not wait for a town to grow by itself. You must make the
town come to you. People don't know what they want until you sell it to
them." Housing becomes the new financial frontier. Real-estate speculation reverses the narrative of westward settlement to make another pass
of economic extraction over the country. The *Business Week* quotation
above focuses on speculation through California-chartered thrifts. In the
novel the "West" is correspondingly positioned as both the engine room
of real-estate speculation and of the consumer demands that would help
drive it, in which the westward gaze is re-marketed to homebuyers as a
desirable West Coast consumer aesthetic.

It is worth pausing on the connection of the Washington–California
circuit to the S&L industry. In S&L history, the name "California" (along
with "Texas") is nearly synonymous with the industry's delocalization.
Analysts have called California the state in which the industry, in effect,

went stateless. As thrifts sought charters in states with the least amount of regulation, the promise to "do almost anything you want"—Marcus's language almost exactly echoes the language from *Business Week*—becomes synonymous with the "Californianization" of the industry. This "Californianization" of real-estate speculation follows and extends postwar demographic shifts from the Rust Belt to the Sun Belt. Historian Michael Schaller writes: "Even as Reagan spoke of 'morning in America,' the sun began to set on traditional Northeast and Midwest industries such as steel, rubber, machine tools, and automobile manufacturing."[8] Indeed, California— which was already benefiting from the defense spending enhanced under the governorship of Ronald Reagan from 1967 to 1975—was one of the first states to experience a construction boom resulting from a "spigot of easy commercial mortgage money."[9]

The results of these demographic shifts in the postwar era and late twentieth century have been extensively analyzed in studies of urban renewal and the development of suburbs and "edge cities." Complex narratives of race and class have informed critics' attention to the geographies of sprawl. One urban sociologist argues that real estate functions as the "primary economic vehicle of neoliberalism at the local scale."[10] Smiley's novel takes up the same politics of neoliberal spatialization that inform these critical accounts—but from a distinct point of view that is neither city nor suburb. In focusing on the semirural small town, it suggests the need to reconceive the narrative of finance capitalism from a series of much more localized vantage points. Moreover, it suggests the need to take into account how homeownership changed ordinary Americans' level of entanglement with finance.

It was the thrifts that helped to establish the culture of homeownership in America. According to *Fortune* magazine, the S&L industry did "more than any other kind of private enterprise to convert the U.S. from a nation of renters into one in which two out of three families own their own homes."[11] Lending primarily to local and first-time buyers, a role they filled in the forty years from the New Deal to the Reagan presidency, the S&Ls made possible the meanings of stability and community associated with postwar suburbanization and single-family homeownership. The "thrifts," according to Pilzer, "made homeownership possible on an unprecedented scale, revitalizing an American dream that had been shattered by the Depression."[12] By 1970 a majority of American householders had become homeowners, making the S&L industry, arguably, inseparable from the meaning of real-estate ownership itself.

Catherine Jurca, in her study of the literature of the postwar American suburb, has argued against the critical commonplace that home and market operate as separate and opposed spheres. Instead of the home as a sentimental space that protects and compensates individuals from the injuries of the commercial space, postwar suburban fiction posits "a beneficial fluidity between homes and businesses," an affinity that is not based on "an outworn tension between home and market."[13] In Smiley's text the home is not only inseparable from the market but is also, beginning in the 1980s, a key site for the redistribution of social wealth and the consolidation of class power. Rising property values were, for homeowners, one of the tradeoffs that made Reaganomics politically sustainable—counterbalancing the destabilizing effects of deregulation, anti-union policies, and declining real wages. The S&L context thus speaks directly to the transformation in the United States from an economy based on concerns about social distribution to an economy based on the protection of wealth. Homeownership is one of the means to measure being *in* the market as much as representing security *against* the market.

Sociologists have explained the development of a "local" aesthetic in relation to an increasingly integrated global market. In an analysis of land preservation battles in a wealthy New York suburb, in which community members made strenuous efforts to retain the feel of an "undeveloped" landscape, Duncan and Duncan write: "In the United States, among other things, globalization has produced a nostalgia for small town communities. It is a longing for simpler, quieter, more wholesome places that have an air of historical authenticity and an aura of uniqueness about them, without forcing oneself to be divorced from the many benefits of globalization enjoyed by the more privileged members of society."[14] The conservative politics, class protectionism, and entrenchment of inequality that such nostalgia fosters have been described by David Harvey as exemplifying "the reactionary politics of an aestheticized spatiality."[15] While Smiley's novel focuses more on the generation of an upper-middle-class production/consumption cycle rather than on the rise of exclusionary NIMBY politics or homeowner voting blocs, one can nonetheless trace an aesthetics of class consolidation in the production of these new styles and tastes. A passage near the beginning of the novel describing a local housing development, for example, retraces an entire geography of American social ascent, with the three "Phases" of the development representing the chapters of an aesthetic-historical narrative. The starter homes of "Phase One" begin with the colonial models: "Maryland," "Virginia," and "South Carolina." Phase Two looks westward with the "Sonoma," "Mendocino," and "Santa Rosa." Phase Three concludes with WASP nostalgia and the reconcentration of class power around old-money centers of the Northeast (the "Greenwich," "Ardsley," and "Hastings"). Through these phases the ideological cycle of American ascent can be endlessly reproduced: "At this point the ideal couple was expected to finance the down payment of their eldest child and his or her spouse in one of the Phase One houses, which now had mature landscaping and the individuality born of age and idiosyncratic property ownership" (28).

The financialization of homeownership and the financialization of class are thus two sides of the same coin. Deregulation of the S&Ls can be seen as one of the first chapters in the narrative of the neoliberalization of the middle class. In the following section, I will discuss a second major feature of the structural "adjustment" of the American middle class to meet the demands of Reaganomics: tax politics. Indeed, deregulation and property rights are twin features of the neoliberal engagement with the real estate market. Since real estate is for the middle class the site of greatest opportunity and risk exposure, owning a home is not just a matter of security or status but a primary site of wealth concentration. Taxes, as we will see, speak to the same class protectionism but through the different discourse of property rights.

The Taxpaying Classes

Based on his previous career working at the IRS, Marcus has developed a far-reaching theory about the impact of demographic transformations on the economy: "And here's the key. More people means scarcer resources, scarcer resources mean inflation, and inflation means property and interest-bearing capital have a higher value and work has a lower value. It's as simple as that" (147). Marcus here articulates—accurately of course—an entire paradigm shift in which property will increasingly become the basis for the widening distinction between a laboring class and an asset class. Apparently untroubled by oil-crisis-era anxiety about population growth, resource scarcity, increased social competition, or problems of environmental impact, Marcus anticipates (again, correctly) the end-of-century inversion of values of nonproduction over production and financialized accumulation over work earnings. "You know what I hate the most?" Marcus asks Joe. "I hate paying taxes." If S&Ls represent financialization from the deregulatory side, Marcus's strategy of (not) taxpaying represents the supply side:

"You know the simplest way to avoid paying taxes?"
  "Obviously not."
  "The simplest legal way that takes no cheating and no creative bookkeeping and passes every audit?"

"No."

"You live on borrowed money. You sell the property piece by piece to pay the interest and you keep borrowing more. . . ."

"That's assuming that—"

"That the value of the property keeps rising. And it does."

"I don't know, what with interest rates so high—"

"It does. That's the lesson of the Beatles. More and more people who like things nice, who are educated and have good taste, are just starting to come into some real money. Families with two ambitious adults in the workforce instead of one. Gay couples." (150)

Here is a condensed narrative of the subsumption of post-sixties class politics into status-driven "lifestyles." Gay couples equal two incomes and no kids. The lesson of the Beatles is the "maturing" of cultural rebellion into consumer identities: "Record buyers. Burger buyers. Blue jeans buyers. *Hmm mmm.* Customers. I mean, in this last election, everyone breathed a sigh of relief. Finally the sixties were over and the revolution had ended and something bad had happened to all those kids—they, or we, got our just deserts. We disappeared or grew up or something. The Carter years taught us the long-awaited lesson" (147). In connecting taxes, borrowing, and the mechanics of class mobility, Marcus's lecture anticipates the upscaling of consumer spending that would take place in the 1980s even as the bases of the working classes were being dismantled.[16] Barbara Ehrenreich famously described the U.S. middle class of the 1980s as marked by a "fear of falling"; meanwhile, *Newsweek* called 1984 the "Year of the Yuppie."[17] What one critic has called the "financialization of class" describes, in part, how class anxieties are made increasingly leverageable in the consumer marketplace.[18] Yuppie consumption becomes one of the most visible cultural effects of the reorganization of accumulation. A theoretical account for this expansion of a consumer-driven class-consciousness can be found in David Harvey's description of capital's hoped-for "consumption solution," in which the rising contradictions of global overaccumulation supposedly would be addressed through a general "mobilization of all the artifices of need inducement and cultural transformation that this implies."[19] As capital seeks solutions to structural contradictions through American buying power, consumers embrace "everyday" financialization through personal debt, investment retirement plans, and the leveraging of homeowner equity.[20]

It is vital to note that the cultural transformation of consumption in the 1980s is not founded on wages, which were steadily decreasing in real terms, but on rising property values. Real estate becomes the focus of a range of entitlements and protections as rising property values—together with an economic conservatism that favors homeowners—make a whole new consumer aesthetics available to the property-owning class. Retailers sell upscale antiques and Scandinavian bedding. The diner renovates into a self-referentially postmodern "diner." On inspecting a new "luxury" housing development, the narrator remarks, "Looking back, I would have to say that that's when the eighties began, as far as I was concerned—the first week in June, 1982, when modest housing in our rust-belt state got decked out with Italian tile" (71).

Here again the novel looks west. If Washington is the metonym for politics happening on the right, California stands for the consumer side of Reaganomics to the left. The West Coast is where deregulatory and cultural aspects of the 1980s converge. No character ever travels to California (just as the name "Reagan" is never used in the novel), but buyers admire kitchen tile that looks like "my sister's house in California." The new restaurant has a "chef from California." Marcus casually refers to the "golf course at Pebble Beach" as a model for his development deal. The West Coast, uniting business interests with consumption patterns, is where the real-estate market and consumption demographics converge.

What cultural accounts of 1980s consumerism tend to overlook, however, is the context of the rise of antitax discourse. When homeowners embrace tax resistance movements in the name of individual property rights—as they did beginning in California in the late 1970s—tax politics become, in effect, another front of middle-class protectionism.[21] Taxes are a means for individual homeowners to position themselves to benefit from the neoliberal push to greater privatization and to serve as a bulwark against the instabilities of the economy. Maintaining downward pressure on property taxes offsets the risks endemic to an increasingly speculative and financialized economy. Together these protectionist and speculative flanks of real-estate culture demonstrate how housing has become the primary site to manage the mixed symptoms of class security. Or as Toporowski puts it, "in an era of financialization, the mass of the middle class is sedated and deprived of the need to think by escalating property values."[22]

It is particularly useful in this context to consider the history and politics of California's Prop 13. This antitax voter initiative of 1978 has been extensively analyzed by political scientists, tax scholars, policy experts, and journalists. Championed as a grassroots movement, the measure was a direct response to a dramatically rising real-estate market in which property taxes, which were based on a house's market value, could inflate much more quickly than incomes and potentially force longtime residents out of their homes. Prop 13 supporters framed rising housing prices as a threat to "community stability" (although the measure was heavily sponsored by businesses and corporations that derived far greater benefits).[23] Highly controversial and nationally publicized, Prop 13 spawned similar tax limitation initiatives in other states such as Massachusetts and Colorado, and caught the attention of national politicians. It arguably set the stage for development of the supply-side ideology of the 1980s. Immediately following the passage of Prop 13, market libertarian Milton Friedman wrote in *Newsweek*: "To politicians around the country, the message from California should be clarion clear. The wave of taxpayer protest can carry politicians who learn to ride it to the highest offices in the land."[24]

In sum, it is not a stretch to see Prop 13 as one of the cornerstones of the domestic architecture of neoliberalism. Though scholars dispute whether antitax sentiment of the late 1970s and early 1980s actually represented the popular will—or even delivered any coherent political message at all—it still became a core part of the mythos of Reaganomics. Reagan himself was elected, in part, on the strength of his conversion to California-style tax resistance and his effort to spread its appeal on a national level. Critics have persuasively shown that the former governor of California—who was not originally interested in taxes as a political issue—found a platform that would help usher him into the White House, as well as a model for his later campaigns to reduce capital gains and inheritance taxes.[25] Historian William Martin writes, "What matters is that politicians *thought* Reagan owed his victory to the tax revolt, and they took Reagan's victory as a mandate to cut taxes."[26]

Marcus's antitax speech in the novel thus marks the moment when taxes are first being politicized in ways that would ultimately serve neoliberal ends. To say that taxes are political may seem tautological from the standpoint of the 2010s, in which antitax and antigovernment discourse is widespread, and when even mainstream media, not just Tea Party activists, view tax resistance as an American tradition. However, the antitax politics of 1970s were a distinct historical development. In the postwar period, during what Judith Stein calls the "consensus" years of American economic policymaking, taxes were not considered particularly burdensome and tax cutting was not a big political issue.[27] Martin similarly rejects the argument that tax resistance is a "timeless cultural trait," observing that tax rates had been much higher at other periods in U.S. history than in the late 1970s. He argues that "the distinctive antitax constituency that is characteristic of American politics today" was specifically inaugurated by the Reagan-era "right turn" of public discourse about taxes.[28]

To argue that the Prop 13 movement represented a reassertion of traditional American values is therefore greatly to underestimate the complexity of this political shift.[29] Tax-cutting mandates can, and often do, express a conservative and/or libertarian withdrawal from the shared costs and responsibilities of public citizenship. Indeed much popular discourse about the suburbs takes as a given the argument that homeownership tends to make people more conservative. (Politicians assume that "a sense of property rights and a concern for tax rates comes with the key to a suburban home," observed the *New York Times* in the midcentury.)[30] The emergence of a "suburban bloc" of the American electorate has been described as a shifting of allegiance from urban to small-town "values," from a public or state-oriented notion of citizenship to a private one, and from liberal ideals of social inclusivity to neoliberal assertions of property rights. Critics have observed the ways in which the discourse of "property rights" tends to operate as code for white racist protectionism.[31] Historical analyses have illuminated the ways conservative postwar politics tended to be articulated in moral terms—often, as reactions to the perceived urban ills of blight, poverty, and crime. Whether or not a racially inflected social conservatism is always inherent in fiscal conservatism (the prime example is the 1980s politicization of the phrase "family values," which operated as an ideological index for white, middle-class values), there is no doubt that property taxes, like real-estate development itself, are deeply entangled in social and class politics. Neil Smith writes that "revanchism is in every respect the ugly cultural politics of neoliberal globalization."[32]

But although tax sensitivity can represent an antistatist withdrawal or resistance—conservative in the small "c" sense—it can also represent a highly proactive engagement with neoliberalism. Tax privileges, as critics observe, are as much a form of social policy as tax expenditures. From this perspective, the conventional wisdom that "the tax revolt, in its gut-level expression, is a throwback to the most primitive nineteenth century individualism"[33] gets it exactly wrong. What often passes for a backward-looking, conservative response to the issue of property taxes can be more accurately understood as a forward-looking entitlement movement (forward-looking in the sense of future-oriented, not as socially progressive). Marcus himself makes the class agenda clear with the opportunity for the middle class to seize a piece of the economy:

> I started really looking at the tax returns I was going over, and you know what? I saw other sorts of lives there, perfectly legal lives, lives where the government backed a little risk, and the risk paid off, and it wasn't that these people were just making lots of money, it was also that they were having fun. And believe you me, the way things are going in Washington, there is going to be more fun, more more more fun than anyone has ever had since God knows when, because the tax

code is transforming before your very eyes, and everyone is perfectly
happy to see it happen. (109)

Marcus's fun seeking obviously does not sound protectionist in the same
way that homeowner language of "community stability" does. Compared
to the more usual conservative discourse that tends to advocate restrain-
ing public spending—and to moralize about welfare reform (the famous
Reagan-era epithet was "welfare queens")—Marcus's enthusiasm for fun
is hardly antistatist. In fact, it is the reverse of antistatist to cast tax reform
as an entrepreneurial opportunity, since it makes evident that the redistribution of the tax burden is simply a less visible form of government
spending. Isaac Martin argues, for instance, that far from being antistatist,
the antitax movement is about defending a giant federal housing subsidy
to the middle and upper classes. Taken with the most significant giveback
to homeowners—the mortgage-interest deduction—real estate operates as
an enormous social program aimed at the middle classes—no less than an
entire "invisible welfare state." "On the eve of the tax revolt [in Califor-
nia]," Martin writes, the mortgage deduction "was providing more benefits
than any other social policy in America, except for the twin blockbusters
of the federal budget, Social Security and Medicare."[34]

Tax resistance is thus a rent-seeking movement *concealed* in the language of protection against the market. Under Reaganomics, the discourse
of individual rights and liberties camouflages what might otherwise plau-
sibly be seen as a shift in national housing policy. Moreover the relationship works both ways. A growing resistance to taxes among middle-class
homeowners was not just a result of neoliberal ideologies at work but a
movement that anticipated and softened the ground for the Reagan school
of supply-sideism to come. Certainly the references to Washington suggest a political shift that is as much top-down as bottom-up ("My God,
look at what happened in the last election"). Thus, the novel shows how
political interests combined with class anxieties to create the "Reagan
revolution." The tax resistance discourse of the period represented a historically specific eruption of class protectionism in the language of neoliberal individualism.

California politics are not mentioned in the text—"California" is simply shorthand for consumption, as I have discussed. But the Proposition 13
history is a necessary reminder that tax policy is fundamentally political in
the same way that real estate is fundamentally political: both represent the
distribution of resources in a given population. Both are indices to the late
twentieth century's wealth redistribution from nonowning to the owning
classes. Exempting homeowners from rising taxes puts a disproportionate

burden on newcomers, reinforcing a hierarchy of property ownership that strongly favors existing communities, and their social and political interests, over new ones. The contradiction would become even stronger in the national-level antitax movement of the 2000s, which specifically rejected government "interference" while, of course, refusing to recognize any distinction between active and passive formations of social policy. To "not tax" is easier to misunderstand and misrepresent as a form of noninterference, concealing the fact of its regressive social restructuring.

From this angle, the ways in which the housing economy is a moral economy become obvious. As David Graeber has argued, debt and land distribution determine nearly all other structures of wealth and social justice. Constance Perin observes that shelter determines "access to many other necessities: education, work, social life, and political participation."[35] Land-use regulations, which are "decisively man-made factors" that "represent an exercise of social choice," are the means by which the population allocates its resources and in turn becomes sorted into hierarchies of ownership. These include spatial hierarchies (based on distance to places of education, work, and social life), economic ones (with renters at the bottom and owners and landlords at the top), and moral ones, in which property owners are seen as representing more stable and long-term community interests and, in turn, as more responsible persons. (Such moral value judgments at the level of the individual are made explicit in bank lenders' evaluations of mortgage applicants' personal characters.)

The strong cultural preference in America for homeownership is made possible, Perin points out, by a long history in the United States of "pervasively low land prices."[36] An abundance of seemingly free land enabled the original flourishing of American cultural preferences for single-family homeownership over apartment housing or other higher-density forms of shelter. As a result, "America's most widespread cottage industry is the house itself as small business, the household's credit rating providing for each generation's economic well-being, the location for the children's public education, and its eventual resale and profit-taking for the parents' future."[37] The novel invites us to consider real estate as a primary "text" of American social distribution as it becomes the basis of a new range of middle-class entitlements and protections in the 1980s. As Reagan-era anxieties about class reproducibility go hand in hand with changing racial and ethnic demographics, population growth, and decreasing land availability, real estate becomes a vehicle of the new fiscal and cultural conservatism. Even at times when the housing market is clearly no haven against the vicissitudes of the stock market, the demands of risk-taking and the anxieties of class positioning under neoliberalism have continued to ensure that property ownership and property values serve as twin anchors of social entitlement. The middle-class dependence on what might be called homestead economics enables—and provides cover for—the more generalized late twentieth-century wealth-transfer that David Harvey calls the "class project" of neoliberalism, and that leads Fredric Jameson to only semi-ironically state that in the era of finance ideology suddenly the "guiding thread of all contemporary politics seems much easier to grasp: namely that the rich want their taxes lowered."[38]

Reading Character

"An investment in character can teach us about the character of investment," writes Sara Ahmed.[39] Investment here refers to the affective attachment to an *idea* of character, one that tends to prevail even when contradicted by actual evidence. This idea of consistency—a set of expectations, or a sense of genre, as Ahmed points out—makes it possible to judge what is "in character," allowing us to distinguish how a character is like or unlike itself and how it evolves over time. A change of character is the opening of a space between one set of expectations and another—a space that demands a new way of reading and, potentially, a new idea of what it means to read character realistically.

Arguments have been made elsewhere about the characteristics of personality demanded and rewarded by "flexible capitalism." Despite what has been described about new forms of personality that accommodate (or fail to accommodate) postindustrial restructuring, the point here is not whether character *changed* in or around the 1980s but about the misalignment between "realisms" of character and "realisms" of structural abstraction. Journalists certainly struggled to find epithets vivid enough to meet the requirements of the S&L narrative. Thomas, the critic mentioned at the beginning of this chapter, writes, "The foxes—the crooks, fools, swindlers, and charlatans—took over the chicken house." Thomas's inclusive sampling of con artists is, I suggest, a symptom of a narrative inability to escalate the terms and dimensions of realism beyond the inside/outside dimensions of character.

Which brings us back to the word *hearty*. This word demonstrates that Joe is reading like a realist: measuring the alignment between inside and outside. With this descriptor he submits Marcus to analysis of what Leo Bersani calls the "expressive function" of character ("the relation of a narrative surface to a typological deep structure"), in which the "most casual word, the most trifling gesture, the most tangential episode all submit easily to the discipline of being *revealing* words, gestures and episodes."[40]

John Frow describes a similar view that "behavior and action in the novel *exemplify* moral and psychological qualities which it is then the reader's task to retrieve (to put a name to, finding what was there to be found)."[41] *Hearty* indicates a depth model of reading, one that seeks to penetrate the surface to assess the true interior. In effect, Marcus appears to Joe as a nineteenth-century problem of authenticity.

Authenticity—in the sense of real versus fake—is precisely the concern that the con man has traditionally represented in American literature. Critics have analyzed the tricksters, speculators, and scoundrels who abound in many periods of U.S. literature as signaling anxieties about personal deception in times of fluid social and economic self-redefinition.[42] In the late nineteenth century the problem of character reading changes as self-formation becomes more implicated in a potentially deceptive or misleading commercial environment. Instead of the con man as a figure of dishonesty and as an antisocial exception, as in the earlier, Melville type, the problem of the representation of "realness" becomes a more generalized feature of subjectivity. Mary McAleer Balkun, for instance, focusing on the fiction of Henry James, argues that there is a new relationship to "realness" in the late nineteenth-century commercial environment in which this quality is determined in inverse not to fakeness but to the logic of commodification. The counterfeit, in this view, represents not a problem of identifying the real but in assigning value to it. James Salazar similarly approaches character as a "site of a profound hermeneutic anxiety," in part because its relationship to the inner self was sometimes illegible and in part because of its vulnerability to misrepresentation particularly by the "skilled manipulator of signs." The structural abstraction of the commodity becomes the model for the alignment of internal and external. And just as the "real" becomes a performance fully informed by the substitutions of the commodity, so too the problem of properly *valuing* the real becomes thoroughly personified.[43]

More theoretical accounts of literary character agree on the need to address *conditions* of legibility as much as character itself. John Frow argues that our understandings of character depend on the conditions of possibility of reading. Quoting Ian Hunter, he writes that it is within "the practical deployment of a public apparatus of reading" that "what is to count as character is determined."[44] Deidre Lynch argues that it is only within particular reading formations that character becomes visible. And in her examination of the textuality of eighteenth-century character, Lynch, like Frow, quotes Ian Hunter on the need for attention to alterations of "the historical surfaces on which the content of a text can appear."[45] Character became conceived as reading matter in the first place, Lynch observes, because new modes of looking were required that could capture a radically transforming field of social distinctions. Once traditional hierarchy could no longer be relied upon to map the social, "faces" replaced "places" as sources of legibility.

In effect, character *arbitrates* between what counts as realism. At any given moment, and in any defined field of reading, personified figures always express a tension of character reading between the allegorical and the representational. Typological abstractions (Lynch cites "vanity" and "altruism") are the basis for allegorization, whereas the representational aspires to infinite historical particularity and detail. These two modes of signification work in dialectical fashion such that, as Frow writes, "allegorical typifications are both drawn from and fed back into the social text."[46]

We have seen how the stock figure of the con man does not readily align with the structural demands of a late twentieth-century economic narrative. What may look like a revelation of false character (an exposure of personal inauthenticity) may be seen, instead, as a consequence of redistribution in the available modes of reading. In this way, it might be argued that *Good Faith* models the ways that the moral character function has been *redistributed* in contemporary textual space. I borrow the term *distribution* from Alex Woloch, who argues that nineteenth-century social realism is the "key site" of the tension between a historical/referential and a structuralist/textualist view of character.[47] For my purposes here the point is not the way characters compete with each other, as Woloch discusses, but the way that the character function competes among other elements within the textual field under changing conditions of legibility. In *Good Faith* it is houses that become reading matter and landscapes that become textual as character becomes "flattened" into the allegorical. The novel's historical and economic indexing competes with this flat character as a text for realist scrutiny. Between the structural imperative—balancing of deposits and loans—and attachment to a moral-characterological assignment of responsibility, a crisis of reading is produced.

Seen in this light, Joe's "investment" in character, in Ahmed's sense, only deepens and complicates the novel's attachments to narrative realism. His story is about the values and responsibilities he is able (or unable) to assign:

> [Marcus] "Crosbie is the real villain, you know why?"
> [Joe] "Why?"
> [Marcus] "Because a big loan is an asset. All those deposits he's got, those are the liabilities, and those loans are assets. Crosbie's new. He

came in to transform the savings and loan from money loser to
moneymaker, and he's got to make the books look good, so he's making
big loans, which go on the asset side and cover old loans that aren't
making any profit." (149–50)

The "villain" is summoned into existence by a structural imperative ("he's
got to make the books look good"). Of course it can also be read psycho-
logically as a displacement of Marcus's (future) guilt. But either way, the
abstraction of type papers over a shortfall in realism—the fully detailed
economic realism of "the books." The word *villain*, which is drawn not
from realism but from the typology of melodrama, marks the incoherence
of the demand for structural *realism* of capitalism and for moral clarity
at the same time. The typologization of character signals the crisis of an
inward/outward mode of moral realism. A fully structuralist reading might
have been one that juxtaposed the instability of the trickster against the
presumed stability and long-term interest of the homeowner, as Perin sug-
gestively proposes. Arguing that the trickster is a middleman similar to
that other quintessential transitional figure, the renter, she observes that
the trickster exists in social spaces of limbo such as apartment buildings
and motels, and that like renters, tricksters "behave as if there were no
social or moral norms to guide them."[48]

The abstraction of character to the level of the allegorical or typological doesn't make it any less powerful, however. Even if the Reaganomic
moment seems to inaugurate a capitalism too mutable for character to
function as a site of moral accountability, the demand to read *as realists*
persists even to the point of interpretive distortion. Joe is invested in the
"good faith" rubrics of trust, commitment, and loyalty that his own parents represented in a generation of stable passbook savings accounts. We
might compare the novel's title—which suggests a moral crisis on the level
of the individual—to a phrase equally relevant to the 1980s: "full faith and
credit," the motto of the FDIC. The FDIC, a New Deal insurance program, was created to reassure the public about the safety of the banking
system in the wake of the failures of the 1920s and 1930s. By the 1980s,
however, this blanket federal protection of savings on one hand combined
with S&L deregulation on the other all but guaranteed the speculative
frenzy that would follow. Confident the government would step in to cover
for their excessive risk-taking, S&L lenders had nothing to lose.

Taken together, the two phrases are symptomatic of the conflict between
a character-driven and a structural narrative. The turn to type is essentially a gesture of old habit, a crutch for when one is at a loss to evaluate
tax policy and deregulation in any but typological terms. The same crutch

can be seen in S&L journalism. Journalistic accounts of the banking crisis make particularly visible the clash between narratives of personified criminality and those of inverted risk. Both S&L critiques and apologias usually agree on the same starting point: that the lending market was incompetently regulated, turning risk and reward upside down. The apologias, logically, remain focused on the system, even if they concede the existence of a few bad apples. The critiques confront a different problem. Even the harshest of critics must decide whether an individual or structural approach produces a more powerful condemnation. Writers who denounce S&L criminality as "outrageous accounting" and "atrocious theft" are forced to concede that lenders' risky behavior was only to be expected considering the perverted incentives created by deregulation. It is hard to avoid the implication that the industry was functioning *too well*, such that it might be difficult to pinpoint exactly what combination of standard lending and accounting practices crossed the line.[49]

If the definition of *crime* therefore feels unstable in S&L accounts, surely it is because the definition of *capitalism* is unstable. Even relatively sophisticated analyses are caught in the dilemma of identifying what activities are acceptable. For instance, one team of "forensic" analysts argues that in order to emphasize systemic incentives in the industry without absolving large numbers of participants of moral responsibility, the S&Ls should be understood along the model of an organized crime ring.[50] Organized crime, rather than corporate crime, they argue, offers a model to analyze criminal behavior structurally, through a combination of intention, opportunity, and risk tolerance. But this analysis does not consider the possibility that *all* forms of capitalism, not just the more obviously illegal ones, behave like organized crime. The deregulation of the S&L industry in the early 1980s simply provided an exceptionally glaring example of a moral hazard that is endemic to the system.

Following this logic it might be argued that the novel cops out at the end by allowing Marcus to flee the country as a fugitive. The structural conflicts would have been far more glaring if Marcus had stayed, and if his wheeling and dealing had remained in the legally ambiguous area that much S&L lending actually did. His absconding with a suitcase of unambiguously stolen funds permits Joe's retroactive reading of him as a villain. Joe's effort to reinterpret events in terms of personified intentionality and moral responsibility requires summoning up a con man from the character "archives." This borrowing of a figure from the literary archive shows that our reading of unstable and changing social texts remains tightly bound up in characterological terms of motives, intentions, and action. To read character as a primary moral text exposes the inadequacy of these terms—

even while demonstrating a more intimate dependence on the "character-function" than ever.

Salazar, in a study of the American rhetoric of character, observes that the history of character from the nineteenth century to the twentieth has typically been told as a history of decline. The conventional scholarly view of the rhetoric of character, he writes, is that it "has been commonly understood as a theory of self-formation, cultivated by the novel form, whose ideological function was to inculcate those forms of economic agency and social discrimination essential to the formation and regulation of a liberal, democratic public sphere in the United States." Salazar argues against this critical assumption that political and demographic changes led to character's "increasing obsolescence as a cultural and regulatory ideal," or that an interiorized, essentially disembodied view of character was replaced by more public and "expressively embodied" form of "personality." In fact, he argues, "such stories of character's devaluation . . . like the laments over character's presumed decline, are what enable and extend character's cultural work and regulatory function."[51] The "reversibility of the relationship between the sign and the referent of character" allowed it to continue to be so powerful into the twentieth century.

In the late twentieth century, in Smiley's novel, this simultaneity of the character function is taken a step further. Even as the novel models the difference in moral legibility between reading character and reading landscape, it shows how interdependent these "texts" remain. Just as critics have shown how an eighteenth-century "surface" form of character textuality was actually quite distinct from a later understanding of character as a projection of a moral self, a comparison between nineteenth-century and contemporary realism allows us to be more specific about the changed "historical surfaces," in Lynch's words, of character reading by the end of the twentieth. The con man expresses the contradiction of economic virtue as a readerly guide or text for an era of neoliberalism. The persistence of a mode of inward and outward alignment, despite its insufficiency as an index to a field of endless consumer differentiation, suggests the difficulty for contemporary realism to accommodate the rise of "interests" as a social formation more important than character or personality. But if the paradox of finance capitalism is that it is more about character than ever, then what does it mean to read like a realist? Short of a new novelistic realism that can accommodate endless financial differentiation, we might see the rise of the typological and allegorical forms of character as an acknowledgment of the limitations of the realist mode to accommodate these structural changes, and as a hedge against allowing "character" to cooperate seamlessly with the terms of neoliberal accumulation.

CHAPTER THREE

Epic Compensations

Corporate Totality in Frank Norris's
The Octopus and Richard Powers's *Gain*

In the age of the epic, according to Georg Lukács, "the world of meaning can be grasped, it can be taken in at a glance."[1] In contrast, according to Richard Powers's 1998 novel *Gain*, "History heads steadily for a place where things need not be grasped to be used."[2] If the epic, for Lukács, stands for a world of unified totality where all meaning is apparent,[3] then, for Powers, modernity increasingly excuses us from needing to know anything about totalities, lost or otherwise: "Plastic happens; that is all we need to know on earth." This statement appears near the end of the novel, in the middle of an extended description of a disposable camera:

> Camera in a pouch, the true multinational: trees from the Pacific Northwest and the southeast coastal plain. Straw and recovered wood scrap from Canada. Synthetic adhesive from Korea. Bauxite from Australia, Jamaica, Guinea. Oil from the Gulf of Mexico or North Sea Brent Blend turned to plastic in the Republic of China before being shipped to its mortal enemies on the Mainland for molding. Cinnabar from Spain. Nickel and titanium from South Africa. Flash elements stamped in Malaysia, electronics in Singapore. Design and color transfers drawn up in New York. Assembled and shipped from that address in California by a merchant fleet beyond description, completing the most heavily choreographed conference in existence. (347–48)

The full camera description covers multiple pages; long paragraphs detail the resources used to produce the cardboard carton, the black plastic casing, the film, the flash battery, the bar code on the label. Bruce Robbins calls this catalog of parts a Whitmanian "prose poem."[4] The culmination of global production, the camera represents "a feat of master engineering under the hood too complex for any user to follow." The finished object is fully disconnected from the "staggering ballet" of systems that produce it: "What makes the sale is transparency. Set to go, right out of the package, and ready to disappear when used. No anything required." To know the origins, relations, or processes of this piece of plastic is unnecessary, even impossible. At the fullest moment of realization—in the clicking of the shutter—these processes are actually canceled out: "The entire engineering magnificence was designed to be pitched. Labor, materials, assembly, shipping, sales markups and overheads, insurance, international tariffs—the whole prodigious creation costs less than ten dollars. The world sells to us at a loss, until we learn to afford it" (348).

This line reads as one of Powers's more enigmatic. If the camera is being sold at a loss, how do we learn to afford it? Capitalism searches the globe for further efficiencies, cost-effectiveness, and divisions of labor. The result is an end-product cheap enough to throw away. Oblivious of the system of production, we are ignorant of the true totality of the object's costs. The "loss" of awareness of production consummates the reification by which objects conceal the living labor that produced them. As the product is autonomized, the narration formally collaborates in the occlusion of making. Ursula Heise has noted that as the shape of the camera gradually emerges from its parts, the "human design, work, and organization that go into this emergence are downplayed." The passage's "lack of inflected verbs and passive constructions foreground its elision of agency; the object seems to be assembling itself before the reader's eyes."[5] If, as Adorno wrote, all reification is a forgetting, then *Gain* invokes an entire landscape of consumer amnesia where the product—a camera, a bar of soap, a packaged snack food or disinfectant spray—renounces its origins.

There is another level of forgetting associated with the camera. The reader soon learns that it has been found in a hospital room by a nurse's aide cleaning out a drawer. Description follows of the undeveloped negatives inside it: "A woman blowing out the candles on a cake, the IV just visible beneath the sleeve of her robe" (348). The patient, not identified, is presumably Laura Bodey, the character whose illness and decline we have been following in the novel. The narrative marks Laura's death by giving over the function of memory to the mechanical object. This event, a fusion of subject and object, is further signaled by the shift from narration to description. Such fusion is no utopian synthesis. The description of the camera is not a recovery of totality but instead an elegy on the split between grasping and using. The "loss" in this passage is no mere economic cost or unreckoned environmental debt but the loss of a subjective recognition or relationality to a world of production—even as the world becomes, paradoxically, more and more epically "unified" under global capitalism.

Franco Moretti in *Modern Epic* calls epic a mode of *attempt* that reacts and interacts with other modern generic categories, particularly the novel. One version of the "epic ambition consists in representing 'the totality' of objects," he writes.[6] What constitutes this attempt is the inevitable failure to develop a new form adequate to totality. The epic mode or ambition thus seeks out precisely the dialectic of abstract and concrete, form and content, or first-order and second-order levels of experience, that constitute the remove from a resolvable, coherent totality at any moment in history. In this argument Moretti follows a Lukácsian conceptualization of epic as an impossible, prelapsarian form, born of and reflecting a world that preexisted modern alienation. Lukács theorized the novel as generically constituted by a perpetual yet futile search for unified origins. Lacking the conditions of organic epic wholeness, the novel is obliged to compensate for the increasing alienation between subject and object. It introduces irony, for example, and develops separate worlds of interiority and exteriority. In arguing that the modern novel "still thinks in terms of totality," Lukács meant that it is the search for the whole, not the achievement of it, that defines the genre, testifying to its necessary failure to resolve its constitutive oppositions.[7]

Fredric Jameson famously describes one of the defining conditions of the moment of "late" capitalism as "the waning of concepts and representations of production," with the effect that "tends to deprive people of their sense of making or producing that reality, to confront them with the fact of preexisting circuits without agency, and to condemn them to a world of sheer passive reception."[8] The apparent absence of labor contributes to the cognition of late capitalism that Jameson describes. As the "real" body of the laborer is automated, displaced, swept out of sight or offshore, our grasp of the concepts of production is weakened. The corporation, the entity that is everywhere and nowhere at the same time, and whose agency is unaccountable, is a figure for the problem of seeking to locate agency and agents within an incomprehensibly complex global economy. As a place of no abode—a body without a body—the corporation accommodates the oppositions between a virtualized or abstract capital and an embodied, productive, and therefore supposedly more "real" capital.

Epic compensation, as I will call it, refers to the narrative overreaching that is demanded by the apparent incommensurability between what late twentieth-century capitalism produces and the complex trail of production that it obscures. The issue at stake in Powers's novel is how to give a full enough account of the loss between grasping and using. *Gain* has been called the "most fully realized contemporary American novel of life in the epoch of corporations."[9] The narrative is divided into three different strands. One narrative is the history of the Clare Corporation, a fictional conglomerate that has been roughly compared to the real-life Proctor and Gamble. This corporate "biography" is coextensive with nearly two centuries of American commercial life, walking us through the pages of American history from the era of the sea merchant to the corporate multinational. Interspersed with this history is a contemporary story about Laura Bodey, a real-estate agent and divorced mother of two in Illinois who is dying of cancer. Laura has no obvious connection to the Clare corporation except that she happens to live near the location of its world headquarters. These two narratives trace a metaphor of growth, benign and malignant, across a wide range of economic and social registers. One is the growth of trade, the other an unchecked overgrowth of leukocytes. The narratives are densely interwoven yet at best circumstantially connected. The formal impulse of the text is not to reconcile the narratives, I argue, but to further their incommensurability. The corporation, in this reading, is the body of production repressed in one history that returns as sickness in the other. Formally and historically, the novel casts and recasts the relationship between these narratives in the context of the "corporate" aspiration to totality.

Jeremy Green, in *Late Postmodernism*, succinctly describes the novel as making a "structural principle" out of the gap between the lived experience of the individual subject and the "large structures and processes" of the postmodern world. By representing Laura as living in a total system shaped by capitalism, he writes, the novel "embodies in its divided form the structural obstacles the novelist faces in representing late capitalist society."[10] In one of the first and still most critically important discussions of *Gain*, Ursula Heise similarly argues that the "narrative nucleus" of the novel is the idea that "large scale systems in to which technologies are embedded have become so complex that they can no longer be easily understood or controlled." Heise raises the term *epic* in this context to link the concern with systems of risk (to environmental contamination and toxic exposure) to an "epic mode" of contemporary fiction's "attempt to grasp the planetary implications of some risks." Heise does not explore the term *epic* further, however, and concludes her analysis by negatively criticizing the novel's structural partitioning between the "self-assured omniscient narrator" of the Clare narrative and the limited perspective of the individual who cannot hope to see the big picture.[11] I will return to this critique below.

In focusing on these two narrative strands, critics have tended to neglect the third. Interspersed throughout the Clare and Laura stories are a series of intertexts, set off visually and typographically from the "main" text, that bridge otherwise apparently unrelated jumps between the two narratives. These textual fragments appear to be a jumble of material from the archive of commerce: everything from advertising pitches, promotional copy, excerpts from histories, an epitaph on a Clare headstone, corporate mottos, product labels, road signs, the text of a stock certificate once owned by an ancestor of Laura's, information on how to see a copy of Clare's latest SEC filing, a poster for the World's Fair, a Clare environmental press release, a flowchart of the company's executive structure, and numerous literary and historical quotations and epigraphs, many from actual sources.

Powers himself has called his style a form of "crackpot realism."[12] This, and various other descriptions of *Gain*—as employing a "stereo view" (Harris), a set of "contrapuntal" narratives or "symphonic" plots, or "triple realism" (LeClair)—essentially describe the same features: the investment in and commitment to multiple modes of narration—realistic, modernist, postmodernist—while self-reflexively attending to their limits and problems.[13] Put together, what these narrative strands yield is not a totality of representation but a recognition of the impossibility and necessity of such a notion of totality. The corporation becomes a figure for the drive to totalization under global or world-systems capitalism. Against the Lukácsian assertion that totality is a feature "lost" in the post-epic era— not to mention poststructuralism's later rejection of the concept of totality altogether—the epic counter-impulse becomes a way to question capitalism's power to invoke and naturalize a projection of the "whole." Far from being irrelevant or anachronistic to late capitalism, then, the notion of totality must be seen as an integral tool to its practices of self-reorganization and self-reproduction.

Epic pretensions are most obvious in the Clare narrative. Certainly this is the most highly synthesizing of the text's different narrative strands. A seemingly omniscient chronicle of the company's history, it begins with the rogue English merchantman Jephthah Clare, who in 1802 flees his debts at home by stowing away to America on one of his own trading ships. The fledgling business set up by his sons in early nineteenth-century Boston struggles through early American industrialism, grows into a tightly run family firm, and prospers through civil war and westward expansion. By the late nineteenth-century "age of incorporation," Clare is ready to take new risks and achieve astonishing leaps of efficiency. It leads the nation's monopolistic consolidation, discovers advertising and promotion, and swells the wave of early twentieth-century consumer credit. It thrives on world-war-era industrialism and promises "better living through chemistry" on the domestic front. Postwar affluence turns it into one of the great forces of multinational capitalism, surviving the deflationary 1970s, the mergers-and-acquisitions 1980s, and even positions itself for the corporate eco-capitalism of the 1990s.

Clare's mythopoetic aspirations are cast into high relief. Language takes on world-historical terms. From the company's earliest days, the language of salvation is closely tied to the Clare brothers' commercial mission, but by the mid-nineteenth-century age of expansion, business and spiritual manifestoes are even more grandly conflated: "Manufacturing, like the very project of civilization that it advanced, was a snaking torrential Shenandoah beyond anyone's ability to dam" (105). Richly metaphorical language exalts the nation's industrial and westward destinies: "Life now headed, via a web of steam-cut canals, deep into the interior. . . . Schuykill, Delaware, Mohawk, and Hudson; every Valley exalted, and every hill laid low. Rail threatened to render distance no more than a quaint abstraction. America at last split open its continental nut" (67). The corporation and the nation become metaphors for each other: "Now the new American race had burst those shackles. Now it could couple its energies in one overarching corporation, one integrated instrument of production whose bounty might grow beyond thwarting" (91).

In the narrative's inflated, mock heroic style, time is foreshortened, events lead over actions, processes over people. "Clare and Sons had only to hold up their hands and let the magic skein of trade loop itself around their outstretched fingers" (12). Even accident is incorporated into the providential narrative of the company's growth, such as Ben Clare's discovery of the plant *Utilis clarea* and his saving of this one specimen from the otherwise total loss of his scientific research in a shipwreck. History is an account of technodeterminist discoveries: "The new, self-propelling engines began to fling mankind outward, and the expansion sucked all business along in its wake" (42). The rails throw themselves down across the continent; the week vanishes into hours. The "automated crank seemed capable of propelling the very engine of history" (68). All growth is teleologized: "Two chemists in Spray, North Carolina, poured the sludge from a failed experiment into a stream, and up from the surprise bubbles of acetylene rose Union Carbide" (237).

Heise argues that the formal flaw in this sweeping history is that it offers *too much* coherence: "Powers' narrative strategies suggest that whatever difficulties the characters may encounter in their attempts to grapple with the global corporate world, the readers can rely on the comprehensive map that the self-assured omniscient narrator unfolds before them." The omniscient passages convey a false sense of mastery and knowability. The "panorama" of systems in the Clare narrative, she writes, is "drawn up by a narrator who knows the corporation in both its historical and its geographical extension down to the most minute details, and who delivers them in an idiom that never questions the reader's ability to grasp and connect these details."[14] Heise would certainly be correct to say that the omniscience of the narrative is never achievable by the characters who occupy the incoherent, postmodern present. If anything, Laura faces the pushback of too much information. The fractures, jargons, and incommensurabilities of knowledge highlight the collapse of epistemological certainty. Laura's ex-husband pressures her to take action—to look up studies, question doctors, monitor statistics, and read ingredients. Next to his consumer activism, her fatalism ("You can't change your number coming up" [40]) feels entirely in keeping with the depiction of a powerless consumer subject.

A state of postmodern indeterminacy is clearly inadequate to connecting the corporate body with the cancerous one. As the repressed materiality of the body returns in the form of illness, it tasks us with the problem of assigning corporate responsibility. The question never answered in the novel is whether Clare is directly responsible for Laura's death. The company's presence in her life is self-evident. The fabric of the community is woven with Clare support: scholarships, bake-offs, and 5K walks. Laura even unconsciously hums the corporate theme song as she gardens. Her house is a virtual exhibit of corporate sponsorship: "Two pots in her medicine cabinet bear the logo, one to apply and one to remove. Those jugs under the sink—Avoid Contact with Eyes—that never quite work as advertised. Shampoo, antacid, low-fat chips. The weather stripping, the grout between the quarry tiles, the nonstick in the nonstick pan, the light coat of deterrent she spreads on her garden. These and other incarnations play about her house, all but invisible" (7). Even the hospital wing where Laura dies was built by the company. Laura's illness exposes the limitedness of our understanding of the forces of production: the corporation's ability not only to make products but to manufacture needs, market risks, and shape worlds. Heise notes that we are never even told the name of the gardening product that Laura uses that is named in the class-action suit against Clare. "The most obvious reason for this elision [of the substance that might have caused Bodey's cancer] seems to be that there is no way of being sure." The intentional uncertainty suggests that "more than any single substance and more even than the whole array of products it delivers, it is the corporation as a social form that kills Laura Bodey."[15] Responsibility is further sidestepped when Clare settles the lawsuit out of court. Laura's children collect the settlement money after her death. The settlement is not an admission of guilt but merely the company's rational management of the costs of prolonged litigation. The realism of cause and effect is hereby trumped by the realism of cost/benefit analysis. In a risk-driven world of complex systems, no cause can be isolated, no measurement can meet a legal standard of evidence. If a "realistic" cause-and-effect mapping were possible, it would have to be a historical realism of accounting rather than of action or intention. It would have had to begin with the mathematical formula of growth itself: "A pound of fat makes two pounds of soap, one of which will trade for the next pound of fat. A simple enough thing, and nothing can keep it from covering the earth" (295).

But although the Clare narrative offers an expansive "epic" coherence, it is not omniscient in any simple sense of the term. Its elaborately self-rupturing language insists that there is no unmediated narrative of history. For instance, the narrative voice at times merges freely with the indirect discourse of Julia Clare, Resolve Clare's wife, who writes jingoistic pamphlets exhorting the United States to war against Mexico: "For how many eons had insurmountable geography impeded man's business?" she writes. "For whom was this continent meant . . . if not those most capable of developing it?" (93). The triumphal representation of American progress indicts the self-glorifying ideologies bound up in it. Irony and contradiction are never far from the narrative's cheerful notice. Resolve's business-minded wife holds "enlightened" views on slavery—meaning that she recognizes its negative market costs as opposed to its human ones. Ben Clare returns from his years at sea to find a world in which "industrialists always managed to escape prosecution on the grounds that their works had done more cumulative good than harm" (68). Other costs of growth are similarly alluded to: "Rail cost outrageous sums to lay, a massive sink of both capital and labor. Trains were slower and less reliable than the creatures they competed with. Locomotives eternally exploded, setting fire to fields, boiling clientele alive by the hundreds per year. Extorted by canal companies, foreign interests, and politicians alike, the start-up railroad companies nevertheless plowed into the frontier, as inevitable as the grave to which all expansion leads" (42). Such passages are not traditional omniscience but a self-disturbing, postmodern form of it. Heise argues that "the self-assurance of the narrator's command of the global and his transparent (though complex) language remain in tension with the scenario of individual powerlessness vis-à-vis the global power networks that the novel portrays."[16] But the language is not transparent. It calls attention to its own complicity in producing a world in which "history called out, above all else, for a better cake of soap" (95). Instead of a traditional extradie-getic omniscience that privileges the narrator's absolute insight and con-trol, the narrative highlights its susceptibility to partial, revisionist, and self-rationalizing historicization. It is the "official" version of history that would appear in an approved textbook. *Gain*'s objectified or (at least desubjectivized) omniscience is reminiscent of E. L. Doctorow's paradig-matically postmodern, flattened syntax in *Ragtime*, the text used by Fred-ric Jameson to theorize the crisis of history, in which Jameson argues that the use of simple, declarative sentences creates a "subterranean vio-lence" of style in which historical events are presented as if forever "sun-dered from any present situation (even that of the act of story telling or enunciation)."[17]

The postmodern condition in *Gain* seems formally and thematically confirmed by the impossibility of recovering the past. In a late incident in the text, Laura, between increasingly debilitating chemotherapy treat-ments, visits a local historical society. An exhibit about the Clare company reveals the fruitless operation of a Lukácsian reified consciousness as it "tries to apprehend a relation between past and present."[18] Display cases are filled with material artifacts, photos, textual fragments—presumably similar to the artifacts described in the intertexts and based on what Pow-ers himself likely researched in the Proctor and Gamble archives while writing the novel. Laura happens to view the display in reverse, but this backward telescoping from the present only reinforces the teleology of Clare's forward progress: "Each glass showcase gets a little older than the last. . . . Time pulls off, layer after layer. The company strips in front of her, like someone getting undressed for the night. Factories shrink; equip-ment goes rickety and primitive; the official company portraits grain and blur. The Oakland addresses on the labels vanish, turn back into Kansas City, then Lacewood, Chicago, Sandusky, Walpole, Roxbury: a reverse Pilgrim's Progress, back toward Plymouth Rock" (294). With such highly conventionalized images and discourses ("The Me Decade reverts to the Summer of Love, which faced back into the Golden Era"), there is no sense that Laura could construct a history nearly as comprehensive as what the reader has encountered. Even recognizing for the first time what the company logo is supposed to represent underscores the unmooring of signifiers: "The famous Clare logo grows backwards before her eyes. The icon unsimplifies. It branches and embellishes itself until finally, after all these years, she makes out what it is: the bud of an ornate plant." Visit-ing the museum does not counteract the alienations of history but con-firms the futility of seeking any unity of knowledge outside the corporate narrative.

The postmodern, contemporary narrative mode therefore *confirms* the unity of the corporate epic. The corporation seeks out conscious and unconscious material in order to reshape our perceptions of reality. Powers's elaborately aestheticized language ("disturbance disrupted distribution" [143]) both fetishizes the world-making power of the corporate narrative and targets its presumptions of synthesis. Again, this is not omniscience in any conventional sense. Here is where a closer attention to the formal possibilities and implications of the epic, I argue, enable a deeper analysis of how *Gain* disturbs the overcoherences of capitalism's self-representation, highlights its troubling drive toward aesthetic unity, and seeks formal opportunities to turn the epic fantasy of capitalism against itself. I will shortly turn to the intertexts, mentioned above, to discuss these formal disruptions. The intertexts, I argue, mediate between the corporate-historical and postmodern-individual narratives in precisely the "compensatory" ways that the camera discussed at the outset does, by using the reified object as a strategy for narrative expansion and prolongation. Before I turn to this formal reading, however, a brief detour into the past will help to highlight its historical stakes. To recognize how *Gain* shifts the representation of a corporate aesthetic totality into contemporary terms, I turn to a comparison with a text often seen as synonymous with the genre of corporate epic, Frank Norris's *The Octopus*.

Epic Rivalries in *The Octopus*

Norris's 1901 novel, which announces its epic aspirations with the subtitle *The Epic of the Wheat,* depicts the struggle between wheat growers and the railroad corporation in turn-of-the-century California.[19] Like *Gain*, the novel associates the corporation with a rising global vision. My interest here is the way in which the text's ambition to develop a scale that would be equal to this "globality" runs into formal incoherence. *The Octopus* was meant as the first part of a projected trilogy. As a narrative of commodity production, it was followed by a narrative of financial circulation (*The Pit,* 1903) and was intended to conclude with a third volume, never finished, of distribution and consumption. The three volumes thus projected would have corresponded to stages in the cycle of production. I turn to *The Octopus*, not *The Pit*, even though the later novel more explicitly deals with finance in its representation of the Chicago wheat exchange.[20] The unfixable coreality of Norris's railroad—at once disembodied and monstrous—has been persuasively interpreted to express the problem of agency upon which nineteenth-century literary naturalism frequently turns.[21] Certainly the body's constant threat of uncontainable generativity suggests the reverse side of the naturalist novel's movement toward, as Mark Seltzer puts it, a "resolutely abstract account of force."[22] The representation of the corporation directly addresses the displacement of individual agency and becomes the proto-figuration of competing causal abstractions within a world-system. To read the corporation as a figure of aesthetic totality, as Norris does—and as I argue Powers does— is to see it as closely aligned with the financial imagination of abstraction. This displacement of any other perspective on the resulting enormous global system takes precedence, in my reading, over issues of corporate malfeasance, greed, or even the impunity of corporate "personhood."

The Octopus is therefore a useful example for comparison because although it sets up a similar challenge to *Gain*, it does so in a different historical situation, and with quite a different formal outcome. My interest is not to hold up one novel as a standard against which to measure the other. Instead, the different historical terms on which each operates demonstrates the recurrence of an "epic" movement in fiction that reveals continuities and discontinuities in the formal aestheticization of capitalism's drive to expansion.

Moreover, although there was once a critical industry centered on *The Octopus*'s use of Homeric and mythological references, my point is also not to measure the text against some objective standard of epic form.[23] The classical allusions that locally dominate the early chapters of the text, such as the nightmare "colossus" of the railroad engine, are less significant to this reading of Norris's epic attempt than the all-encompassing horizon projected for the trilogy as a whole—tellingly, never achieved. Nonetheless, in order to recognize the problem of epic scale as it develops in the novel, it is useful to begin with some of the self-consciously "epic" pretensions of the main character, the poet/observer Presley. From nearly his first arrival in the West, Presley frames his aesthetic quest for a "song of the people" in classical terms: "Ah, to get back to that first clear-eyed view of things, to see as Homer saw, as Beowulf saw, as the Niebelungen poets saw. The life is here, the same as then; the Poem is here; my West is here; the primeval, epic life is here, here under our hands, in the desert, in the mountain, on the ranch, all over here, from Winnipeg to Guadalupe" (40–41). Presley here seizes on the term *epic*—though the word is supplied by another character—to fit his material into a preconceived genre (a "thundering progression of hexameters"). Claire Virginia Eby usefully labels him a "negative example of a would-be epic writer" since in his romantic quest for a song of the people, Presley ironically misses the more obvious subject at hand, the railroad.[24] Presley fails to connect his poetic quest to the "great iron note" of capitalism even as Norris underscores the connection between the metaphors of the iron horse and those of the aesthetic imagination ("Stupendous ideas drove headlong through his brain" and "Terrible, formless shapes, vague figures, gigantic monstrous, distorted, whirled at a gallop through his imagination"). Eby uses the famous scene in which the artist confronts the head of the railroad corporation in his office to argue that the poet's "historical understanding is as flawed as the epic he tries to write."[25] The limitations of Presley's conventional poetics are fully exposed when he cannot fit the executive in front of him into his preconceived forms: "No standard of measurement in his mental equipment would apply to the actual man. . . . He began to see that here was the man not only great, but large; many-sided, of vast sympathies" (575). In an ironic reversal of roles, the railroad head even criticizes Presley's poetry, causing the poet to feel "confused, all at sea, embarrassed." The so-called poet, Eby claims, is unable to recognize the possibility that the businessman is more of an artist than the poet, indeed that the railroad head "is the Homer of *The Octopus* and the railroad his subject" (41).

To read Presley as a flawed artist, and a flawed focalizer, is one way to resolve the novel's awkward split in narrative consciousness, which at times seems to endorse the poet's privileged aesthetic viewpoint and at other times registers the impossibility for any single character, however inspired, to achieve a totality of vision. When Presley stands on a height and gazes across the San Joaquin Valley, he is rewarded with an epiphany that seems in keeping with Norris's own vision of epical enlargement: "And as Presley looked there came to him strong and true the sense and the significance of all the enigma of growth. He seemed for one instant to touch the explanation of existence. . . . It was the mystery of creation, the stupendous miracle of re-creation: the vast rhythm of the seasons, measured, alternative, the sun and the stars keeping time as the eternal symphony of reproduction swung in its tremendous cadences like the colossal pendulum of an almighty machine" (634). Just as the machine of the railroad engine brutally interrupted Presley's earliest poetic reveries in the first chapter, this vision of the expanding firmament is dialectically interrupted by the figure of the particular ("But as he stood thus looking down upon the great valley he was aware of the figure of a man, far in the distance . . . hardly more than a dot"). This dot is a shepherd who meets Presley and articulates the moral vision attached to his perceptual expansion: "What remains? Men perish, men are corrupted, hearts are rent asunder, but what remains untouched, unassailable, undefiled? Try to find that . . . and you will find, if your view be large enough, that it is *not* evil, but good, that in the end remains" (636). For readers it will be difficult to reconcile the idea that "good remains" with the text's conclusion in which good is thoroughly trumped by monopoly capitalism. If there is any justice for the individuals crushed by the railroad, it is projected into a vaguely distanced, future standpoint from which forces even larger than those of the corporation, and capable of taming it, will become apparent. But to achieve the "large enough" view referred to above, within which all injustice and struggle become resolvable, evidently requires redefining the imaginative bounds of the corporation. *The Octopus* is therefore a first step in narratively locating monopoly capitalism within a coherent totality, in which the epic poet's effort to move *toward* a large enough (or "many-sided") view is not ironized, even if he falls short in his ability to "measure" the scene in verse.

Another way to grasp the formal conflict of the novel is through the rivalry between title and subtitle. The shift of emphasis from one figure to another—from the "monstrous" machine that causes the first, early scene of carnage in the novel to the force of the wheat at the end that crushes a man to death in the hold of a ship—makes clear that the unity of Norris's three-part epic is ultimately located in the wheat of the subtitle, not the octopus of the title. Colleen Lye comments that by the end of the novel the wheat "more visibly conveys the specificity of *The Octopus'* representation of monopoly capitalism" than the railroad does. In fact, she argues, it is specifically to counter the power of the wheat that the novel "dreams of a figure of unfulfillable global consumption who could forestall the dangers of American overproduction."[26] This persuasive argument about the text's concluding gaze toward Asia, however, is based on a relatively small portion of a long novel that is elsewhere dominated by the title figure. Other critics attentive to the novel's outward turn similarly privilege the text's conclusion. (Russ Castronovo analyzes the novel's imperialist vision of a "beautiful infinity of global exchange" in ways that emphasize the aesthetic promise of the subtitle.)[27] However, to see the circulation of wheat as the vehicle of the novel's geo-aesthetic is to further aggravate the novel's formal imbalance, in abandoning the five-hundred-plus-page indictment of the violence and suffering inflicted by the railroad. In effect, the awkward shift from the railroad to the wheat as the symbol of a greater and more indomitable "force" affirms an unresolved conflict between two metaphors of epic corporeality. Norris's text circles around the problem of *which* scale more effectively measures the naturalist force of production. The *overcoherence* of globality promised by the wheat weighs against the *incoherence* of the machine.

Both lines of argument appear to be in keeping with the longstanding critical debates about naturalist fiction as a form of failed realism. Indeed, recent critics of *The Octopus* who have deepened accounts of the railroad's

formal disruptiveness continue this tradition of argument about naturalism's narrative failures.[28] Such a reading of the "symbolic overload" of the
railroad harks back to early critical discussions about the power of realism
versus romance—a debate initiated by Norris himself, who saw in it no
less than the future and capacity of narrative realism at stake. Presumably,
Norris intended his three-volume epic to offer an overall canvas of a scale
adequate to contain and proportionalize the mythical "grotesque corporeality" of the railroad.[29] But *The Octopus*'s turn toward the more abstract
metaphor of the wheat only calls even more specific attention to the ways
in which the body of the railroad ("a monster born of the alienation of
labor," according to Meadowsong) resists demystification. It is unlikely
Norris could have resolved this contradiction of his corporate aesthetic.
Nonetheless, the structural divide of *The Octopus* suggests the ambition
to develop an epic standpoint that disables neither realism nor romance.

Gain's Epic Undoings

If *The Octopus* sought to locate monopoly capitalism within a coherent
totality, *Gain* uses the epic gesture to seek alternatives to the totalities
produced by capitalism. While Norris's novel reveals the problem of epic
incoherence at a literary or aesthetic level, Powers's novel attends to the
temptation of overcoherence at the level of capitalist self-representation.
In this way, we might say, *Gain* definitively shifts the problem of the corporate narrative into contemporary terms. The epic remains a problem
of scale. But it also reopens the question of point of view. A brief set of
examples demonstrates the different divisions and unities of the texts:

> My respects to the hungry Hindoo. Tell him "we're coming. . . ." Tell
> the men of the East to look out for the men of the West. The
> irrepressible Yank is knocking at the doors of their temples and he will
> want to sell 'em carpet-sweepers for their harems and electric light
> plants for their temple shrines." (Norris 648)

> The world was still full of unfilled vistas. One simply had to look
> farther afield. The Philippines was awash with people who craved
> Clarity Pore Purifier. Isolated Indonesian villages swarmed the Clare
> Lady who came selling shampoo samples out of her motorboat.
> Already Brazilian Partifest sales were growing twice as fast as North
> American. Eastern Europe had a hundred million young adults ready
> to swap their Trabis for a year's supply of Compleet and Viva-cleanse.
> The Indian middle class would soon outstrip any in the world. In China
> alone, one billion people had never tasted fat-free fruit snacks made

with real fruit. And by the time Clare filled all that map in, even Africa
would be ready to provide additional new markets. (Powers 338)

Castronovo specifically argues that the above scene expresses the "jocular
Yankee optimism for profit that sees commodities as the building blocks
of total cultural synthesis. As the shipping magnate bids farewell to Presley, he licks his chops over the new markets that the poet will encounter
on Asian shores." The text's aesthetic of global unity—or what Castronovo calls its "aestheticentrism"—is driven by expanded consumption:
"Cosmopolitan promise masks Orientalist threat; humanitarian mission
primes the development of overseas markets."[30]

The Octopus thus appears to promise aesthetic reunification through
the global expansions of the twentieth century. In fact, the passage might
be said to invite precisely what Mark Seltzer has elsewhere warned literary
critics against: the temptation to read the nineteenth century as all about
production and the twentieth as all about consumption.

But whereas West speaks to East in the first passage through the proxy
figure of the industrialist, the second is narrated from the self-synthesizing
viewpoint of global capital itself. The horizon has expanded from an East/
West axis of exchange to cover the entire map ("even Africa"!). Markets
reach equilibrium automatically as the Clare Lady is "swarmed" by eager
natives. Expansion is couched in terms of Whitmanian "vistas" of progress and democracy. Labor is swept out of sight. Global brand names are
fully autonomized. There is no direct dialogue. Language ("year's supply";
"fat-free") becomes the free indirect discourse of advertising. In this discourse, *everything* is production and *nothing* is production. The result is an
ideal condition of capitalist self-reproduction to which virtually all relations, spaces, and temporalities become assimilable.

The authority of this vision is equaled by no single individual, not even
the one at the top of the company. In one scene a 1980s Clare corporation
CEO is shown sitting in a "glass-skinned executive aerie" high over the
city of Boston. The view from the aerie could conceivably offer a version
of the Whitmanian "aerial view" that Laura, as Bruce Robbins argues,
has begun to develop as a result of her illness.[31] But instead of the poetic
capacity to imagine beyond the immediate geographies and temporalities
of the present, the CEO's view is of himself as "the corporation's point man,
the passive agent of collective bidding" (349). This particularly *Octopus*-
like scene emphasizes the "subjectlessness" of the corporation—a headless
body with no agents at the helm. With its address everywhere and nowhere,
including offshore tax havens, the corporation is a virtual entity producing

virtual products. (The company advertises financial services such as insurance and retirement and investment portfolio advising through its "Clare Material Solutions" division.) Just like Norris's railroad manager, who denies having any control over the company at all and claims that the railroad serves the natural expression of supply and demand, the Clare CEO is amused, even, "drawing the salary he does, how little say a CEO has about anything" (349).

Here the "subjectlessness" of the epic mode becomes the point of entry for the novel's critique. The intertexts of *Gain*, underdiscussed in criticism of the novel, suggest a resource for rethinking the subject/object unity of the corporate aesthetic. In *The Dialogic Imagination* Bakhtin writes that "epic disintegrates when the search begins for a new point of view on oneself."[32] The movement from epic to novel is a movement toward a point of view that is singular, limited, and subjective. Bakhtin's observation on point of view suggests a corollary for our reading of the novel form today: that a problematic temptation to aesthetic totality is a potential consequence of the *overcoherence* of subject and object. The perspectival unity of the corporate epic makes it impossible to distinguish between them. As the overcoherent narrative of Clare shifts almost without transition between these perspectives, it becomes impossible to say what is and isn't part of a "point of view."

The intertexts, the third mode of Powers's narrative, disrupt the reified unity of the omniscient whole in way that reopens this question. Not quite description and not quite narration, these material and documentary interludes are presented, without commentary, as if samples from an archive of the cultural unconscious. They include visual graphics, such as a stick figure drawing, a company flow chart, or a chart of linked chemical compounds. More often they comprise text set off from the main text not graphically but *typo*graphically with alternative fonts or types. When not set off at all—as in the case of the camera—the "object" in question is described visually. With its emphasis on what is and isn't visible to the naked eye, this mode of visual description narrows the distance between narration and description. There is no way to "read" the camera without at the same time narrating multiple histories of production, such as logo design decisions, necessary legal disclaimers, or the meaning of this global manufacturer's California address. Here in another description, of a postcard, is an example of a *textual* object being read as a *visual* object:

> *At bottom, next to the* Copyright © 1997 Attention Grabbers
> Marketing, *two tiny icons proclaim:* PRINTED WITH AMERICAN SOY INKS
> ON RECYCLED PAPER.

On the back of the card—Bulk Rate U.S. Postage Paid, Lacewood, IL Permit No. 534—*arranged to fall within the recipe card's outline, the* Next Millennium Realty *logo adorns a picture of* Laura Rowen Bodey, Broker, GRI, CRS. More than just an agent. Because your home is more than just a house. Call your friend in the business. (55–57)

A postcard (especially one with no images) might appear to meet the most minimal conditions of being an "object" as opposed to a text. To scrutinize the postcard *as* an object means treating both textual and nontextual elements as likely signifiers. This includes the fine print, the particulars of graphic design, the function of a bulk postal-rate symbol. Here the narrative narrows the distance not only between narration and description but between representation and reproduction. To *represent* is to recognize that different kinds of marks fall into different meaning categories. To *reproduce* is to replicate all marks, whether understood as signifiers or not. In this sense, the passage above aims not to represent the postcard, nor to visually reproduce it, but to *discursively reproduce* it. Like a visual reproduction—a Xerox copy—it captures even seemingly random or unimportant elements. But as a discursive reproduction, it also insists on a minimum level of recognition of elements that we might ordinarily see without seeing.

Such reproduction suggests a mode of as-yet-unrealized close reading. In turning the object into a summary of potentially unlimited signs, this reading might be described as a strategy of avoiding interpretation. In this sense the text performs what Bruno Latour calls the "cultivation of a *stubbornly realist attitude*."[33] Latour actually mentions Powers in a footnote of his widely cited essay "Why Has Critique Run Out of Steam," which addresses the stalemate of contemporary intellectual discourse in which so-called facts become co-optable for any of a variety of ideological positions. Latour argues for adopting a method of analysis that replaces "matters of fact" with "matters of concern." Instead of moving rapidly from questions of fact ("What is it?") to questions of meaning, interpretation, and critique ("What does it mean?"), Latour's method requires situating the object within the entire "complex" of issues it raises and to resist "prematurely naturalized objective facts."[34] Such an analytical method acknowledges that the "facts" are only a small portion of a larger "state of affairs." To slow down and seek a greater roominess in the question "What is it?" is to invite an accumulation of issues, relations, and histories. It is to ask, for instance, how the object came to be understood as such, what participants are involved, and what knowledges and perspectives are required to contextualize it.

Latour's idea that no simple "fact" exists tout court essentially rehabilitates a Lukácsian critique of reification but without the Marxist framework. Latour writes: "Objects are much too strong to be treated as fetishes and much too weak to be treated as indisputable causal explanations of some unconscious action."[35] This suggestion—that objects are too much *and* not enough like subjects—seems to correspond to Lukács's description of the object, as conceived within the epic, as "metasubjective": "Since an empirical form-giving subject follows from the empirical nature of the object seeking to acquire form, this subject can never be the basis and guarantee of the totality of the represented world. In the epic, totality can only truly manifest itself in the contents of the object; it is metasubjective, transcendent, it is a revelation and grace."[36] The "transcendence" Lukács describes is, I would argue, the very projection that Powers's novel works against. In the narrative this fusion or "unity" of interior and exterior points of view is not the prelapsarian innocence that some critics have accused Lukács of mistakenly projecting backward onto the epic world. It is the contemporary mystification conferred by global capitalism, which produces divisions of labor between subject and object and at the same time projects their reunification through the commodity. The formal "gatherings" of the object scrutinize the virtual fusion of subject and object. The postrealism of the narrative here is aimed at disrupting the free indirect "transcendence" between the Lukácsian "form-giving subject" and the "object seeking to acquire form."

In Powers's novel, this mode of resistive reading is a way of both returning to the fetishized and/or reified object theorized by Marxist criticism and seeking in it a new wedge for materialist critique. The epic, we might say, works not to defetishize (nor, importantly, to de-factize) the object by exposing its falseness of appearance. Instead its bulky realism works *additively* to build a field of theoretically unlimited causalities, determinations, and relations. It compensates for the limits of realism by adding more realism. In its gesture toward an encyclopedic accumulation of detail, *Gain* claims the whole of American history as its research archive. This endless gathering is not a movement toward synthesis, however, but toward disruption of the seeming unity of the object (or Latour: "fact") by adding more and more information. Epic detail becomes compensation for the object's tendency to assume reified wholeness and closure. In short, it prolongs incorporation as a process and forestalls it from becoming an end extractable from that process.

Wai Chee Dimock, in the essay "Genre as World System," offers different, but in my view ultimately complementary, terms for reading epic as a problem of scale. The epic, she argues, is a form that expands and contracts depending on the scale of measurement required. By way of Plato and Aristotle's definitions, she describes the epic as "not smooth": "The epic is the most lumbering of genres; its transit through different environments is a slow transit; this slowness opens it up, makes it porous to its surroundings. The epic, in short, is a kind of linguistic sponge. Springing up at contact zones, it is also super-responsive to its environment, picking up all those non-Greek words that come its way, but not necessarily dissolving them, perhaps keeping them simply as alien deposits, grains or lumps that stick." The rough, sponge-like surface of the epic makes it uniquely slow moving, incorporative, and accumulative. It gives it its "special tendency" (Aristotle) toward greater bulk and its own mode for "gather[ing] together the world."[37] Dimock borrows a model from fractal geometry to develop a more global *and* more particular literary account of the epic.[38] Fractals, she argues, is "the geometry of the irregular and the microscopic, what gets lost in a big picture." An extreme close-up, for example, reveals folds, crevices, or wrinkles that are simply not measurable from a more distanced viewpoint. The "scalar recursiveness" of the fractal model, which combines both "finite parameters and infinite unfolding," becomes a model for the kind of morphology that the epic requires.[39]

Gain demonstrates how the epic can be simultaneously a form of accumulation, as in Latour's terms, and a form of prolongation, as in Dimock's. Its epic structure resists premature synthesis in favor of continuing accumulation. Its realist "gathering" is also a delaying, the incorporation of a temporal mediation to its additive structure and disrupting the critical impulse toward closure. I have discussed the ways in which the intertexts can be seen as unassimilated lumps in the epic narrative that *resist* the incorporation of all conscious and subconscious material into a seamless unity of the present. This reading has also suggested that one of the "post-realist" capacities of the epic genre is to resist the conflation of subjective and objective points of view. As the corporation *claims* to narrate a larger subject/object unity, its discourses shift in free transition between subject and object in ways that signal the *would-be* omniscience of capitalism.

To treat the corporation and its productions—commodities and discourses—as matters of concern, then, is to take them as objects *contra* Lukács—not as sites for marking a loss of totality but for suspicion of false unities. Narrative compensation for these epic tendencies is the search to reopen the divisions of labor between subject and object that capitalism has concealed. Powers's elaborately aestheticized omniscience ("Disturbance disrupted distribution") neither proposes a recoverable narrative totality nor elegizes its loss. It acknowledges the fetishization of narrative authority and targets its presumptions of synthesis. Laura's museum visit performs the same function for her that *Gain*'s intertexts perform for the reader: to move us from a passive (or Lukács: "contemplative") relation to the object to a more subjectively engaged one. Such engagement, as discussed above, appears to demand a Latourian realism that can accommodate more data while resisting premature knowledge or assessment.

Gain thus rewrites the corporate epic for late global capitalism, to rethink the divisions of abstract and concrete, wholeness and fragmentation, subject and object. The outward and inward, expanding and contracting scales of the narrative reveal the demand for a narrative form that forecloses neither micro nor macro scales of world making. If we read Norris's formal expansion of the corporate epic as a way to unify and naturalize the cycle of accumulation, *Gain* would seem to affirm precisely the falseness of such aesthetic coherence in the face of the epistemological fragmentation of a fully developed commodity-object world. Powers's novel therefore cannot itself be characterized as an example of "epic attempt" in Moretti's sense but as a formal challenge directed *against* the capitalist epic fantasy in which "things need not be grasped to be used," as the camera at the beginning of this chapter is described. *Gain*'s epic undoing aims to short-circuit the world-system's ability to aestheticize and narrate itself.

Contemporary theorists have sought to rehabilitate the notion of totality for the present as more than an outdated "yearning for some sort of plenitude,"[40] and even to reconceive reification as a problem of subject/object interrelation.[41] If the economic realism of a century ago sought totalizing forms to represent monopoly capitalism, the contemporary novel confronts the problem of totality in a new way. The turn to various realisms in contemporary fiction suggests the novel's ongoing effort to develop modes of representation adequate to an abstract and globalized capitalism while able to disturb its systems of mystification. The contemporary anti-epic *attempt* is an aesthetic mode that seeks to undo, or at least to disturb, the corporate drive toward a unified totality, calling attention to these projected coherences and turning the epic fantasy of capitalism against itself. Instead of seeking to "balance" its internal contradictions, the contemporary novel questions what ends such an aesthetic totality might serve.

CHAPTER FOUR

Financial Sublime

Virtual Capitalism in Don DeLillo's *Cosmopolis*

Mystifications

In his 1997 book *Wall Street*, economic historian Doug Henwood takes postmodern theory to task for its failures to explain the "real world" of finance. Ignoring actual production, he argues, the discourses of global capital promote an understanding of finance so shallow that it could be "derived from capital's own publicists." "Cybertopians and other immaterialists," he writes, "are lost in a second- or third-order fetishism, unable to decode the relations of power behind the disembodied ecstasies of computer trading." Rejecting fantastical descriptions of capital as "weightless," "astral," or able to "launch itself into orbit," Henwood cites the work of Jean Baudrillard as an example of how academic theories of capital have become indistinguishable from neoliberal faith in market self-regulation:

> Marx simply did not foresee that it would be possible for capital, in the face of the imminent threat to its existence, to transpoliticize itself, as it were . . . to make itself autonomous in a free-floating, ecstatic and haphazard form, and thus to totalize the world in its own image. Capital (if it may still be so called) has barred the way of political economy. . . . It has successfully escaped its own end. . . . Money has now found its proper place, a place far more wondrous than the stock exchange: the orbit in which it rises and sets like some artificial sun.[1]

Six years later, in *After the New Economy* (2003), Henwood again criticizes the "partisans of weightlessness," arguing that they "overlook the monetized social relations behind seemingly insubstantial wares." He reiterates his main point that "though financial markets seem very fanciful, appearing detached not only from production but even from social relations, they are actually institutions that consolidate ownership and control among the very rich of the world." And in the wake of the collapse of dot-com stocks, the widespread disillusionment with the New Economy, and numerous accounting scandals, Henwood again quotes the same passages from Baudrillard. But beyond calling them "several years ahead of the accounting profs," he refrains from further critique, as if recent events had made their flaws sufficiently obvious.[2]

The implication is that if we cannot separate the real and the mythical in our accounts of capitalism, and if we fail to reject euphoric metaphorizations of finance, history will at some point have a (painful) correction in store. And Henwood is not alone in calling attention to the overlap between certain leftist discourses about capitalism and neoliberal discourses of the market.[3] But to accuse cultural theory of excessive abstraction from economic reality, as he and other commentators have done, is not simply to echo a by-now standard complaint about postmodernist theory as being essentially conservative and/or nihilistic. Instead, this critique highlights a central contradiction in our understanding of capitalism since the last quarter of the twentieth century: namely, the problem of abstraction itself. Although conceptions of "liberated" capital may have emerged out of an entirely different set of ideological commitments than New Economy discourses in the 1990s, they converged around a shared image of markets as frictionless entities where abstract capital moves freely through barriers of time and geography, information is universally distributed, and the market itself symbolizes a general system of intelligence too flexible and immense for individual control. As globalization narratives became increasingly shaped as financial narratives, finance capital, in particular, has come to define a new level of conflict between the real and the unreal. If the mythical and the real appeared to become exceptionally compatible during certain moments of technocapital advancement (which certainly happened during the rise of Internet and tech stocks in 1990 and continued, except for a brief interruption in 2000 and 2001, in the spheres of housing and global debt financing), how do we discern capitalism's actual operations and effects on the world—except historically, in hindsight? Even as the most recent efflorescence of "new era" exuberance in the mid-2000s (with finance suddenly, again, proclaimed to be unbound by material, national, or temporal constraints) has been punctuated by its own meltdowns and scandals (driven by mysteriously complex debt instruments, subprime lending, Ponzi schemes on an unprecedented scale, and overall regulatory negligence), we can hardly doubt that the cycle will eventually be repeated, heralded by yet another embrace of capital's "emancipation" from reality.

The question at stake, therefore, is our relation to these narratives of abstraction and the power that they exert upon us despite our collective desire to keep capitalism accountable (a desire that I take to be a common denominator among its critics). Henwood concedes that to examine the financial system in terms any less abstract is not easy. "It's a system that seems overwhelming at times, almost sublime in its complexity and power."[4] And it is precisely because "sublime" or "fanciful" conceptions of global finance are so dominant that Henwood aims to resist allowing terms such as *finance*, *capital*, and *money* to become abstractions in the first place. That Henwood, in his first book, frequently takes Baudrillard's use of *capital* and *money* and replaces them with the word *finance*, for example, already indicates an attempt at the level of language to reassert the material relations of power, to counter the loss of agency implied in abstract, semi-autonomous representations of capitalism, and to reframe the discussion in terms of discrete operations and agents.

For all Henwood's acerbity, in other words, perhaps the limitation of his critique is that it fails to take the problem of the sublime seriously enough. It ignores how the discourses and images of an abstract totality help produce a "cognition" of capitalism that, in turn, only further contributes to its financial realization. What I will here call the *financial* sublime refers to the full range of mystifications of capital—technological, political, and otherwise—that make it difficult or impossible to distinguish the actuality of money from the increasing unreality of global capitalism. It acknowledges an ambiguity that is perhaps irresolvable: on the one hand, a troubling aestheticization (which Henwood is right to see as depoliticizing the "real" power of finance), and on the other hand a real symptom or expression of the historical imagination that cannot be simply dismissed as a "false" representation. I propose that we treat the financial sublime as an invitation to theorize yet another level in the processes of "economic mystification" that Marx considered inherent in all capitalist forms of production and that Lukács located as the root of the social phenomenon of reification. The sublime, in this reading, demands more than a well-intentioned contrast with "real" finance. In effect, finance now becomes more "realized" through the accelerating dynamics of instability, circulation, asymmetry, and totalization. Money—the original sign of abstraction under modernity—now signifies an ever-expanding *process* of abstraction across time and space.

The main character of Don DeLillo's novel *Cosmopolis* (2003),[5] in studying the flow of currency information across computer screens, no doubt "celebrates" the transcendence of the material world and the obsolescence of time and space in precisely the way Henwood criticizes. In his romance with capital, Eric Packer is indeed a George Gilder–ish figure. "There's a common surface," Packer declares, "an affinity between market movements and the natural world" (86). (Gilder, who is characterized by Henwood as the personification of conservative cybertopianism, made himself over from a 1980s-era class theorist to a 1990s New Economy promoter by selling subscriptions to his newsletter of stock picks, the "Gilder Report." In *Cosmopolis*, Packer is described as having started his career forecasting stocks on a website.) DeLillo's novel, which has been widely panned as a dissatisfying critique of global capitalism, can be understood to revolve around the convergence discussed above between a neoliberal fantasy of technology and the seductions of "transpoliticized" capital.[6] Its main character appears to endorse the contemporary metaphorization of capital (to use Baudrillard's semi-ironic terms) as "autonomous," "free-floating," and "ecstatic and haphazard." Yet however ironic this representation of the sublime in DeLillo's text, it cannot be easily "de"-abstracted or otherwise unmasked, since it stands in for precisely those virtual systems that, in a global information economy, increasingly evade recognition or accountability.

Packer, a billionaire currency trader and head of Packer Capital, who moves yen around in quantities large enough to precipitate worldwide currency disturbances, loses his fortune (and his wife's) in the course of a day-long trip across Manhattan in his limousine. Although readings of this journey have emphasized, variously, Packer's impulse to self-destruction, the ephemerality of wealth in the global era, or even the Ulyssean pace of crosstown traffic, none adequately accounts for this fable of financialization, in which capitalism is imagined as not only expanding beyond the rules of historical materialism but as liberating itself from the real world altogether. Watching a stream of "soulful and glowing" green numbers, Packer anticipates a high-tech evolutionary leap: an imminent transformation in which capitalism will become "fully realized in electronic form" (24). The money moving across the screen ("numbers gliding horizontally and bar charts pumping up and down" [63]) figures Packer's quest for elusive new formulas of meaning: "He knew there was something no one had detected, a pattern latent in nature itself, a leap of pictorial language that went beyond the standard models of technical analysis and outpredicted even the arcane charting of his own followers in the field" (63).

DeLillo's critics have been quick to declare such descriptions clichéd (James Wood calls the novel's language "already half-mortgaged").[7] And indeed, they appear to derive from at least one of the author's earlier flirtations with cybercapital. When Jack Gladney checked his bank balance at the ATM in *White Noise* in 1985, the scene was no simple banking transaction but a passage between levels of being:

Waves of relief and gratitude flowed over me. The system had blessed
my life. I felt its support and approval. The system hardware, the
mainframe sitting in a locked room in some distant city. What a
pleasing interaction. I sensed that something of deep personal value,
but not money, not that at all, had been authenticated and confirmed.
A deranged person was escorted from the bank by two armed guards.
The system was invisible, which made it all the more impressive, all the
more disquieting to deal with. But we were in accord, at least for now.
The networks, the circuits, the streams, the harmonies.[8]

This is informational feedback that tells everything and nothing at the
same time; it is a prognosis based on the most advanced technology of the
mid-1980s, hovering on the verge of actual information—even confirming
that the presence of information has been conclusively detected—but
unable to deliver it in meaningful form. In *White Noise* the ATM offers
one of the most routinely powerful moments of connection with a system
that lurks beyond the borders of perception. Gladney's "waves of relief
and gratitude" echo the invisible waves, rays, and particles that the novel
everywhere invokes. To be blessed, authenticated, and accepted means not
to be "deranged" in the sense of disarranged, disordered, or incompatible
with the system.

But something has changed. In 1985 the moment was about "something
of deep personal value, but not money, not that at all." In 2000 it *is* about
money. Gazing on the yen, Packer is absorbed in the promise of systems.
"There is an order at some deep level," he insists. "A pattern that wants
to be seen" (86). The streams of numbers, the rises and falls of currencies,
the "roll and flip of data" are now openly self-referential. "Money has lost
its narrative quality the way painting did once upon a time," a character
in the novel reflects. "Money is talking to itself" (77). The electronic data
contains the "eloquence of alphabets and numeric systems . . . the digital
imperative that defined every breath of the planet's living billions" (24). If
the networks, circuits, and streams of the ATM represented our primitive
perception of the incommunicable, the screen of cybercapital now promises full-fledged transference to the "technology of mind-without-end"
(208), to the possibility of immortality, of infinite circulation, of living
"outside the given limits, in a chip, on a disk, as data, in whirl, in radiant
spin, a consciousness saved from the void" (206).

With a central image that appears hardly adequate to bear the weight
of signification that the novel puts onto it, *Cosmopolis* would seem to
offer a paradigmatic example of the postmodern sublime. Through Packer
we see the utopian convergence of capital and information that Henwood

criticizes, yet his lyric flights about cybercapital also locate a formal failure of representation. The further capital's "flight" into increasingly spectral realms, the more the numbers and charts symbolize its de-narrativization, its striving toward the altogether nonrepresentational. Reaching the limits of representativity is not a problem *of* the novel, therefore, but a problem *for* the novel, one that it locates, adopts, and inscribes into its narrative structures. Even if these lyricizations only represent a particular point of view, they still raise questions about the novel's frame of possibility. What kind of political critique do these aesthetics of the sublime enable? What new systems of meaning do they produce? Unlike *White Noise*, where money shapes our most intimate consumer identities—the mall a temple of commodity worship, the supermarket a modern Taj Mahal—*Cosmopolis* appears less concerned with any social nexus of consumption than with an image of technocapital that is ever less mediated and ever more nakedly self-referential. The more ephemeral capital becomes, the more brightly the numbers glow, as the trace of the representational within the system as it moves toward greater and greater levels of abstraction.

The image of a seamless, timeless global network, a frictionless system of exchange that can dispense with real-world referents, is by now a common one in contemporary discourse. It has circulated not only in theories of global systems—Arjun Appadurai's "financescape," David Harvey's time-space compression, Fredric Jameson's analysis of the "logic" of multinational capitalism, and Manuel Castells's view of financial globalization as an "Automaton" controlling human lives, as well as borrowed from the world-systems analysis of Immanuel Wallerstein and Giovanni Arrighi—but also as part of a common idea of capitalism as a *force majeure* that organizes a vast network of relationality around the planet.[9] The idea that this immense system has become (or is on the verge of becoming) fully elaborated through cybertechnology in ways that shape our lives on a heretofore unimaginable scale has thus become both a popular shorthand for the economic complexity and interdependence of the world as well as a powerful theme in postwar cultural and literary narratives. Emily Apter uses the term "oneworldness," for instance, to describe the condition for which conspiracy and paranoia constitute the most recognizable literary response. "Oneworldness," she writes, "refers . . . to a delirious aesthetics of systematicity: to the match between cognition and globalism that is held in place by the paranoid premise that 'everything is connected'."[10] As critics have grouped contemporary fictions through the tropes of systems of conspiracy, paranoid subjectivity, global surveillance, and postmodern techno-determinism, then what Joseph Tabbi has called the "postmodern sublime" can be understood as a response to a dystopian sense of connectedness, an anxiety about the all-encompassing reach of the "system" and resistance (however futile it might be) to its totalizing power.[11]

If this image of an unfathomable global system is already clichéd, what possibility of critique does it offer? This is the question that I suggest we understand *Cosmopolis* to have appropriated as a narrative preoccupation. What work do the sublime aesthetics of abstraction and global connectivity perform? Which recognitions of capitalism's real-world operations do they produce—and which do they foreclose? The novel does not examine any specific financial innovations, for example, or even aim to defamiliarize our assumptions about what Bruce Robbins calls "the outer reaches of a world economic system of notoriously inconceivable magnitude and interdependence, a system that brings goods from the ends of the earth."[12] Instead, the very familiarity of the image suggests how it has already been reified in the imagination, or, in other words, how our historical understanding of so-called late capitalism is inevitably conditioned and limited by the "sublime." In the absence of a viable counternarrative—one that would enable a kind of political or ethical critique that the sublime itself appears to negate, and that many critics have found the postmodern novel in general and *Cosmopolis* in particular to lack—we might understand the text's financial mystifications as a diagnosis of the absence or failure of representation to rise to the "oneworlded" level.

Thus, although DeLillo's text articulates the same problem that Henwood's does, it refuses the notion that the sublime can be in any simple way "demystified" by a sufficiently rigorous and penetrating socioeconomic analysis. Where the text turns its attention toward the ineffable, the mysteriously significant, the looming sense of meaning that lies beyond our normal capacities of perception, it also marks the failures or inadequacies of its history. The novel refuses, in the first instance, the narrative analyses of class relations or moral examinations of self-interest that are the familiar themes of American economic realism. In this sense, readings of the novel framed in terms of Packer's ethics of selfhood—Jerry Varsava calls Packer a "rogue capitalist" and a "diabolical sociopath,"[13] and media reviewers similarly describe him as a monstrous figure—actually obscure the politics of the novel; in order to press DeLillo into a more vigorous critique of capitalism, they must reduce the text to a denunciation of self-interest and laissez-faire economics. The novel is both subtler and more far-reaching if we see it as an experiment into how capitalism's virtualization at once excites and impoverishes the historical imagination. In my view the novel is not about failures of market regulation, for instance, or the growth of rogue capitalism (as if "rogue" and "legitimate" could be meaningfully separated in the world-economic present) but the withering of these frames of critique in the face of this new cognition of the market. The thinness of the novel's history and the abstractions of its narrative form reflect precisely this new condition: the sublime imagination of capital literally does not reach into the thickness of historical material relations. As wealth comes and goes in the blink of a cursor, *Cosmopolis* suggests, our representational techniques may be limited to historicizing the forms of alienation that are *produced* by such contemporary cultural fantasies of global technocapitalism.

Certainly modern technology has often been described in the terms of romantic sublimity, with critics suggesting that one or another innovation represents the latest mediation between self and object, or between perception and imagination, just as nature once served for nineteenth-century writers.[14] Joseph Tabbi writes, "One could hardly find a better contemporary occasion for the sublime than the excessive production of technology itself. Its crisscrossing networks of computers, transportation systems, and communications media, successors to the omnipotent 'nature' of nineteenth-century romanticism, have come to represent a magnitude that at once attracts and repels the imagination."[15] Suggesting that Kant's sublime object, "a figure for an infinite greatness and infinite power that cannot be represented" (ix), has been supplanted by modern technological forces and processes, Tabbi describes the failure of representation in contemporary literature as if it were coextensive with a larger failure of recognition—our inability to conceive of the full dimensions of these processes operating upon us: "Now, when literature fails to present an object for an idea of absolute power, the failure is associated with technological structures and global corporate systems beyond the comprehension of any one mind or imagination."[16] Similarly, Vincent Mosco, discussing the "digital sublime" of the computer age, argues that the 1990s constituted a "strong mythic phase" of cybertechnology's existence, on a par with the early days of telegraph, radio, or television. Arguing that the "mythmaking" stage is integral to the eventual social realization of any new technology's power, he summarizes the 1990s self-narrative of the digital revolution as follows: "Powered by computer communication, we would, according to our myths, experience an epochal transformation in human experience that would transcend time (the end of history), space (the end of geography), and power (the end of politics)."[17]

As DeLillo's work evidences, however, the politics of this "techno sublime" or "postmodern sublime" are more politically dynamic and contradictory than most critics have acknowledged. Mysterious networks and systems have long permeated his fiction: the mystical waves and rays of *White Noise*, the cosmological balances and patterns of conspiracy in

Libra, the global corporations and intelligence systems of *The Names*, or the deterministic coincidences of history in *Underworld*. Technology in his work is a moving target of meanings and associations. As its forms evolve, its meanings, objects, and associated historical consciousness also shift. As history "catches up" to the novelist's imagination (a development frequently remarked upon by DeLillo readers), the stakes of the representation change. The "clichéd" technology in *Cosmopolis*, by intensifying figures that predated (even predicted) the new technology in earlier texts, thus represents at once an emptying and a doubling down. As the unfathomability of DeLillo's familiar networks is now literalized in *Cosmopolis* by the rise of digital globalism, we might therefore need to ask new historical and political questions about how the real-world gap between the literal and the figurative has been tightened. If the digital technology of the 1990s merely overtakes and validates the images of capital already in circulation, then the novel suggests paradoxically that this overdetermination has not made capital more representable—quite the reverse. In its confrontation with financial unrealism—a projection of capitalism as evolving beyond time, space, or history—DeLillo's work also confronts the adequacies of the novel form to meet our present-day imaginative capacities.

Technological Consciousness

Let us note another important feature of *Cosmopolis* carried over from *White Noise*: an odd, peripheral figure hanging around by the cash machine. The "deranged" person that Jack Gladney saw removed from the bank recurs here as an anonymous (but still "strangely familiar") figure occasionally spotted by Packer at different cash machines around the city. We learn his name (or names) when his first-person journal entries interrupt Packer's third-person narrative. Benno Levin is an assumed name of a onetime employee of Packer who is stalking and threatening to kill his former employer. He reveals that he was once an assistant professor of computer applications at a community college, until leaving to "make my million." At Packer Capital he analyzed the baht until he was "demoted to lesser currencies" and then fired without warning or severance. Left by his wife and child, he squats in an abandoned West Side building, stealing electricity from a lamppost like Ellison's invisible man and writing "The Confessions of Benno Levin," a "spiritual autobiography" that he expects to run for thousands of pages. "The core of the work will be either I track him [Packer] down and shoot him or do not, writing longhand in pencil" (149).

Levin travels at the dystopian edges of the system. Despite his marginal existence, he does not reject the circulation of technology—indeed, this is not possible—but has failed to activate himself within it. For Levin technology is not a source of transcendence but of paranoia, contagion, and dysfunction. He claims to suffer various strains of global illness "contracted from the Internet," namely, *susto*, or soul loss, from the Caribbean and *hwabyung*, or cultural panic, from Korea. He keeps a bank account "for the ongoing psychology of it, to know I have money in an institution. And because cash machines have a charisma that still speaks to me" (60). Levin's compulsive need to check his account several times a day signals a formal link between subjective and economic systems. Picking up where the ATM incident in *White Noise* left off, Levin says he uses the cash machine outside because the guard won't let him inside. "I could tell him I have an account and prove it. But the bank is marble and glass and armed guards. And I accept this. I could tell him I need to check Recent Activity, even though there is none. But I am willing to do my transactions outside, at the machine in the wall" (151). The money in the account is beside the point; it is the ATM card, and having access to the nerve system of capital, that authorizes a kind of minimum balance of subjective functioning.

Wherever DeLillo's novels take up the figure of the paranoid or the isolated outsider, the problem of technology becomes linked to consciousness and agency. Levin's soul loss and cultural panic, contracted in the form of a Web virus, might be considered what Timothy Melley calls "agency panic," or an "intense anxiety about an apparent loss of autonomy, the conviction that one's actions are being controlled by someone else or that one has been 'constructed' by powerful external agents."[18] In the conspiracy framework Melley analyzes, to be a subject in postwar America is to conceive of oneself as monitored by forces of surveillance, manipulation, and control. It is to assume the existence of operations—governmental, technological, scientific, or corporate—that circumscribe one's movements and are manifested in one's conscious processes. "This is the age of conspiracy," Melley quotes from DeLillo's *Running Dog*. "The age of connections, links, secret relationships."[19] Indeed, the "deranged" man from the ATM encounter in *White Noise* reemerges here with a paranoid anxiety about the loss of control that is entirely familiar. Levin is defined not by his lack of money but by his phobia of daily capitalism: "I'm helpless in their system that makes no sense to me," he says. "You wanted me to be a helpless robot soldier but all I could be was helpless" (195). He is overwhelmed by the complexity of ordinary functioning in the modern world: "I thought all these other people. I thought how did they get to be who they are. It's banks and car parks. It's airline tickets in their computers. It's restaurants filled with people talking. It's people signing the merchant copy. It's people taking the merchant copy out of the leather folder and then signing it and separating the merchant copy from the customer copy and putting their credit card in their wallet. This alone could do it" (195). By way of the institutional rules of subjectivity demanded by modern systems—how to buy airline tickets, to use credit cards—Levin's basic failure is his inability to keep up. "It's all I can do to be a person," he protests (196). "I loved the baht," he tells Packer. "But your system is so microtimed that I couldn't keep up with it. I couldn't find it. It's so infinitesimal. I began to hate my work, and you, and all the numbers on my screen, and every minute of my life" (191). Levin claims to aspire to a temporality beyond the reach of capitalization: "I don't own a watch or clock. I think of time in other totalities now. I think of my personal timespan set against the vast numerations, the time of the earth, the stars, the incoherent light-years, the age of the universe, etc." (59–60).

But the effectiveness of a conspiracy framework is limited here, since Levin is a thin and minimally developed character whose point of view never seriously rivals Packer's. Even though Levin's "Confessions" are written in the first person, the text is as strongly dominated by a third-person perspective as White Noise—where, Frank Lentricchia has insisted, there is really nothing outside of Gladney's aestheticization of everything he sees.[20] (Like much of DeLillo's third-person technique, Packer's point of view resembles an unusually objectified form of first-person.) As an indeterminate first-person voice, therefore, Levin is perhaps better understood as a figure for the kind of social analysis that the sublime disables. In the era of financial unrealism, alignments with or against rich or poor no longer make sense—at least right now. "You're not against the rich," Packer tells Levin. "Nobody's against the rich. Everybody's ten seconds from being rich. Or so everybody thought" (196). Although Levin disrupts Packer's narrative of the technosublime, he hardly offers a viable or coherent counternarrative. In essence, standing for the diminished power and status of an Other, who nonetheless cannot be written out, Levin is the figure of the sublime.

In a review of Cosmopolis, John Updike suggests that DeLillo's natural allegiance to marginalized persons interferes with his representation of the rich. "How much should we care about the threatened assassination of a hero as unsympathetic and bizarre as Eric Packer?" he wonders. "DeLillo has a fearless reach of empathy; in Mao II he tells us just what it's like to be a Moonie, and how the homeless talk. But for what it's like to be a young Master of the Universe read Tom Wolfe instead. DeLillo's sympathies are so much with the poor that his rich man seems a madman."[21] Updike's comparison to Wolfe reveals more about his default expectations for social satire of the rich than about what *Cosmopolis* actually delivers. And he is hardly alone; references to *Bonfire of the Vanities* abound in the novel's reviews.[22] But if Packer initially appears to have wandered over from the pages of Wolfe, with his high-rise apartment, security team, custom-armored limo, technological toys, daily medical checkups, and other trappings of privilege, DeLillo's descriptions—in contrast to Wolfe's focus on status detail—instead inform us of the *loss* of precisely those techniques of socioeconomic analyses that Updike would presumably characterize as "sympathy." The über-elite in *Cosmopolis* is as generic as the limousines and uniformed drivers that wait at the curb: It consists of the "investment banker, the land developer, the venture capitalist, for the software entrepreneur, the global overlord of satellite and cable, the discount broker, the beaked media chief, for the exiled head of state of some smashed landscape of famine and war" (10). DeLillo's serial lists—some of the most expressively ironic moments of the novel—distill these figures into two-dimensional, tabloid images (no doubt hawked by the media chief), replicating a process of social abstraction where images of power replace relations of power in the global financial constellation. These figures are not individual objects of Wolfean satire; the list as a whole stands in for the unnarrated process of the deterritorialization of capital (from the "smashed landscape") and its reconcentration at the highest levels (of Manhattan high-rises).

I suggest, therefore, that it is *Cosmopolis*'s formal split between rival narrators rather than its social analysis of wealth that opens up the theme of how subjectivity is shaped by modern technocapitalism. The anxiety of agency is dispersed across two figures, in two directions: the paranoid who fears losing control over his world and the post-humanist who gladly anticipates his technological leap into the future. Levin's disruptions, such as they are, fail to generate a counternarrative that might enable a recognition of alterity. And although the Other may interfere with the story on a narrative level (Levin describes writing the "Confessions" while Packer's corpse lies on the floor, though the reader has not yet reached the scene of Packer's death), we do not know which narrative frames which. The shifting point of view from third to first person only further underscores the loss of subjective authority. Packer's occasional tendency to narrate his own actions in the third person (he refers to Levin as "the subject" during their final encounter, as in "the subject fired his weapon") reads as a wishful shedding of agency, a reversion to some originary code or pre-social script.

The desire to see and refer to oneself as an object rather than a subject, as an image on screen instead of as an actively shaping point of view is a theme traceable back to *Americana*, DeLillo's first book, where the main character says, "In this country there is a universal third person, the man we all want to be."[23] The promise of the third-person point of view "came over on the Mayflower" (271) and is now located in the objectifying image: the advertisement, the eye of the camera, the screen of cyberspace. As Packer seeks to disperse himself into the universal consciousness of technology, this rumbling symptom of agency (which lurks wherever DeLillo characters aspire to third-personhood) ruptures the surface of form. Where Jack Gladney's first-person narrator offers a kind of comic overcompensation for his anxiety about a world over which he has little control, Packer's third-person literalizes a desire for self-dissolution. Packer represents less the threat of extreme self-interest (as he might have represented in traditional economic realism) than the aspiration to *de*formalize the self, a yearning for "fatedness" through the power of the network. Levin's death threat is a promising opportunity that "spoke to [Packer] most surely about some principle of fate he'd always known would come clear in time" (107). He feels "disinterested and free" (136). He throws away his gun because he prefers "to trust the power of pre-determined events" (147).

What I read here as Packer's desire for *systematicity* is also a desire to merge with history. If an ATM card enables access to basic systems of personhood, then full entry into technological circulation and self-reproduction promises a whole new relationship to temporality. Already, the global flows of money have had a leveling effect over historical and political realities:

> [Packer] thought of the people who used to visit his website back in the days when he was forecasting stocks, when forecasting was pure power, when he'd tout a technology stock or bless an entire sector and automatically cause doublings in share price and the shifting of worldviews, when he was effectively making history, before history became monotonous and slobbering, yielding to his search for something purer, for techniques of charting that predicted the movements of money itself. He traded in currencies from every sort of territorial entity, modern democratic nations and dusty sultanates, paranoid people's republics, hellhole rebel states run by stoned boys.
>
> He found beauty and precision here, hidden rhythms in the fluctuations of a given currency. (75–76)

Against a backdrop of political disintegration and financial reorganization, the "monotonous and slobbering" details of history now represent the residual traces of particularity within the expansion of the global economy; here is a moment where we see the movement toward abstraction in process, becoming realized against some preceding experience of historicity.

A further result is that actual relations of production are made *historical*; they are vestigial forms from a past that has not yet caught up to the financial present. What we get is not exactly a loss of history but a *tour* of potential new temporalities. The future exerts a strong pull on Packer. He "liked knowing what was coming. It confirmed the presence of some hereditary script available to those who could decode it" (38). "He is always ahead, thinking past what is new," says Levin. "He wants to be one civilization ahead of this one" (152). On the closed-circuit security screen in the car, Packer sees his mouth move a second or two before he actually speaks. We only learn that he recently got married when he happens to catch sight of his wife in a nearby cab. We don't find out any past details of the relationship. In a series of coincidental encounters they discuss the future possibility that they might have sex. Packer recoils from a bomb blast before the shock wave hits the car. He sees his own death happen on camera in advance. Through images of past and present Packer actively narrates overlapping time. Sitting in traffic and watching the street vendors, he thinks about "the amassments, the material crush, days and nights of bumper to bumper, red light, green light, the fixedness of things, the obsolescences, going mostly unseen." An old Chinese man gives sidewalk massages, under a handwritten sign promising "relief from fatigue and panic" (83). Fatigue and panic are the symptoms that Packer's assassin later claims to suffer as a result of his exposure to futuristic technology. Reading the Chinese man's sign, Packer marvels, "How things persist, the habits of gravity and time, in this new and fluid reality" (83). In the sensory richness of street life (as opposed to the sensory richness of electronic data), Packer interprets a jostling of images of residual and emergent history. This is not a rejection of the past but an astonishment at its continuing presence.

As Packer passes through the diamond district, for instance, he contemplates an older economy that somehow still flourishes within the modern: There are "Hasidim in frock coats and tall felt hats," "exempt from the tremor of the street," "men who only saw each other" and deal in "a form of money so obsolete Eric didn't know how to think about it" (64). But the "obsolete" money of the past has not actually disappeared—it is more present than ever, by virtue of being so far removed from the virtual. ("It was hard, shiny, faceted. It was everything he'd left behind or never encountered, cut and polished, intensely three-dimensional.") A lengthy meditation on the scene connects forms of exchange across time:

He knew the traders and gem cutters were in the back rooms and wondered whether deals were still made in doorways with a handshake and a Yiddish blessing. In the grain of the street he sensed the Lower East Side of the 1920s and the diamond centers of Europe before the second war, Amsterdam and Antwerp. . . . He saw a woman seated on the sidewalk begging, a baby in her arms. She spoke a language he didn't recognize. . . . She seemed rooted to that plot of concrete. Maybe her baby had been born there, under the No Parking sign. FedEx trucks and UPS. Black men wore signboards and spoke in African murmurs. Cash for gold and diamonds. Rings, coins, pearls, wholesale jewelry, antique jewelry. This was the souk, the shtetl. Here were the hagglers and talebearers, the scrapmongers, the dealers in stray talk. (64–65)

A mythic past ("the souk, the shtetl") is connected with the universality of exchange. "Stray talk" is an earlier information economy. The advertisements survey the history of forms of value: rings, coins, stones, scraps of junk. FedEx and UPS are metonyms of circulation among these different temporalities. But it is not a nostalgic scene. The stark image of a beggar with a baby adds to the confusion of past and present, blending them synchronically. The racial hierarchy of these economic activities—the Jewish diamond trader, the African street barker, and the as-yet-unidentified new ethnic supplicant—suggests (but does not let us pause to examine) an ongoing history of global migration and displacement.

From this perspective, we can see the entire city as a palimpsest of capital traces semi-visible across time. The cosmopolis is inscribed with the history of money. At dawn the "whores were all fled from the lamplit corners" as "other kinds of archaic business" begin to stir (6). Narratives of past and future are written on façades. The names of financial institutions are "engraved on bronze markers, carved in marble, etched in gold leaf on beveled glass" (38). On the corner of Sixth Avenue is a brokerage house, "cubicles exposed at street level, men and women watching screens" (75). Its older, industrial, even pre-industrial histories are written onto the buildings: "An old industrial loft building stood on the southeast corner, ten stories, blocklike, a late medieval sweatshop and firetrap" (171). A repair crew "passing fiber-optic cable down a manhole from an enormous yellow spool" (83) sends the roots of future technology into the most archaic levels of urban infrastructure.

Technology promises to "universalize" all this history—to make possible a constant circulation of past and future within the present. If the technosublime in DeLillo's work stands in for displaced spiritual yearnings and desires, it also extends the sense of "oneworldedness" across temporalities. The literalization of a worldwide virtual network not only makes impossible a novel of moral accountability or class consciousness but also threatens to dissolve a narrative version of history into a system of universalized time, causality, and agency. To recall that the Internet's arrival is already anticlimactic in DeLillo's work—its effects having begun to appear long before the technology itself does—is to recognize how world-historical developments have tended to appropriate the author's best metaphors. When the Internet is first named as such—in the conclusion of *Underworld* (1997)—it consummates the technological intimacy that Jack Gladney had already rhapsodized about in the pre-Internet year 1985. Gladney's early vision of systematicity in the "networks and circuits" of the ATM is realized in cyberspace as a "glow, a lustrous rushing force that seems to flow from a billion distant net modes." Near the end of *Underworld*, Sister Edgar experiences an afterlife that illuminates technology as the connective substance of time. "There is no space or time out here, or in here, or wherever she is. There are only connections. Everything is connected. . . . [S]he is in cyberspace, not heaven, and she feels the grip of systems. This is why she's so uneasy. There is a presence here, a thing implied, something vast and bright. She senses the paranoia of the web, the net."[24] The Internet becomes the massive digital center of all the correspondences of history, which in turn is theorized as a set of unexplained "affinities" or connections across time whose revelation at any given moment is limited by our present technologies.

But whereas Sister Edgar wonders, "Is cyberspace a thing within the world or is it the other way around? Which contains the other, and how can you tell for sure?"[25] Packer suffers no such ontological uncertainty. Revising her spiritual transcendence as a financial transcendence, he identifies money with vast, cosmic processes and connections accessible through a cybernetic afterlife. Going broke becomes "blessed and authenticated" (136) (the exact words used by Jack Gladney at the ATM). Death represents a summons to universal memory: "The technology was imminent or not. It was semi-mythical. It was the natural next step. It would never happen. It is happening now, an evolutionary advance that needed only the practical mapping of the nervous system onto digital memory" (206–7). Packer's existential reckoning—is capital contained within the world? Or the other way around?—is a Pynchon-like question. But whereas Levin could fit easily into a Pynchon world, in which doubt and distrust are reasonable responses to a universe of unstable meanings, Packer is the opposite. He willingly abandons the agency that the paranoid is so suspicious of losing. The forces operating just beyond the edges of perception are associated positively, not threateningly, with the dissolution of the self in a joyous death drive toward a disembodied future of information: "It would be the master-thrust of cyber-capital, to extend the human experience toward infinity as a medium for corporate growth and investment, for the accumulation of profits and vigorous reinvestment" (207).

In effect, the novel's splitting of first- and third-person perspectives can be read as a division of labor. As technology makes possible capital's "oneworldedness," and as the subjective self—of classic liberal autonomy and self-possession—is disabled in favor of an increasingly technologized third person, agency becomes expressible in terms of circulation, self-reproduction, and even post-humanist systems.[26] Theorists of culture remind us that such systems of objectification have a basis in the dialectic of capitalism itself. In fact, as Benjamin Lee and Edward LiPuma have argued in their work on cultures of circulation, the market *demands* an asymmetry of first- and third-person agentive perspectives. In *Capital*, they note, Marx "creates a model of collective agency in which objectification and fetishism embed a third-person perspective on exchange relations within a first-person dialectical model of social totality."[27] (Labor being the agentive subject, and price the third-person objectification of labor.) This asymmetry of subject and object thus constitutes, in traditional production-based Marxian analyses, part of the "deep structure" of capitalism and that which continues to drive its dynamic of expansion even as old forms of production are abandoned and capital takes "flight" into global financial networks.

Packer reflects that "there was something about the idea of asymmetry. It was intriguing in the world outside the body, a counterforce to balance and calm, the riddling little twist, subatomic, that made creation happen" (52). With asymmetry as a recurring theme in the novel—Packer is concerned about an asymmetry in his prostate, he walks out of a barbershop with half a haircut—we can recognize the obvious hubris, perhaps, in his search for order, for the systems and patterns of the universe, for his insistence that the yen *has* to chart. But asymmetry is not merely a reminder of the human, the flawed, or the irrational; it is also a force of creation. Profit is generated in the discontinuities of capital's circulation (which drive Packer's currency arbitrage) and the disjunctures of time (which create debt instruments such as derivatives). If the reality of asymmetry is confirmed by Packer's death at the end of the novel—the reality of pain, the inescapability of mortality, inevitability of flaws or mutations in abstract patterns—it is also preserved in the world of social and economic inequality, the historical conditions that invite capital's restless self-discipline, its movement toward cheaper labor, fewer political barriers, more profitable markets. The uneven divisions of labor in the subject, which recapitulate the uneven divisions of labor around the globe, thus further underwrite capitalism's "systematicity"—its ability to incorporate all time, space, and history—and assert its power to remake subjects in its own image.

History's Resistance

Writing in the *New Republic*, critic James Wood reports finding in *Cosmopolis* the latest evidence of the decay of the "Novel":

> *Cosmopolis*, so eager to tell us about our age, to bring back the news, delivers a kind of information, and delivers it in such a way that finally it threatens the existence of the novel form. For in what way does this novel tell us something about the world that only the novel form could tell us? As long as writers such as DeLillo fixate on cultural analysis as the chief mode of novelistic inquiry, so the novel will be thought of as merely *unus inter pares*, one form among a number of forms (theory, cultural studies, journalism, television), all of them equally qualified to analyze postmodernity.[28]

What "threatens" the novel in this view is the degradation of form in relation to content, a refusal of the genre's responsibility to supply a higher authority over the glut of cultural matter. In embracing an aesthetics of information rather than holding off the atomization of forms, the novel— or "Novel"—becomes interchangeable with any and all modes of postmodern discourse, fictional or otherwise. Wood's attachment to traditional forms of realism is well known (his *Cosmopolis* review is littered with references to nineteenth-century novels), and his resistance to the genre's formal and historical evolution has been taken up by critics elsewhere.[29] The shortcomings of his normative view aside, however, Wood's diagnosis of fiction as overly driven by "information" returns us to the contemporary problem of realism. What Wood calls *Cosmopolis*'s lack of "perspective" pinpoints what is missing in Henwood's critique of financial realism: recognition of the cognitive mediations necessary to the representation of abstraction—and, indeed, the emergence of a whole new historical "cognition" of capitalism.

We need not elevate an older mode of realism over the purportedly fallen condition of postmodernist narrative, therefore, in order to ask what cognition of capitalism actually emerges through what Sven Philipp calls *Cosmopolis*'s "strangely disconnected and disconnecting" form.[30] It is more useful to ask how *Cosmopolis*'s formal limitations chart the fantasies of capitalism that it diagnoses. How do we map the novel's resistance to this totalizing history? Henwood warns that claims of capital as breaking historical rules, transforming markets, turning "hard" money into "spectral" information, and leaping beyond the barriers of space and time, can only serve the politics of neoliberalism. And, indeed, such ideological harnessing is neither unique to the "new economy" (in the brief period when it passed for new) nor to its later chapters of corporate malfeasance (Enron being one of the most notorious). It also belongs to the ongoing processes of globalization and their accompanying structural agendas: the opening of new trade zones, the minimizing of business regulation, the privatization of public and national resources, the disempowerment of labor and political suppression of indigenous groups, the delegation of former state functions to NGOs and for-profit interests, and the enforcement of these policies by banks and financial institutions through the global leveraging of debt in cash-poor but resource-rich countries. (Packer, in his trading in "currencies from every sort of territorial entity," represents precisely this enforcement arm of global finance.)

To expose obfuscations in the operations of the market and, wherever possible, to make visible the stakes of power and profit, is therefore only one necessary task. Another is to account for the dimensions and strength of free-market ideologies by *historicizing* the conceptions (some might say fetishizations) that underwrite them. To fail at this is to ignore the power of the representation to shape its own political reality. From here we can understand a whole range of analyses of postmodern narrative— such as Tabbi's examination of the sublime and Melley's genre of conspiracy fiction—as responses to the elusiveness of the "system." Fredric Jameson, most famously, characterizes the sublime as a mediative figuration, however inadequate, for this systemic abstraction: "Our faulty representations of some immense communicational and computer network are themselves but a distorted figuration of something even deeper, namely, the whole world system of a present-day multinational capitalism." The sublime, in this view, is a specifically contemporary problem of representation, with technology standing in for our "degraded attempt" to understand the whole: "The technology of contemporary society . . . seems to offer some privileged representational shorthand for grasping a network of power and control even more difficult for our minds and imaginations to grasp: the whole new decentered global network of the third stage of capital itself."[31]

The financial sublime can be understood as a response to the contradiction between a systemic view (a "network" with its own "deeper" logic) and a historical view (finance as a "third stage" of capital), in which capital is understood to be reaching a crisis and/or inevitable transition. In "Culture and Finance Capital," Jameson builds on the world-systems narrative, in which capitalism is conceived in terms of long historical cycles of accumulation. "Incalculable" movements of money and "new kinds of political blockage" are part and parcel of various "new and unrepresentable symptoms" in everyday life.[32] Chaos in global markets is understood not in terms of politics but of an internal contradiction. The "systematicity" of capitalism, in this view, is thus hardly ahistorical. Quite the reverse, it becomes the engine of a new grand narrative of history. Popular histories of "oneworldism" have also drawn upon world-systems assumptions. William Greider, for instance, describes finance as appearing further and further "unhinged" from reality and the global revolution in commerce and finance as reaching a "pathological" stage. He characterizes capital in the same self-agentified terms that Henwood would reject (capitalism has "leapt inventively beyond the existing order and existing consciousness of peoples and societies" and is "fast constructing a new functional reality for most everyone's life" [Greider 15]) and predicts that history will follow the same cycle as earlier world-financial revolutions ("Like Britain's before it and for roughly the same reasons, American hegemony will be ended" [193]).[33] In this world-historical narrative, the apex of American financial power will soon be visible, in retrospect, as the beginning of its structural and historical eclipse.

Notions of systematicity thus also accommodate a historical conception of capitalism as undergoing a major transformation—even, perhaps, to the point of a reversal in our assumptions of what constitutes the "reality" of the economy. Under these circumstances the task of representation—for the novelist as well as for the theorist—lies in this confrontation between the narratives of system and history. For some postmodern writers, the "impossible" relation of representation to reality is registered as an experiment in metafictional historical consciousness. Through the "historiographic metafiction" or "metahistorical romance" of post-1960s fiction, critics have identified the self-reflexive quality of the new historical aesthetics. Amy Elias, for instance, argues that the sublime offers a metahistorical figure for the *recuperation* of the historical; the sublime *is* the postmodern desire for history.[34] However, in DeLillo's novel, I would argue, the desire is not to recuperate past history but to recognize the present *as* historical. The metanarrative of the novel—as of the financial era itself—is now the de facto explanatory power of capital's role as an historical agent.

In his insistent focus on the novel's contemporaneity, Wood oddly sidesteps the challenge to read *Cosmopolis*, first and foremost, as a historical novel. What if we view DeLillo's forays into novelizing recent history not as playing with information and theory but as an experiment in acknowledging the intensification—or a whole new round of *realization*—of the unrealism of money? The sublime in this sense signals how both image and language become part of a historical condition. There is the NASDAQ ticker, for instance, which is literally too big for the eyes. Packer and his Chief of Theory leave the limo and step out to the sidewalk for the full effect:

> This was very different from the relaxed news reports that wrapped around the old Times Tower a few blocks south of here. These were three tiers of data running concurrently and swiftly about a hundred feet above the street. Financial news, stock prices, currency markets. The action was unflagging. The hellbent sprint of numbers and symbols, the fractions, decimals, stylized dollar signs, the streaming release of words, of multinational news, all too fleet to be absorbed. But he knew that Kinski was absorbing it. (80)

The meaning of these decimals and dollar signs are no more available to us than the harmonies or pulsing stars of *White Noise*. In fact, as referents disappear into pure spectacle, meanings have become more *un*available than ever. Technology does not advance our understanding but resists our attempts to keep up:

> Never mind the speed that makes it hard to follow what passes before the eye. The speed is the point. Never mind the urgent and endless replenishment, the way data dissolves at one end of the series just as it takes shape at the other. This is the point, the thrust, the future. We are not witnessing the flow of information so much as pure spectacle, or information made sacred, ritually unreadable. The small monitors of the office, home and car become a kind of idolatry here, where crowds might gather in astonishment. (80)

Streams of data are hieroglyphics, "ritually unreadable." The "idolatry" of these crowds echoes a scene in *Underworld* in which crowds gather to witness a sacred apparition on a commercial billboard in the Bronx and one of the final scenes in *White Noise* in which postmodern sunsets turn a freeway overpass into a site of spontaneous communal gathering. But where those scenes suggest an eruption of an archaic and authentic impulse into a modern context, the ticker celebrates no miracle beyond its own illegibility. Reviewer Walter Kirn even holds up this scene as an example of what happens when "fossilized academic futurism" is substituted for authentic-sounding dialogue or characters with real "souls."[35] This is a common criticism of DeLillo, whose characters often read as the temporarily borrowed effects of their own words. But does the point of view in this scene really depend on who is speaking? Packer's indirect narration supposedly takes place for his colleague's benefit, yet—since she says nothing—is self-contained. DeLillo's detached narrative style yields a form of language that is always already self-contained—dissociated from any particular speaker even as it is uttered—as if discourses themselves ran like data along discrete tiers, jumping from one level to the other without a flicker of distinction. If there is a relationship between the levels, it is specified only in that all of these discourses are universally available at once. All discourse here is always free and indirect.

In this sense language becomes another symptom of money's new historical unrepresentability, a way of tracing the formal processes of abstraction over various cultural economies. With technology changing so much faster than the word, language becomes a real-time archive of technological obsolescence. David Cowart, among others, has noted that nouns and phrases such as *skyscraper, cash register, ambulance, phone, hand organizer, stethoscope, computer, airport, vestibule,* and *ATM* are tainted with irrelevance to Packer.[36] The automated teller is "antiquated" and "anti-futuristic," a term "aged and burdened by its own historical memory" and "unable to escape the inference of fuddled human personnel and jerky moving parts" (*Cosmopolis*, 54). Some authenticity from the past seems to erupt in the speech-forms Packer hears in the barbershop—where "elapsed time hangs in the air" (166), an older cadence and accent that contrast with the general destabilization of language that is elsewhere collected, consumed, discarded. Packer's obsession with the latent obsolescence in language indicates how the destabilization of values has spread across social, cultural, and subjective registers. The financialization of discourse is not simply an instability between sign and signifier but an accelerated circulation of discourse: a speculative inflation of contexts, correspondences, and meanings.

A comic riff on the speech of a finance minister plays on the use of language as an economic indicator:

> "There's a rumor it seems involving the finance minister. He's supposed to resign any time now," she said. "Some kind of scandal about a misconstrued comment. He made a comment about the economy that may have been misconstrued. The whole country is analyzing the grammar and syntax of this comment. Or it wasn't even what he said. It was when he paused. They are trying to construe the meaning of the pause. It could be deeper, even, than grammar. It could be breathing."
> (47–48)

As in the hyperanalyzing of the phrase "irrational exuberance" following a 1996 speech by Federal Reserve chairman Alan Greenspan, the performance itself becomes the site of the negotiation of value.[37] DeLillo plays this incident for a joke about the lure of "deeper" economic indicators—somewhere in the grammar, the pause, the breath, the body. A word is no longer an indicator of value; it indicates nothing but its inadequacy to stabilize value. Discourse inflates into a bubble of competing indicators. The episode echoes another notorious example of linguistic parsing: the furor caused by President Clinton's evasive response to questioning in 1998 about a sexual relationship (Clinton: "It depends on what the meaning of the word 'is' is"). The subsequent focus on the legal defensibility of the president's statement, by supporters and critics alike, again invited speculation on the manipulation of language as an indicator of the manipulation of deeper values, on discourse as a form of risk management.[38]

The novel thus occupies these correspondences between discourse and history without settling down into direct historical referentiality. Take the word *haircut*—Wall Street lingo for taking a hit in the market. Packer's whim to visit an inconvenient barbershop recalls the apocryphal but widely reported news story of 1993, in which national air traffic was supposedly delayed while the president received a haircut aboard his plane.[39] The story of the story's circulation furthers DeLillo's theme of the autonomy of discourse, as the haircut (the word that came to signify the story) became dissociated from anything but the secondary sound bites attached to it (the cost of the haircut, the vanity of the president, the disruption of air traffic) rather than to the actuality of the event. In the novel, the "cost" of Packer's haircut includes an expensively customized stretch limo, which is later ruined, several bodyguards, one of whom is killed, and the over-clogged streets of Manhattan. His assassin suggests that one of his reasons for killing Packer is "the limousine that displaces the air that people need to breathe in Bangladesh" (202). Again, however, DeLillo uses the haircut not as a political comment but for its historical features: discourse becomes a self-reflexive event, dissociated from speaker or situation and free to circulate in contexts of its own choosing. In borrowing an essentially manufactured rumor and rewriting it here as fiction, DeLillo circulates the event yet again. In this discursive space, the word or phrase—*haircut*, *irrational exuberance*, *is*—becomes the sign of a speculative overabundance of signification, an uncontrolled proliferation of meanings around specific events.

For many readers, such self-reflexivity is precisely the symptom of literature's critical disabling, the collapse of reality with representation that Jameson associates with the "crisis of historicity." Yet DeLillo's work confronts not the *loss* of the real, the authentic, or the historical but the return of history with a vengeance, catching up to and even overtaking the author's vision. Readers have remarked on the connection between DeLillo and terrorism, focusing on the declaration in *Mao II* that the act of terror may be the only meaningful act. We might also note the premonitory, recurring appearance of the World Trade towers in the novels *Players*, *Mao II*, and *Underworld*, in the great glass bank towers of *Cosmopolis* that appear strangely empty and hard to see, and of course in the novel *Falling Man*, DeLillo's first fictional treatment of 9/11. That *Cosmopolis* did not mention the World Trade Center attacks was one of the major disappointments to critics, since these events loom ominously over a novel that was drafted before September 11 and revised in the months immediately afterward. (DeLillo's more direct historical comment on the events appears in his nonfictional *Harpers* essay in December 2001, which provocatively compares the "Genoa, Prague, Seattle" protestors' desire to hold off the "white hot future" with the terrorists' desire to return to an unaccelerated, anticapitalist form of time.)[40]

When DeLillo does write directly about September 11, moreover, in *Falling Man*, the novel's relationship to, and ability to respond to, recent history is hardly clear-cut.[41] The text circles around an event that is, again, too big and significant to see. Although the narrative begins with a man walking away from the towers, covered in dust and ash, and periodically flashes back to his spiraling descent down the stairwell of the North Tower, the text focuses less on the event itself than on its uncanniness and un-cognizability. The Falling Man is an Icarian figure—literally a performance artist dressed in a business suit who jumps off buildings around New York City and hangs, suspended, a visual reminder of the bodies falling from the towers. He is a figure for the traumatic and the sublime, that which remains unprocessable and psychically unassimilable into the narrative of history. "There was the awful openness of it," thinks Lianne, a character who witnesses two of the Falling Man's performances. "Something we'd not seen, the single falling figure that trails a collective dread, body come down among us all. And now, she thought, this little theater piece, disturbing enough to stop traffic" (33).

The image of a freely falling body—repeated, circulated, iconic—refers both reader and character to a well-known actual photograph of a man falling headfirst from the North Tower.[42] Later in the novel, Lianne searches the Internet for information about the performance artist and learns there is "some dispute about the issue of the position he maintained in his suspended state. Was this position intended to reflect the body posture of a particular man who was photographed falling from the north tower of the World Trade Center, headfirst, arms at his sides, one leg bent, a man set forever in free fall against the looming background of the column panels in the tower?" (221). As she reads this description, Lianne realizes "at once which photograph the account referred to. It hit her hard when she

first saw it, the day after, in the newspaper." As with the circulation of discursive mediations in *Cosmopolis*, DeLillo here refers without referring—
returning us to the historical event, which remains both insistently real
and mediated, with the image standing, as always, for its own impossible
relationship to historical events. Lianne first remembers the photo ("Headlong, free fall, she thought, and this picture burned a hole in her mind and
heart, dear God, he was a falling angel and his beauty was horrific" [222])
before searching for it online. But the actual photo is too disturbing to
see. Clicking forward, she cannot bring herself to look at it. Trying to connect the "burn[ing]" photo with the live performance, she realizes that she
herself has become the medium of transmission: "She was the photograph,
the photosensitive surface. That nameless body coming down, this was
hers to record and absorb" (223).

In the 9/11 aftermath "we really needed time to think," writes John
Leonard, in his review of *Falling Man*. "DeLillo returns us to that parenthe-
sis," the silence after the catastrophe, before "the event was hijacked . . . by
putschniks."[43] The process of "recording and absorbing," as Lianne puts it,
is the real event, a fragile and temporary state of suspension before meaning and narrative begin to cohere. The silences and absences, ungraspables
and ineffables, of the event are large enough to call art's representational
capacities into question. "Nothing seems exaggerated anymore," says a
character (41). And indeed, several critics have read *Falling Man* as symptomatic of the crisis of the novel, speculating that recent history has trumped
the power of metaphor. The work "inadvertently exposes the limitations
of the 'nonfiction novel' that Mailer and Capote and Wolfe unleashed on
the world," writes James Ledbetter, which "cannot accomplish more than
a semi-public revisiting of grief."[44]

Such observations might seem to confirm diagnoses of postmodernism
as an aesthetic dead end. Timothy Bewes, for instance, describes the determinative approach of recent criticism that is based on the periodizing logic
of Jameson and Harvey as "having had the effect of closing down discussion of contemporary literature, contributing to a sense of political, artistic and subjective impotence by focusing on the tragic, impossible relation
of postmodernity to representation."[45] Arguing that postmodern fiction
"is read largely in terms of banality, depthlessness, cynicism, alienation,
nihilism, political defeat, the totality of commodification—in short, as a
form that incarnates failure, endemic impossibility," Bewes links such
approaches to the claim that the postmodern "announces the end of the
possibility of the event."[46] In contrast, Bewes argues for an understanding of the work as the *occasion* of the event—a marking of the absence of
narrative wholeness within a form that remains "indisputably" the form
of a novel. In representing the Falling Man as, at once, a reference to the

incomprehensibly real event and to an endlessly metastasizing reproduction of the event ("this picture burned a hole in her mind and heart"), DeLillo's sublime opens out into this question of representational possibility. The *impossible* relation between reality and representation is not simply assumed or incorporated into the novel but is constantly theorized by the text itself. DeLillo's attention to events of history, together with the narrative's conspicuous failures and inadequacies of representation, does not simply mark the end or "exhaustion" of the novel but becomes the site of its most vital politics. The tension between the formal and the representational elements in the text, as Bewes writes, "signal the status of the text as irreducibly an event, rather than, say, the *representation* or *imagination* of an event."[47] Perhaps most significantly, this angle of engagement does not suggest a retreat from politics into aesthetics; instead the novel's concern with—and experiment with—its own status reflects its commitment to the ethics of representation.

The image of a falling man resonates across both of these texts. "Icarus falling," Levin tells Packer in their final confrontation. "You did it to yourself. Meltdown in the sun" (202). (Coincidentally, Packer happens to have studied ornithology: "He'd been interested once and mastered the teeming details of bird anatomy. Birds have hollow bones" [7].) The hubris of an Icarus, whose aspiration and audacity cause him to melt his own wings, meets with the falling man of history. Each represents a profound reckoning of losses inherent in our global narratives. The convergence of capital, technology, and virtuality both occasions and limits the imagination of global systematicity. The performance artist's re-creation of the trauma of the towers confronts the incommensurability between the historical event and aesthetic representation—history threatens to evacuate the possibilities of narrative altogether. Does such an event clear a space for new counternarratives to global capitalism? Within the texts, this seems as yet wholly undecided: DeLillo focuses not on the alternatives to the neoliberal global imagination but instead on the constant, restless, and indeed sometimes fruitless search for new modes by which such alternatives might be articulated. The novel form becomes, in the process, the sensory realization of this exploration—an exploration of what Bewes calls a sense of the impossibility of the novel form as such. A novel such as *Cosmopolis* becomes considerably more interesting when we treat it as an experiment in form, an investigation into the adequacy of our representations of capitalism in its dimensions and effects. If the results are sometimes formally unsatisfying, this reveals less about the text's shortcomings than about the nature of the problem the text confronts: the abstractions of capital in our own time and the aesthetic repercussions of these abstractions that contemporary fiction is only beginning to assess.

CHAPTER FIVE

Liquid Realisms

Global Asymmetry and Mediation in Teddy Wayne's *Kapitoil* and Mohsin Hamid's *How to Get Filthy Rich in Rising Asia*

Leerom Medovoi argues that world-systems literature is constituted by relationality. It expresses a "broader network of relationships across the unequal exchanges that striate the globe." The genre is both spatially and systemically dynamic: "World-systems literature is not simply a literature that 'maps' the scales and coordinates of the globe for us as might a chart of gross domestic products, oil consumption rates, or ballistic missiles. Rather, it is a literature that maps the dynamics of the system as an interplay of subject and object—power and desire, force and affect—as they are propelled by the spatial dialectics of territory and capital." Conceiving of global economies through these multiple dialectics is extremely useful for the project of making visible the existing asymmetries between subject and object. But Medovoi acknowledges that such visibility does not guarantee political change, as in the production of new subject positions or new forms of resistance. Thus, even while world-systems literature represents a "textually complex symptom of a world-system in transition," he concedes in a footnote that it remains unclear whether it "has a means of invoking any sense of collectivity through its allegorical function."[1]

In the previous chapter I read the split of first- and third-person perspectives in *Cosmopolis* as allegorizing the financial imaginary's fantasies of "one world" and "systematicity" against the realities of highly unequal divisions of labor. DeLillo's novel does so from the limited perspective of New York, as if one world-city could be sufficient to synechdochize global relations. In this chapter I read Hamid's *How to Get Filthy Rich in Rising Asia* and Teddy Wayne's *Kapitoil* as exploring global relationalities as the inequities and blockages between first-world and third-world subject positions are intensified.[2] Without in any simple way imagining the elimination of asymmetries, these texts formally highlight the world-system's "interplay of subject and object."[3]

Both texts turn to the literary in a way that might seem more self-referential than political, more textual than realist. Second-person narration, for example, which I will discuss in Hamid's case, is often associated with the postmodern novel; Brian Richardson has argued that the second-person point of view "threatens the ontological stability of the fictional world."[4] If a new global realism stands in distinction to first-world postmodernism (or in allegorical relation to it, as has been controversially proposed in the past),[5] it is true that these two novels do not offer clear resistance to geofinancial fluidities. Politically and aesthetically, they question capitalist relations from within narrative forms that refer to realism's mimetic, accumulative, and subsuming impulses while never "realist" in any uncomplicated sense. In reconfiguring postmodern modes and repurposing Western narratives for a radically uneven, circulation-driven global economy, in which the persistence of inequality and the violence of real abstraction are posited at the outset, they seek to resist capitalism's tendency to narrow realism to its most instrumental forms. In highlighting narrative asymmetries between subject and object, Wayne's and Hamid's texts are less about demonstrating the inadequacies of the realist novel than about radicalizing certain of its formal features.

Oil Aesthetics

Kapitoil is about a developer of financial applications from Qatar who comes to New York to work for an American investment bank. A nonnative speaker of English, Karim Issar narrates the novel in a highly sympathetic, humorous first-person combination of grammatically formal English and global business jargon of "enhancing" his "skill sets." Karim's robot-like voice sounds like a computer programmed to build new data sets out of the English language. (A character refers to his "steel-trap mind" [239].) His highly logical speech errors—the misuse of "deletes" as in "her smile deletes," or "careless" for "not caring," for example—are textually playful but also highlight a formal attentiveness to language. Indeed, printed at the end of each chapter are lists of unfamiliar words and phrases that Karim has compiled for further study—a kind of running vocabulary list that maps the nonnative speaker's journey into the idiomatic. If we read these lists not as just interruptions of the narrative but as representing a temporal backlog of as-yet-unprocessed data, they open up for the reader deeper levels of interiority and affect than Karim's uninflected narrative style at first suggests.

Karim is rapidly promoted at Schrub Equities after he writes a success-ful financial program that predicts vacillations in oil prices. The program works by searching the daily *New York Times* for keywords predictive of outbreaks of political violence in stories about oil-producing countries of the Middle East. The unique aspect of the program is that beyond obvious keywords such as "terrorism," "attack," or "gunfire," it also searches for terms such as "bitter," "weary," or "resigned"—language described by Karim as "tangential" to violence (as in "the oil minister sounded weary after talks" or "the diplomatic corps was resigned to the treaty"). Karim draws the parallel between using these tangential variables and his own position as a foreigner, an outsider: "Because I am a tangential foreign banker in the U.S., possibly I will have a greater chance of locating these tangential data, e.g. as a parallel, because I am not a native English speaker I must pay closer attention to its grammar" (19). Karim's encounter with the idiomatic—for instance, he notices when American-English speakers use "data" wrongly as a singular instead of a plural—thus generates more raw information to incorporate into his analysis. Just as Kapitoil the pro-gram refines its predictive power over oil prices, so too does Karim con-tinuously refine his internal algorithm for understanding and interacting with Americans.

For a 2010 novel with "oil" in the title, and that concerns the index-ing of global oil prices to geopolitical instability, it is surprising how far around the political the narrative steers, particularly since Kapitoil's suc-cess is tied to the tracking of rising anti-American sentiment around the globe. The only millennial event on the horizon for Karim and his col-leagues in the late 1990s is the Y2K virus, which represents a "golden opportunity" if markets are gripped by the fear and panic that experts anticipate. Other political critiques are similarly sidelined, as when Karim passes the time by calculating how much gas a plane flight or car trip has consumed or how much petroleum was used to make a couple of towers of compact disks. The development of any link between oil and first-world consumption is restricted by the narrator's narrowly focused attention. Even the compressed events of the final chapters that hospitalize Karim's sister after a bombing incident in Qatar, and precipitate Karim's ethical crisis, raise the specter of violence only to refuse to shift from a personal health scenario into political concerns. Karim's sister is not injured by the bombing, but while at the hospital she is coincidentally diagnosed with a chronic disease that would have become debilitating if not discovered in time. This development reverberates with the years-earlier death of Karim's mother from cancer and clinches his decision to repurpose Kapitoil for humanitarian ends. At the novel's end he refuses Schrub exclusive control over the oil program, successfully bluffs him about having copyright ownership, and returns home resolved to expand Kapitoil as an epidemiological, disease-predicting program instead of a capitalist, price-predicting one.

Kapitoil thus does not stage the kind of geopolitical allegory more obvious in other recent novels similarly centered on neoliberal moral hazards such as Peter Mountford's *A Young Man's Guide to Capitalism*, James Scudmore's *Heliopolis*, or Hamid's *The Reluctant Fundamentalist*, set respectively in Bolivia, Brazil, and Pakistan.[6] Though the topic of oil is an inherent reminder that issues of distribution and scarcity are concretely political, the novel appears little concerned with questions of resource scarcity, global competition, or even the environmental limits of consumption. The novel would not, for instance, be easily assimilated to the emerging critical analysis of "petromodernity," a category that critics have developed to help "map the violences that constitute global capitalism" and to "better understand the social relations of US empire."[7] Karim's crisis of conscience instead models the generic tendency of the novel to reframe structural conflicts as personal ones—in this case, the conflict of an employee whose job, visa status, and career are threatened when he refuses to sign away ownership rights over his creation. In fact *Kapitoil* is striking in its cultivation of geopolitical innocence. Its remove from the violence of neoliberalism is due in part to its pre-2001 setting, after which 1990s utopianism about globalization would no longer be possible. Karim's narrative is thus a kind of Bildung that sets a naïve idealism of market abstraction against a corrupt "realism" of United States financial interests personified by Schrub. If oil is the novel's geopolitical unconscious, its conscious preoccupation is the rationalizing and narrowing logic of financialization that, while obviously linked to political questions about the global distribution of resources, is suspended within a closing moment of political deniability.

Well aware of the uneven distribution of risk over the globe, Karim nonetheless appears at the beginning of the novel committed to a cooperative, even collective, view of global development. He corrects his father when his father uses the phrase "American economic policy of imperialism," insisting that "globalization" is a fairer and more appropriate term since it actually "creates more trade and jobs for everyone, in both the U.S. and Qatar" (9). Again, the history of the financial imperialism of the global North on the global South inflicted through neoliberal structural adjustment programs is here refused in favor of an abstracted, textbook economic model of "how markets work." While not naïve about the leveraging of violence for profit, Karim rationalizes that the violence will happen in any case with or without his making money from it. If nothing else, Kapitoil "produces at least some positives from a very negative situation," he reflects. On the face of it, of course, such logic of salvaging "some positives" cannot be distinguished from the most predatory forms of capitalism for which it does in actuality often serve as an ideological alibi. But since the violence will happen anyway, Karim reasons, at least Kapitoil "turns the violence into a zero-sum game, because the money and violence cancel each other out, instead of producing exclusively a negative game" (42).

Karim's abstract zero-sum calculation contrasts with Schrub's predatory "realism" according to which someone has to lose for someone to win. Schrub (the name sounds like an amalgam of Schwab, the investment bank, and Shrub, the nickname of soon-to-be-president George W. Bush) argues that to be ruthless is to be realistic: "If we don't do it, someone else will. . . . those are the rules of the game" (262). Pointing out that Kapitoil's success has created jobs for Karim's colleagues and more financial opportunities for the company, Schrub insists, "Look, I want to help people, too. But I'm a realist. . . . You don't cut open the goose that lays golden eggs" (262). For Schrub, then, a zero-sum game is not the salvaging of a lose-lose game but an ordinary strategy of optimization. Whereas Karim sees himself as recuperating some positives from a flawed global situation beyond his personal responsibility or control, Schrub—a player who bears a great deal more personal responsibility for a world of inequality—counsels taking a narrower view, ironically reducing Karim's world-systems-level imagining in the name of a more immediate, partial, and self-interested realism.

Zero-sum thus contradicts the logic of endless global expansion. A similar conceptual narrowing of the narrative of the "systemic" is presented by Giovanni Arrighi, who uses the term *zero-sum* to characterize the third or financial stage of the cycle of capitalist accumulation, in which "an overaccumulation of capital leads capitalist organizations to invade one another's spheres of operation; the division of labor that previously defined the terms of their mutual cooperation breaks down; and, increasingly, the losses of one organization are the condition of the profits of another. In short, competition turns from a positive-sum into a zero-sum (or even a negative-sum) game. It becomes cut-throat competition."[8] Zero-sum thinking thus signifies the turning of systemic imbalance against itself. The logic of externalization becomes one of internalization, where existing players and markets compete for dominance within a "closing" system. Zero-sum is thus a figure for capitalism's global contraction, exhaustion, and self-cannibalization. It is a manifestation of organizational breakdown in the same sense that Medovoi has used the term to characterize the development of a "terminal crisis" literature. The "cut-throat" logic of global competition belies Schrub's fairy-tale figure of the goose that lays endless golden eggs.

In beginning to question the limits of zero-sum thinking, Karim resists the Schrubbian binary narrowing of realism. This questioning begins in the area of interpersonal relations, such as when he tells a coworker that she does not owe him anything for helping her at work: "We are coworkers and coworkers are parallel to family members in that you do not incur debts" (47). The logic of loss/gain does not hold up for sexual relations either, which he decides are a "true example of something that wasn't a zero-sum game" (251). It is binary logic that Karim ultimately rejects in his confrontation with his employer. Schrub's final put-down is to call Karim a cipher, a person of no value or significance: "You are a nothing. A nobody. You don't exist" (284). With this insult Schrub extends the principle of zero-sum calculation to its logical extreme, the dehumanization of the other.

It is through the politics of language, I argue, that the novel resists this binary foreclosing of alternative social perspectives. *Kapitoil* suggests language has resources to disrupt the hardening of subject/object asymmetries. Schrub calls Karim a cipher, but most of the work Karim performs in the novel is actually *de*-ciphering. Operating much in the role of a literary critic, he detects and predicts patterns of textual meaning through close reading. As part of his study of English, Karim records conversations on a voice recorder to play back later. ("I listen on my voice recorder . . . multiple times to decipher it, because frequently it is not the words themselves that matter but the way they are said.") His analysis of the difference between "the words themselves" and the "way they are said" makes possible the final scene in which Karim analyzes a casual utterance of Schrub's to decide that his employer is negotiating in bad faith ("there was something about his 'Why don't you' sentence that bothered me besides the fact that it was less a question and more a statement" [236]). Karim's task over the course of the novel is to become less literal and more literary, learning to operate on the level of metaphor, allegory, irony, and subtext. Just as Kapitoil's predictions improve the more its data set expands, Karim becomes a more subtle social actor as he accumulates examples of English going beyond its conventionalisms. He assumes the "peripheral" status of an ethnographic observer on American culture: "As someone whose native language is not English, I must pay closer attention to the words to produce logic from them, and sometimes I observe things others do not about English" (41). His abstract model of grammatical correctness (like his abstract model of globalization) combine with the vicissitudes of real usage to produce a different model of the "real" than capital's zero-sum realism, one that is not reducible to a set of binary choices and does not require that "one party's victory always causes another party's defeat" (285).

Karim's level of close reading manifests itself formally in the narrative's accumulative structure. *Kapitoil*'s structure is not the same as Powers's epic mode of attention to commodity histories, as examined in chapter 3, but is instead trained on relations and contexts. I have already mentioned two ways in which an accumulative form is built into the narrative: Karim's glossary lists and voice recorder. A third mode of data collection— Karim's journal—is coextensive with the novel itself. All three tools imply a recursive structure of reading as Karim analyzes earlier conversations through his vocabulary notes, digital recordings, and acts of re-narration in his journal. Many of the words and phrases that puzzle him have to do, for example, with managing after-hours social relations; he humorously defines "pre-game" for instance as: to "drink alcohol in the apartment before external parties to reduce panicked feelings" (129). Karim's definition of the key terms is belated, appearing at the end of a chapter and sometimes well after the scene in question, inviting the reader to consider his revised or deepened affective reaction to earlier events. Since the reader doesn't know until the end of the chapter which phrases have caught his attention, a recursive temporal flexibility is required on our part as well, as we reconsider the relation between the "data" Karim offers and the narrative of internal development that we construct around him.

In an essay about the emergence of globalizing tendencies in American fiction, Caren Irr describes a new subgenre of "triangulated narratives." Such narratives work by "staging a collision of 'worlds' that throws the institutional and political specificities of the US into sharp relief." Irr mentions *Kapitoil*, among other recent novels, as "treating expatriates from elsewhere in the world as they encounter conditions in the US."[9] These new expatriate fictions, as reworkings of the modernist American-abroad genre, follow a pattern in which a non-American narrator-protagonist provides new "clarity" on the U.S. scene, and to the relationship of third-world or developing-world actors within it.[10] Often, as the emerging world-novel pushes away from familiar, nationally rooted identities and toward a new globalism of the subject, it presumes to "collect reflections of the livelier dramas surrounding protagonists from the developing world before absorbing both into a new synthesis at the level of the technologi-cally mediated global image."[11] Irr acknowledges that the triangulation of subjects and global spaces risks simply reconstituting familiar asym-metries of exploitation for purposes of literary credibility. Situating the developing world as an as-yet-untapped resource that serves to revitalize the first world may appear to be "an attempt to steal some reflected glory from the purported authenticity of the third world subject while containing the potentially disturbing political effects of genuine solidarity."[12]

Triangulation thus implies a seeking of synthesis, a dialectical resolution. The "metaphors of triangulated flight" to which Irr refers signal the ways in which nationality potentially becomes resolved at a "higher" level of globality. I suggest that Karim's tangentiality offers a different politics of encounter between the literary and the political than triangulation. Tangentiality is a model not of synthesis but of impermanent and limited connection. (A tangent is the single point at which two independent lines touch but do not cross.) It shares the formal properties of metaphor, a construction of temporary analogies and parallels. It preserves the independence of separate "lines" of flight while illuminating relations between them. Karim thinks about "how one object can mirror another one not because they look precisely equal, but because something more tangential feels similar" (210). Tangentiality suggests a mode of comparison that is not reducible to perfect exchange.

Language, in its movement between the literal and the literary, becomes a model for tangential resistance against the capitalist preemption of the real. The aesthetic impulse of the novel is associated with a process of a re*animation* that resists the static realisms of zero-sum. The novel's epigraph is from *Capital*: "There is a definite social relation between men that assumes, in their eyes, the fantastic form of a relation between things." Karim's literalism exposes the social relations hidden in conventional language. When he calls the shared office with his colleagues the "laboring room" (13), he draws attention to the ways that their high position in the global structure of capitalism blinds them to their role as laborers. Similarly, when he mistakenly substitutes "careless" for "do not care," he draws attention to the different meanings and affects associated with a lack of care. Karim destabilizes the idiomatic, disrupting euphemisms and penetrating reified figures of speech to reassess the vitality of social relationality underneath. When Rebecca, Karim's romantic interest, at one point says, "You're turning into a real postmodernist" (273), this does not mean that Karim, in his fascination with language, has learned to indulge like a Western theorist in the play of language and the undecideability of meaning. But it does suggest that the political stakes of his intervention are inseparable from the aesthetic. In contrast to the postmodern view of language as always already commodified and derivative—recall how quickly words become obsolete technology in *Cosmopolis*—language is here a potential site for an aesthetic revitalization of value. In other words, what is politicized about language in *Kapitoil* is not, as one might assume, the neocolonial imperialism of English over other languages in the global economy but about the unique position of the outsider in holding the dominant language to *account*.

Thus the politics of Karim's position as a nonnative speaker, I would argue, are not simply those of a postcolonial Other holding up a mirror to the West. Daniel Worden reads the tangential as the novel's figure for center/margin relations, but I suggest that the Other in Karim's case even more immediately reflects the outsider position of the artist.[13] Karim models the development of a new "global subject" not through his political insights but through his literary-creative ones. If Kapitoil is Karim's literary work—perhaps as *Capital* was Marx's novel—then Karim must be understood as a creative producer. Kapitoil is copyrighted in Karim's name. It is his literary-aesthetic creation. He decides at one point that it is a work of art since there is nothing parallel to it ("I don't believe anyone else could write a parallel program, even launching from [my] proposal . . . and it angered me that he thought other people could" [282]). The copyright detail conveniently allows the merging of the artistic and capitalistic, permitting the novel to indulge at its conclusion in a romantic conception of the artist as an independent creator who autonomously creates and retains full legal control of his work. (Karim's statement that he did not write the program on company time would not, most likely, forestall a legal struggle for control.) The improbability of Karim's being able to defend his intellectual property rights against such a deep-pocketed and aggressive opponent affirms the "innocence" of the novel mentioned earlier, just as Karim's return to Qatar to work in his father's shop feels to some extent like a wishful retreat from the negative encounters with globalization. Nonetheless, the creative fantasy of the novel is that Karim would be able to take the fruits of his labor and remobilize them for humanitarian ends, using the master's tool of copyright protection to redirect—if not dismantle—a zero-sum logic that produces no redeeming social good.

Ultimately, the political problem that the novel runs into, therefore, is not that it inadequately attends to the violence inherent in the control of global oil resources, or that it only glancingly represents the impact of financial neocolonialism on "peripheral" economies. Instead the problem lies in its own representation of the financier as a creative worker. The troubling "synthesis" suggested here is not necessarily the synthesis of first-world and third-world global subjects, as identified by Irr, but instead between the abstractions of finance and the abstractions of the aesthetic. By turning language data into art, the financier is essentially a poet, located within a highly individualized creative economy (i.e., one that recognizes and rewards "authorship"), with no implied responsibilities beyond those of his art. (Ironically, the idea that language data might lead away from rationalized methods of analysis and toward philosophical reflection inverts a trend in literary criticism toward quantitative methods of "reading.") Karim's immersion in the poetics of language happens to have positive social consequences, implying that attention to the social relations underlying reified language can reinvigorate social impulses and even lead to political action. But it would be difficult to extend Karim's example more generally to see how a social aesthetic could emerge from the individualized economy of intellectual property and ownership protection. The problem is not that the novel fails to demonstrate "genuine solidarity" in the political domain, to borrow Irr's phrasing again, but that the only basis for building solidarity that it can imagine, within its own formal confines, belongs to the copyright-holding and thus rent-extracting class. It is, then, perhaps the inadvertent "realism" of the text to expose that the parallels between financial and aesthetic creativity are as likely to serve the narrower purposes of the financial imaginary as not.

Liquidity Preferences

Mohsin Hamid's *How to Get Filthy Rich in Rising Asia* (2013) begins with a cheeky disclosure about the contradiction of a self-help book: "Look, unless you're writing one, a self-help book is an oxymoron. You read a self-help book so someone who isn't yourself can help you, that someone being the author" (3). But when you take the expansive view, the narrator points out, what book isn't self-help? "Why, for example, do you persist in reading that much praised, breathtakingly boring foreign novel, slogging through page after page after please-make-it-stop page of tar-slow prose and blush-inducing formal conceit, if not out of an impulse to understand distant lands that because of globalization are increasingly affecting life in your own? What is this impulse of yours, at its core, if not a desire for self-help?" (19). With this direct-command form, maintained throughout the novel, the narrator establishes an unapologetically instrumental relationship with the reader. The text at once announces its genre conventions and also punctures the naiveté of the reader's expectations, the extradiegetic narrator cynically exposing the real terms of the exchange: "Any self-help book advocating allegiance to an ideal is likely to be a sham. Yes, such self-help books are numerous, and yes, it's possible some of them do help a self, but more often than not, the self they help is their writer's self, not yours" (57).

The self-help form of Hamid's novel, I argue, develops the simultaneously collaborative and exploitative relationalities of global capitalism. In

its hybrid form, the novel takes on not only the self-help genre but the Bil-
dungs narrative, the business advice manual, and the "global" or "world
novel." This last category is currently understood by critics as, variously,
the inheritor of the mantle of postcolonial novel, the latest stage of development of the American novel, the aesthetic manifestation of the contemporary one-world system, or the marketable form of "cosmopolitanism
lite" that reflects the structures of a publishing industry increasingly
geared to produce English-language bestsellers from certain kinds of geo-
politically "peripheral" writers.[14] None of these definitions adequately
captures Hamid's book, I would argue, although all of them apply to it in
one way or another. Like Wayne's *Kapitoil*, it affirms the contemporary
global novel's negotiation between postmodern or "literary" metafictional-
ity and "realist" political concerns. *How to Get Filthy Rich in Rising Asia*
uses genre as an ironic mediating strategy to "contain" the novel within a
highly consumption-ready form while at the same time highlighting the
inequalities of the global system it depicts.

The novel's metaphorical mode of narration—filled with descriptions of
systems, networks, bodies, organs, cities, data flows, and planetary orbits—
may in fact seem to subsume the movement of the plot. But the chapter
titles assert a forward teleology by way of the classic stages of Bildung
("Move to the City," "Get an Education," and "Learn from a Master").
They include cautionary advice ("Don't Fall in Love" and "Avoid Idealists"), advanced Realpolitik calculation ("Befriend a Bureaucrat" and "Be
Prepared to Use Violence"), and core tenets of management philosophy
("Focus on the Fundamentals"; "Have an Exit Strategy"). By recasting
the novel of development into an instrumental, self-help mode, the text
affirms that competitive conditions require more intensified tools of indi-
viduation even if such self-Bildung is ultimately more destructive to collective welfare.

The plot follows the life of an unnamed male character from an impov-
erished childhood in the rural countryside through his rise in the unevenly
globalized city (though the country is unnamed in the book, the city is
presumably Lahore).[15] Some of the main character's early entrepreneurial
efforts include filling empty water bottles with boiled tap water and resell-
ing them. From repackaging water and re-dating expired canned goods, he
moves up to providing water-mining plants for private customers (which
drain off from municipal supplies): "You have thrived to the sound of the
city's great whooshing thirst, unsated and growing, water incessantly
being pulled out of the ground and pushed into pipes and containers"
(121). As the head of his own company he meets violence from competitors with violence, learns to pay off corrupt officials, and becomes rich

and powerful with many employees. At the height of his career he is one of the bidders to build a private water system at a gated housing development so luxurious that well-heeled residents will be able to drink straight out of the tap.

Mediating thematically among the financial and material circulations of the globe is water. Water becomes the metaphor of all systems, networks, contexts. It is convertability from material resource to immaterial accumulation. It is the original medium of global circulation between first and third worlds ("the shipping lanes binding rising Asia to Africa, Oceania, and beyond" [152]). Traces of older seafaring modes of travel are updated through the ship of a modern telecommunications center, whose "red and white masts soar mightily, towering above satellite dishes like electromagnetic spars built to navigate the clouds" (207). Water is concrete and abstract, literal and metaphorical. Water makes financial circulation possible. Convertible between more and less liquid forms, it becomes the "cloud" of value abstraction as well as the "flight" of debt: "Leverage is a pair of wings. Leverage is flight. Leverage is a way for small to be big and big to be huge, a glorious abstraction, the promise of tomorrow today, yes, a liberation from time, the resounding triumph of human will over dreary, chronology-shackled physical reality. To leverage is to be immortal" (180). The easy metaphorical associations here between financial liquidity, global connectivity, and the promise of "liberation" from material limits, are not simply to demonstrate that water is a useful vehicle for metaphorizing global capital flows. Nor the reverse—that water has some prior material ontology that resists a tendency toward abstraction. In fact I see neither the abstract nor concrete being privileged here. Instead, the text's demetaphorizing and remetaphorizing of liquidity tends to foreground a set of rival conceptual demands. How do we shift, in the text and in life, between the "cloud" of data and information on one hand, and the swelling population and crumbling infrastructure of the city on the other, in such a way that recognizes the realities of the former, while inoculating against the de-mediations, or de-socializations, of the latter?

Even as the self-help form of the novel calls attention to the competitive individuations of modernity, therefore, I argue in what follows that Hamid's second-person "you" becomes a more particular mediating form for the "liquidities" of global capitalism. The novel imagines ways of thinking about the "flows" of the world system that are not just metaphorical—or to put it differently, that highlight metaphor as part of the world-making, imaginative power of the literary. To explain this argument I first discuss the metaphor of liquid modernity and the politics of Hamid's invocation of it. I then examine more closely the "you" of the novel, which works very differently than the "you" of *The Reluctant Fundamentalist*, even though the previous novel exploits the same narrative device to mediate the politics of global relationality.

"Liquid modernity," according to Zygmunt Bauman, describes the contemporary condition in which the barriers to capital accumulation are thoroughly and systematically swept away.[16] Liquidity refers to the factors of speed, mobility, transgression, and inconstancy that allow capitalism to achieve its most effective state of domination. Max Haiven calls Bauman's liquid modernity the situation in which we are "all adrift from social relations and at the mercy of rapacious and uncaring economic forces."[17] Arguing that we "need to think of liquidity more broadly," as not only financial but social, he writes that "liquidity names the success of capital in converting social values into economic value, the pliability of social life to the dictates of capitalist accumulation."[18] Richard Godden quotes LiPuma and Lee on liquidity as the "unconditional, non-conscious, state-of-the-world social ontology."[19] Godden argues that, under financialization, as risk replaces money as the substance being exchanged, liquidity can be understood as the new "monetary figure for the general equivalence without which money's transition from idea to practice could not occur."[20] Liquidity represents the "life-processes" of financial connectivity (David Harvey's term) that lead, in Harvey's famous description, to the financialization of almost everything.

But if liquidity is a social ontology, it is also, more technically, that which facilitates circulation with a minimum of interference. Haiven specifically refers to the degree of "friction" of circulation between the financial and the social. To put this circulatory process in Marxist terms, specifically Marx's $M–C–M^1$ formula of capital accumulation that leads from money to commodity to more money, we might say that friction, or resistance to capital's easy movement, is measurable in the degree of viscosity between the hyphens. The related $M–M^1$ formula (or $M–M^1–M^2$) presumably makes circulation even easier, as money generates itself (as in the form of investment returns) and ostensibly does away with the trouble of the commodity. But Hamid's fiction insists on the ways that this process remains frictional. It reminds us that the $M–C–M^1$ formula of accumulation is always materially—and thus relationally—embodied: "For wealth comes from capital, and capital comes from labor, and labor comes from equilibrium, from calories in chasing calories out, an inherent, in-built leanness, the leanness of biological machines that must be bent to your will with some force if you are to loosen your own financial belt and, sighingly, expand" (119). The labor of the "biological machine" becomes the abstraction of exchange only when bent with "some force." Violence is required to convert the leanness of some laboring bodies into the expanding waistlines of others. (Elsewhere roads in the city are described as "belts" past which the "urban belly is already beginning to bulge" [82]; the upwardly mobile are described as the "hypertrophying middle class, bulging from the otherwise scrawny body of the population like a teenager's overdeveloped bicep" [150].) Since an embodied systematicity requires labor, it is never equalizing but tends to produce the inequality—the imbalance—that turns the cycle of accumulation forward.

Embodied frictions thus counter at all levels the circulatory pressure toward abstraction and liquidation. For instance, the economy may be increasingly global but the social body is hardly postnationalized. The (again, unnamed) nation is simply developing ever more terrible circulation problems. Cities are metastasizing uncontrollably while poorer and more peripheral limbs wither away. The rural countryside has liquidity problems of the very first order, namely flood and drought. Cattle and crops die of thirst; people die from monsoon flooding and from diseases that follow from "stagnant water." In the city, crumbling public infrastructure means a lack of clean public drinking water. "Neglected pipes are cracking" and the "contents of underground water mains and sewers mingling" (99). These deteriorating conditions underscore rising competition and privatization. (In *The Reluctant Fundamentalist*, the main character sends home money from the United States to repair a water pipe in his parents' house in Pakistan.)

Water is just one of the many unequal systems of circulation and connectivity. Urban infrastructure is being updated—not to fix broken water and sewer systems but to connect to the communications network: "Cabling is going in, seemingly everywhere, mysterious cabling, black- or gray- or orange-clad, snaking endlessly off spools into the warm, sandy soil." A character "wonders what on earth it binds together" (195). The fiber optic cabling becomes, on a subsequent page, an umbilical cord that pulls the character "with a soft finality" and that "emanates from the city of her birth" (197). Across the novel the circulations of the city and of the body increasingly converge. The narrator describes the "increasingly mythological space" of the city, a "networked" and "systemic" world ("this city . . . bound by its airport and fiber-optic cables to every great metropolis" [224]). In old age the main character uses Internet cafes to communicate with his son in the United States. He navigates an often "perilous" (212) city, with its uneven circulations of "power and gas outages, traffic noises, and airborne particulates that cause you to wake wheezing in your bed" (223).

Networks of circulation not only affirm social and economic inequality but the failure of the social itself to cohere in any recognizable form ("what on earth it binds together"). In one of its most explicitly politicized descriptions, the text uses the circulatory system of the social body to demonstrate how capitalist liquidity draws down the resources of the social: "The aquifer below the city is plummeting and becoming more contaminated every year, poisonous chemicals and biological toxins seeping into it like adulterants into a heroin junkie's collapsing vein. Powerful water extraction and purification equipment will be needed, plus, in all likelihood, a plan to draw water from canals intended for agricultural use, fiercely contested water itself laden with pesticide and fertilizer runoff" (165). This spiral of extraction and enclosure depletes the commons, contributes to the pollution of what remains, and ensures the further privatization of what is left. Liquidity here is not just convertability; it is also the liquidation of an emptying or close-out sale. The junkie's body metaphorizes the restructuring of the social around the self-cannibalizing processes of rent extraction and resource exploitation. At this level collective politics seem fated to wither. Circulation becomes the addict needing a fix. The "dessication of the soil," Hamid writes, is also a dessication of social relations. It is the "thirst of many millions driving bore after steel bore deeper and deeper into the aquifer, to fill countless leaky pipes and seepy, unlined channels" (205).

In mimicking the individualizing popular genres of the self-help book and the get-rich-quick guide, the novel appears to confirm the liquid situation diagnosed by critical theorists, in which the dissolution of the social—its networks, institutions, and public spaces—increases our exposure to the promises *and* contradictions of individualism. According to Bauman, to seek individual self-realization becomes a "fate not a choice."[21] Jiri Pribán writes: "It seems that the first collective pressure of liquid society is to act according to individual interest. The paradox of individualization is recognized by all living their lives in liquid modernity, from single mothers and unemployed workers to top managers, politicians, and even social scientists. It generates an unprecedented number of opportunities for self-creation and self-satisfaction together with troubles and anxieties arising from the need to cope with and materialise these choices."[22] The self-help form thus appears poised to critique ironically the autonomous individuality that is paradoxically fostered by increased global connectedness. But, I would argue, it is the "you" mode of the narrative—for which the self-help conceit is in some ways merely the generic excuse or occasion—that reveals a more radical ambivalence about the contemporary politics of liquidity. The "you" form of the narrative engages connective relationalities without uncritically assuming that they will destabilize the calculations of self-interest. It negotiates the gaps, inconsistencies, and incompatibilities of relations between self and other(s) without promising fluidly exchange-able subjectivities. It might be said that the "you" form maintains the *socially necessary friction* between subject and object under conditions of liquidity.

Many narrative theorists accept Brian McHale's assertion that the "second person is *par excellence* the sign of relation." "Even more strongly than the first person," he writes in his key work, *Postmodernist Fiction*, "it announces the presence of a communicative circuit linking addressor and addressee." "*You* is shifty," McHale argues. It is a "shifter in Jakob-son's sense, an empty linguistic sign whose reference changes with every change of speaker in a discourse situation: every reader is potentially *you*, the addressee of the novelistic discourse."[23] "You" is thus temporary and replaceable. (When the teenaged main character is left heartbroken by a character known only as "the pretty girl," the narrator informs us that "fortunately for you, for your financial prospects, she thinks of her second man as the one between her first and her third" [54].) "You" is both an abstraction (a role that can be filled by anybody) and the embodiment of the particular (whoever happens to be in the time and place). It shifts between anonymity and particularity, subject and object, depending on the situation.

In Hamid's novel, the shifting discourse situation between narrator and reader is ostensibly collaborative ("For our collaboration to work, in other words, you must know yourself well enough to understand what you want and where you want to go. Self-help books are two-way streets, after all. Relationships" [77]). But the "you" also repeatedly calls atten-tion to the asymmetry between addresser and addressee. Even as the nar-rative constructs a supposedly mutually lucrative relationship, it raises the question of who is working for whom: "Readers don't work for writers. They work for themselves. Therein, if you'll excuse the admittedly biased tone, lies the richness of reading. And therein, as well, lies a pointer to richness elsewhere. Because if you truly want to become filthy rich in ris-ing Asia, as we appear to have established that you do, then sooner or later you must work for yourself" (98). The "you" being addressed here is the autonomous entrepreneur of economic and political neoliberalism. Like all "you" forms, it exists in an unbreakable relation with an implied "I." (Mieke Bal notes that "It is only as (potential) "I" that the "you" him- or herself has the subjectivity to act.")[24] But the individualistic "you" quoted above does not aspire to join the social or contribute to formation of collective or group identities. Although it produces a circuit of depen-dence and recognition between self and other, as the "you" form inevita-bly must, it does so without promising any equalization between them or even necessarily to escape the destructive singularity of the "I."

Although the (unnamed) main character of the novel demonstrates the ambitious, risk-taking, and "creative" qualifications of entrepreneurial individualism, the novel also insists on the relational diffusion and distribution of the modern subject. In one sense, then, the "you" of *How to Get Filthy Rich in Rising Asia* affirms the same neoliberal selfhood that Sarah Brouillette characterizes, in a discussion of Aravind Adiga's *The White Tiger*, as "an exaggerated version of the entrepreneur as ruthless solo-agent" and as "a flexible, dynamic, self-regulating, entrepreneurial engine, willing to engage in constant reassessment and destruction of past beliefs and allegiances in pursuit of a more fulfilled and productive existence."[25] But compared to the pathologically antisocial "I" of Adiga's novel—where the main character, according to Brouillette, is trapped in the "therapeutic" terms of self-development and models "an inability to imagine a collective political response"—Hamid's "you" examines a far more fluid sociality. Its second-person relationality invokes an entrepreneurial imperative while appearing to suggest the conditions for a more collective sensibility. While *How to Get Filthy Rich* goes further than Adiga's novel in examining the persistence of a relational impulse, it also continuously redirects this impulse through capitalist channels of circulation.

In this way, let us pause to note, the "you" of *How to Get Filthy Rich* works very differently from the "you" of *The Reluctant Fundamentalist*, where it mediates between first- and third-world perspectives on U.S. financial and military imperialism. I use these theoretically unfashionable terms instead of central/peripheral or dominant/marginal to emphasize the space of inequality between them. It is this gap of inequality rather than a continuum from more to less centeredness that the second-person negotiates, formally and thematically. It could be argued that *The Reluctant Fundamentalist* achieves its most salient political effects by exploiting one of the most powerful features of the second-person form, namely causing the reader to forget that "I" is not "you." The reader is allowed to mentally translate uninterrupted pages of direct discourse into the first person as the frame narrator, a Pakistani man, tells an American ("you") about his life in the United States as a college student and then as an employee of a high-powered financial valuation firm in New York. When the narrator interrupts his long monologic stretches to address the present-day "you" (the person with whom he sits and converses in a marketplace in Lahore), the breaking of the "I" illusion is all the more disruptive, startling the reader into renewed awareness of the story-discourse distinction. The novel's unstable story-discourse unity thus formally allegorizes the fatal limitations of an American perception unable to focalize beyond the United States. "You" becomes a conflicted target of narrative surveillance. It is "our" own fault if "we" misidentify "you" as a friendly hailing rather than a form of intimate manipulation. "You are right," one of Changez's most ominously polite phrases, is a double-edged assurance that flatters his listener's cultural prejudices. Changez rewrites the Scheherazade plot, luring "you" into accepting his service and hospitality ("Allow me to pour you another cup of tea"), slyly mirroring Western orientalist assumptions ("Your shrug is inscrutable" [17]), and prolonging the encounter to a likely fatal point of confrontation. The "Other" turns out to be even more violently "other" than an American point of view is likely to realize.

The narrator of *How to Get Filthy Rich*, though neither as duplicitous as Changez nor as threatening, builds a similarly complex relation of intimacy and estrangement with the reader. As mentioned above, he revels in crude language, knowing asides, and authorial insinuations. He presumes to know "your" mercenary motives. But the narrator's self-congratulatory voice alternates with a more depersonalized one. It aspires toward a kind of totalized omniscience not available to any single person. Description shifts from subterranean perspectives to aerial views ("Atop the bank's skyscraping offices are blinking lights meant to ward off passing aircraft, lights that glow serenely, high above the city") and camera's-eye views ("Below, as seen through helipad security cameras, parts of the metropolis are in darkness, electricity shortages meaning that the illumination of entire areas is turned off on a rotating basis") (173). An alternating interiorization and exteriorization of views, as if focalized through the high-tech eye of a camera or a drone, or alternately through secret online tracking software, culminates in a kind of global surveillance perspective:

> From the perspective of the world's national security apparatuses you exist in several locations. You appear on property and income-tax registries, on passport and ID card databases. You show up on passenger manifests and telephone logs. You hum inside electromagnetically shielded military-intelligence servers and, deep below pristine fields and forbidding mountains, on their dedicated backups. You are fingertip swirls, facial ratios, dental records, voice patterns, spending trails, e-mail threads. (161)

"You" are an object of surveillance, then, much as the American listener in *The Reluctant Fundamentalist* turns out to be. Though such a high-tech surveillance perspective might bridge various world-systems, it does not hold out the "utopian moment" that critics have sought. The omniscience of big data in this passage does not lead to a commons but to a form of intimate colonization. The anxiety of a dehumanizing circulation of information is evident in one of the few passages in the novel to use "I" and "we"—ironically, in the moment in which individuality threatens to dissolve into data: "We're all information, all of us, whether readers or writers, you or I. The DNA in our cells, the bioelectric current in our nerves, the chemical emotions in our brains, the configurations of atoms within us and of subatomic particles within them, the galaxies and whirling constellations we perceive not only when looking outward but also when looking in, it's all, every last bit and byte of it, information" (159). Even as the subject is universalized, it is reduced to strands of information. The novel responds to this paradoxical situation neither by embracing or rejecting the posthuman omniscience of data, nor by regressing to a humanist "we." Instead, "you" asserts the wills and desires of a subject located within relational politics and circulatory blockages. The relational self here is both anonymous and particular, atomized and universalized. It circulates among multiple, asymmetrical singulars, becoming not a "we" but remaining an "I" among "I"s.

Any social and political "we making" that takes place under these conditions is likely to be in the negative sense of the term used by Arjun Appadurai to describe the reactionary formation of national or group identity (usually out of the group's sense of "frustrated purity").[26] The novel indeed cites a "rising tide of frustration and anger and violence," attributable partly to "the greater familiarity the poor today have with the rich, their faces pressed to that clear window on wealth afforded by ubiquitous television" (205). It notes the "paramilitary forces" deployed to protect commercial property, particularly of international corporations and banks (172). During his time at the university, the narrator joins a fundamentalist political organization that threatens students who violate codes of religious behavior. ("You are part of something larger, something righteous" [61].) But, tellingly, "we" is invoked not in this chapter (titled ironically "Avoid Idealists"), but at moments in which private capitalist and security interests converge, as in the bidding for the development of private water systems: "No, the brigadier thinks, you are wary because you know full well that when we military-related businesses advance into a market, the front lines change rapidly. We get permissions no one else can get. Red tape dissolves effortlessly for us. . . . And in this case we are going ahead whether you partner with us or not" (165). In sum, "we" appears at the service of a totalizing perspective that affirms both the exploitative logic of capitalism and the biopolitical need to manage plural bodies and to regulate whole populations that because of wealth concentration, resource extraction, and global asymmetries, are threatened with becoming surplus populations.

Thus, even as the narrative foregrounds the problem of the multitude, it ultimately points back to the politics of singularity rather than the development of a communal or collective voice. The idea that the literary novel is complicit in individualization is hardly surprising; a primary investment at the level of the subject is, after all, in keeping with the form of the modern novel. The Bildungsroman, a regulatory form aimed at bringing the desires of the individual into line with the demands of society, works to prop up the necessary fictions of selfhood even when these are most unstable ("the idea of self in the land of self-help is a slippery one" [3–4]). If novels are, in essence, a genre of self-improvement narrative that have historically been fictionalized for the tastes of polite company, then Hamid's self-help novel works in reverse, making visible the ways in which advanced global subjectivities require more direct instruments of propping-up.

Yet the novel's historical investment in the individual subject also makes it a form uniquely positioned to critique these proppings. The mediations of fiction are not abandoned; at no point is the reader likely to mistake *How to Get Filthy Rich* for something other than a novel, such as the popular business journalism that it parodies.[27] Instead, as fiction, it models the acts of literary imagination that mediate between the limited perspective of the one and the expansive demands of the many: "When you read a book, what you see are black squiggles on pulped wood or, increasingly, dark pixels on a pale screen. To transform these icons into characters and events, you must imagine. And when you imagine, you create. It's in being read that a book becomes a book, and in each of a million different readings a book becomes one of a million different books" (97). Since one of the functions of the literary is to reinvest in the imaginative resources of the individual, reading a book becomes a form of working for oneself. Books become exchangeable for subjects, reading for the labor of subjective self-development. Reading also means becoming one of a million, which might seem to promise the literary and social richness of a collective imaginary. But "the million" also allows third-person anonymity and distancing, group de-subjectification and dispossession. The proliferating political claims of the "million" evidently require a different collective "we" imagination than the abstract model of "social mind" that some narrative theorists have proposed. It requires one that can encompass both the utopian and exploitative extremes.[28] Literary form becomes a resource for the development of the global subject not because it is unique in being able to imagine the Other but because it foregrounds the mediations required for toggling between the one and the million in ways attuned to the potentially instrumentalizing, even pathologizing, tendencies in each.

Again, even as *How to Get Filthy Rich* projects a more expansive, world-making function for the literary imagination than *The Reluctant Fundamentalist*, its metafictionalized second-person may seem less politically directed than the earlier novel's double-edged realism. For instance, there is a clearly political moment in *The Reluctant Fundamentalist* that explicitly thematizes language as a device for regulating the "frictions" of globality. The narrator, Changez, says, "If English had a respectful form of the word *you*—as we do in Urdu—I would have used it to address them without the slightest hesitation" (98). Changez is referring to the waiters and staff serving a group of American college graduates on vacation in Greece. It is implied that the young tourists, who take the service relation for granted and are at ease in their assumption of being able to buy whatever they want, would never address servers using the formal "you." One conclusion might be that English, with its insistence on a single, equalizing form of the pronoun, is sometimes too blunt a language to capture finer nuances of global relationality. The democratizing English "you" absolves the speaker from responsibility toward the other. It is both individualizing and presentizing; a pronoun that refuses any prior claims or unpaid debts.

In contrast, *How to Get Filthy Rich* appears to conclude on a note of optimism about the development of a relational subject. The main character, it is implied, having lost all his wealth and advantages, has become a more empathetic version of himself: "And how strange that when I imagine, I feel. The capacity for empathy is a funny thing" (220). He has a sense of responsibility for his ex-employees (in contrast to the father's employer's insistence that the mother's medical treatment be the family's own responsibility). Despite his age and relative poverty he seeks to help out kinsmen new to the city, out of "lingering desires to connect and to be of use" (204). Because his affective attachments to other people have expanded his basis of selfhood ("you have been beyond yourself"), the narrator explains, the main character is able to face the moment of his death with "courage," "dignity," and "calmness" (228).

But to expand "beyond" oneself is not a reliable or permanent state of self-transcendence. (The novel undercuts its semiromantic conclusion by uniting the main character and the pretty girl together in companionship rather than sexual passion; at the end of the novel they live together to pool their dwindling resources and do not share a bedroom.) Neither a breakdown of self nor a romantic unity with another, this self-beyond-oneself is the culmination of a process of temporal circulation: "At times the pretty girl feels shocked looking at you, the shock of being mortal. . . . But quickly other data begin to accrue, likely starting with your eyes and your mouth, her image of you resolving itself into something different, something timeless, or if not entirely timeless, still beautiful. . . . She sees you as a boy and as a man" (212–13). Mediated by time and memory, the self is, "if not entirely timeless," nonetheless affirmed through its circulation through past and future versions, or in comparison to the next generation. When the main character's adult son visits, "he kisses the pretty girl's cheek, and she too perceives time ripple as she sees a reflection of your younger self, albeit a better dressed version with a mincing walk quite unlike your own" (222). The son's "mincing walk" further suggests that this circulation of temporalities does not eliminate subject/object differences but refines them. Indeed the son's sexuality, which is only indirectly alluded to, appears to play no other role in the novel but to invoke the different and additional kinds of frictions that the production of global subjects is likely to effect. The son earlier left home and sought protected asylum in the United States from, presumably, homophobic persecution in his home country. The narrator's comment that "we are all refugees from our childhoods" would seem to minimize this conflict—the metaphorization of "refugee" diminishing the son's experience as a literal refugee in favor of an abstracted, depoliticized truth of temporal experience. I read the "mincing walk" as a discordant note, however, an objectification and reminder of the material body of the other that resists incorporation into an entirely seamless, universalization of experience, however much the son's presence at the end may appear to invite a different kind of cosmopolitan synthesis between first-world and third-world subjects in the name of human rights.

Pheng Cheah, in his book *What Is a World?*, argues for a conception of world literature as one that "attempts to remake the world against capitalist globalization." He attributes to literature a special world-making capacity that goes beyond the conventional powers typically attributed to realist literature to constitute a possible alternative to the existing world or to "map" the world's flows cartographically. Instead, he argues, "worlding" literature exerts a normative force through its capacity to reveal and actualize its temporalizations. "Worlding," he argues, "is a force that subtends and exceeds all human calculations that reduce the world as a temporal structure to the sum of objects in space."[29] This capacious, and ambitious, definition of literature's anticalculative and antireductive qualities in my view demands a more sustained analysis of realism's alternating functions *within* literature: its resistance to and its accommodation of capitalist globalization. In foregrounding the frictions of temporality, *How to Get Filthy Rich* emphasizes that literature draws on the same comparative, temporal resources that finance does in constructing value. The novel's use of the second person cannot simply be seen as a form of resistance to capitalism's imaginary, therefore. But it suggests the novel's role in thinking through the subject/object asymmetries that such global circulation helps to produce. Cheah argues that "the world's reality is neither objective nor subjective because it is a process grounded in the force of temporalization."[30] The novel's production of subject/object relations, and its insistence on their oppositions, must be seen as modeling literature's role in re-temporalizing these global circulations of value.

Monika Fludernik claims that "second-person radicalizes—as all written language and especially literature, tends to do—tendencies inherent in the language itself."[31] Hamid's second-person radicalizes the contradictions of relationality. It heightens the frictions between self and other while insisting on their dependencies. It mediates between singular isolation and the imaginative reduction of entire populations to undifferentiated masses. It invokes both the relational side of globality—the development of new intimacies, proximities, and opportunities—and the redistributive side, which tends to produce new incompatibilities, hierarchies, and dispossessions. "You" may move around to occupy multiple and different subject positions, but it does not promise equality or presume to transcend the exploitative relations produced by uneven economies, in which inequality and the violence of real abstraction are endemic.

Without unambiguously disrupting the realisms of finance's imaginary, therefore, Wayne's and Hamid's novels nonetheless expand and thicken them. In questioning the entrepreneurial subject, adding friction to the relations of liquidity, and rewriting the temporalities of calculation, these texts highlight the double edge of literature's mediations of capitalist circulation. I have argued that they aim to develop literary forms adequate to global relationality that are not those of abstract exchangeability and do not erase social distinctions. Their efforts to resist capitalism's narrowings of realism appear to require going beyond the analytical resources of postmodernism or those of "peripheral realism."[32] They suggest the need for a global realism that trains its sights on the problems and possibilities of mediation for grasping and interfering with capitalism's own drive to represent.

Literary Realism and Finance Capital

In a 2015 review essay titled "The Fictions of Finance," Toral Gajarawala asks, "What happens to the fictions we create when money—harnessed by a range of new, sophisticated, and increasingly abstruse financial instruments—begets money on a scale that Marx could scarcely have imagined? As the production of wealth is further and further removed from the production of things, billions of people's lives are tied up in financial markets shrouded in a haze of mystery."[1] While fiction has long been engaged with money and morals, she argues, "the scale now seems vaster," the world of finance less necessarily corrupt than merely indifferent. The problem of financial intelligibility invites the modes of "translation" offered by literary realisms. "As the epistemological divide between finance and everyday life yawns ever wider, fiction has stepped into the gap."

The above diagnosis of capitalism's vastly increased scale and the startling realization of its indifference could easily have been written about the nineteenth-century economic novel. In particular, the shift in the late nineteenth century from realism toward the "systems" representations of naturalism, as I have discussed in the cases of Dreiser and Norris, seem particularly resonant today, compared not only to the contemporary "systems" novels that in many ways take up the legacy of naturalistic-scientific thinking about suprahuman "forces"—recast today as decentered, posthumanist, and object-oriented networks—but also to the quasi-determinisms of "New Economy" discourses that insist that markets must be freed to obey their own internal rules and logics, in effect updating nineteenth-century natural law as today's neoliberal market law.

The question remains whether there is a specific quality of "later" abstraction that engages fiction on different terms than it once did. Has the era of financialization since the 1970s produced new or different historical

realisms? Have the terms of realism changed? Some partial and tentative
conclusions.

As chapter 5 demonstrates, the problem of abstraction, conceived in
financial terms, expands the contemporary novel beyond what can be
clearly identified as "American." The more capital is conceived as abstract
and systemic, the less clearly it is confinable within the category of the
national. Hamid's novel in particular may appear to take this book beyond
its announced focus on American literature and into something more properly defined as the global or world novel. But this is simply to acknowledge
what is true for all the late-capitalist texts discussed here, namely that
their American "localisms" demand situating in relation to historical, geographic, and structural globalisms. It is the insight of the world-systems
approach, even at risk of overreaching, to connect the seemingly uncon-
nected. Franco Moretti's definition of a new "world" literature has served
as a point of departure for many critics to theorize that a heterogeneous
literary landscape is in fact part of one unified formation.[2] The conception
of a world literature as reflecting a "system that is simultaneously *one,*
and *unequal,*" with its parts "bound together in a relationship of growing
inequality," like Arrighi's argument about finance capitalism, invites both
structural and historical methodologies for analyzing its object. These analyses are not limited to representations of literary globality at the level of
form or content, nor limited to the historical-materialist approach to tracing the "flow" of literary works between periphery and core, except insofar
as these contribute to the analysis of the production and mediation of what
Jameson calls a "singular modernity." If the category of "American" fiction
under certain circumstances still appears internally coherent, this has to
be acknowledged as an illusion produced by the highly selective historical
rootings or selective geographical imaginings within specific texts. In this
sense, all the contemporary novels I discuss form part of a world-system
literature—not just the texts by Hamid and Wayne that represent the global
"flows" of finance but the fantasy of unified systematicity in *Cosmopolis,*
the global epic aspirations of capital's narrative in *Gain,* and even the deter-
minedly "local" real-estate market in *Good Faith,* poised to soon become
both a driver of 1980s post-industrial economic growth in the United
States and a refuge for international investment from global financial volatility. From the angle of a financial analysis, even the most locally focused
text, however bound up in the particularities of American cultures and
subjects, presses the novel in outward, less nationally definable directions.

Thus, if this book undoes its own premise as a study of American fiction, it is precisely because taking "finance" as a methodology confirms
the by-now-obvious truth that the boundaries of a national literature are

increasingly difficult to sustain. At the same time, however, one of the contributions of a financial approach is to underscore that any "American" cultural dimension is likely to overdetermine the new global homogeneity for as long as major world financial institutions and organizations remain so closely tied to U.S. political and economic interests. In short, we might say that the financial imaginary is where American and world "realisms" tend to meet. It is where they negotiate the terms between finance's universalizing abstractions and its local realizations, between the logics of differentiation and systematization, between the different meanings and formal operations of "realist" value.

Another distinctive feature of realism today is the rise of its speculative and dystopian forms. This development includes both new critical attention to genre fictions often considered outside the literary domain as well as the turn to genre by established literary authors such as Cormac McCarthy, Colson Whitehead, Jennifer Egan, and Chang-Rae Lee, whose recent narratives of disaster and collapse allegorize contemporary social breakdowns. In their desire for unalienated world-making, apocalyptic fictions address the opposite side of the financial imaginary. In no sense, therefore, can the rise of apocalyptic literary realism be divorced from the capitalist realisms that I have discussed in this book. Both speculative and nonspeculative types of realism offer theorizations of the ways in which, as Cazdyn and Szeman have argued, "capitalism itself now constitutes a very real limit to thought."[3] The complete destruction and elimination of what is becomes the only way to accomplish what political revolution appears unlikely to do. The forms of unalienated labor, re-envisionings of community, and primitive systems of exchange explored in these texts represent a kind of "restart" of the narrative of human production, a fantasized release from the determinations of a late capitalism rendered both illegible and irretrievably compromised by financialization. The sense that it is too late to change the system or to reverse the damage it has done becomes the "final determining instance" of capitalism in realism's more speculative and disaster-projecting modes.

However, apocalyptic scenarios are but one way the contemporary novel seeks to fill in the negative space of abstraction. Fiction has also turned directly to the disconnections of class and to the imagination of its concrete effects on everyday lives and subjectivities. Texts about the restructurings of the working-class subject (such as the short fictions of George Saunders or Stewart O'Nan's *Last Night at the Lobster*) or about middle-class precarity and decline (Jess Walter's *The Financial Lives of the Poets*, Sam Lipsyte's *The Ask*),[4] texts that explicitly link finance to sites of domesticity and family (Jonathan Dee's *The Privileges*, Martha McPhee's *Dear*

Money, Jonathan Franzen's *The Corrections*), and texts about the affects and subjects produced by immaterial labor (Walter Kirn's *Up in the Air*, Dave Eggers's *The Circle*) all work through late-capitalist restructurings at an affective level. Each of these realist fictions in some degree confirms the suspicion articulated by sociologist Richard Sennett that "the old work ethic revealed concepts of character which . . . no longer find expression in labor."[5] Moreover, the outpouring of cross-genre or genre-experimental texts and films—the novel *Predatory Lending*, the film *The Big Short*, and many examples of memoir and autobiography—not only frame finance as a problem of formal legibility but remind us that the novel competes with many other narrative realisms today. Here it is useful to think of Lauren Berlant's argument about the "waning of genre." This is not necessarily a claim that fiction is waning in cultural importance (though that may also be true), but about the weakening of "older realist genres" that structured a relation to the ordinary and everyday in ways that promised forward movement. Berlant has described a new, "emerging set of aesthetic conventions that make a claim to affective realism." Realism is thus expanded in this account beyond a formal literary genre to include any of a generalized set of affective markers. "Any object/scene could belong to a realist genre," she writes. "What matters is the presence of a relation that invests an object/scene with the prospect of the world's continuity."[6] This waning of genre, in contrast with Jameson's postmodern waning of affect, signals an attrition of familiar explanatory narratives (e.g., upward mobility) and a reattachment to scenes or objects of affective investment, even when such attachment contributes to the production of stasis, frustration, or discontent.

Yet such newer scenes or objects of realist investment nonetheless coexist with the afterlife of "older" structures of genre, as in texts such as those named above, in ways that continuously interrogate genre's formal adaptability (or non-adaptability) to the crises and dislocations of the present. It should be clear by now that my point is hardly to idealize the "older" realisms of the past as stable models. Quite the reverse: instead of assuming that the nineteenth century offered an unconflicted, uncontested realism that was perfectly adequate in its time to the task of representing capitalist reality, the juxtaposition of different "financial" moments demonstrates the ways in which even the original economic realism was always already a vexed enterprise. The point is neither to look back nostalgically out of a desire for legibility and moral guidance (although inevitably some writers propose exactly this),[7] nor to assume contemporary realism is better equipped and less theoretically naïve in engaging the problem of abstraction. Instead, the imperfect and adaptive hybrid realisms in circulation today highlight realism's paradoxical commitments: to a mode of indexical, referential representation *and* to a heightened emphasis on narrative mediation.

Ultimately then, we are concerned not with a prescriptive point about whether the novel is or isn't the form most likely to "solve" a contemporary narrative crisis—an outcome about which I remain mostly agnostic—but a descriptive one, to register how its familiar formal categories make sense of the relation between abstraction and representation. Literary realism both expresses and mediates the representational dilemmas of finance capitalism. In so doing, realism promises to reveal more deeply the narrative structures of finance itself. Under financialization, representation replaces labor as a source of value. And the more nonproductive value gains ascent over productive value, the more the representational logic of finance appears historically identical to the representational logic of the literary. A historical analysis of the novel at such moments of financial ascent thus reveals the ways that the realist novel, in its hybrid, absorptive, regulating, retemporalizing, and evaluative (both valorizing and value-measuring) forms, becomes a tool for imagining finance capital, and one that mediates and disrupts its systemic abstractions.

The senses of contingency, impasse, and loss of the good life that characterize the affective landscape of the twenty-first century are not those of the nineteenth century. In many ways, financial crisis seems more likely today than ever before to intensify the weight of the status quo, or the sense of things being "just the way they are." At moments in which finance seemed less clearly ascendant over labor, or capital seemed more restrainable, as in its long mid-twentieth-century détente with labor, critiques of capitalism appear much less bound up in representational dilemmas. Thus, it is not that the middle of the twentieth century did not produce the material for "economic" fiction, for example, or that its crises did not lend themselves to realist representation. But the ends-of-century manifest particular conditions of abstraction in which the nonproductive appears to gain ascent over a productive order of value, and capitalism becomes aesthetically visible as a structurally and historically expansive "system." Both historical moments therefore demand similar adjustments to the idea of capitalism as a "limit to thought." The result is a historical moment in which capitalism appears to be broadening and narrowing at the same time, able to produce value out of nothing, to prioritize the imaginative domain, dictate the terms of "realism," and to confirm the sense of its own inevitability. As capitalism appears to become more systematically and historically encompassing, the novel continues to seek conceptual tools to critique finance and to resist the narrowings of its imaginary.

Introduction

1. Fredric Jameson, "Culture and Finance Capital," *The Cultural Turn: Selected Writings on the Postmodern, 1983–1998* (London: Verso, 1998), 136–61. Blanton, Lye, and Puckett, in their introduction to a special issue of *Representations* on financialization and the culture industry, essentially re-pose Jameson's question: "How . . . should we understand the formal and cultural effects of a world economy ever more dependent on finance's increasingly abstract calculations of value?" C. D. Blanton, Colleen Lye, and Kent Puckett, "Introduction: Financialization and the Culture," *Representations* 126, no. 1 (2014): 1–8. Other critics have also called for a cultural analysis of financialization in special issues of *Cultural Critique* 65 (Fall 2007); *American Quarterly* 64, no. 3 (September 2012); and *Topia* 30–31 (Fall 2013/Spring 2014).

2. Jameson, "Culture and Finance," 142.

3. Much recent popular and journalistic writing about finance focuses on the rise of complex and specialized instruments of speculation. See Robin Blackburn, "The Subprime Crisis," *New Left Review* 50 (2008): 63–106, for a thorough summary of the factors contributing to the credit crisis of 2007–8, including the rise of financially engineered forms of high-risk debt, the operations of the hidden banking system, the deregulatory backstory, and the proliferation of financial intermediaries. Blackburn argues that even the subprime crisis by itself should be properly understood as a "financialization" crisis because it represented a "banker's nightmare in which key assets could not be valued" (67).

4. On fantasy valuations, see Blackburn, "Subprime Crisis." See also John Bellamy Foster, "The Financialization of Accumulation," *Monthly Review* 62, no. 5 (2010): 1–17. On crisis, see Robert Pollin, "The Wall Street Collapse and Return of Reality-Based Economics," *Monthly Review* 62, no. 4 (2010): 1–9. Pollin describes financial crises as a "regular feature of the United States and global landscape since the push to deregulate began in earnest in the late 1970s": "Consider

the scorecard over the twenty years prior to the 2008–09 disaster: a stock market crash in 1987; the Savings and Loan crisis and bailout in 1989–90; the 'emerging markets' crisis of 1997–98—which brought down, among others, Long-Term Capital Management, the super hedge fund led by two economics Nobel laureates specializing in finance—and the bursting of the dot-com stock market bubble in 2001" (1–2).

5. Edward LiPuma and Benjamin Lee, *Financial Derivatives and the Globalization of Risk* (Durham: Duke University Press, 2004), 17. See also "Cultures of Circulation," in which LiPuma and Lee write: "From 1983 to 1998, daily trading in currency markets grew from $200 million to $1.5 trillion, with 98 percent of the 1998 figure intended for speculation; the growth was due in great part to the use of complicated currency derivatives. Trading in derivatives grew 215 percent per year from 1987 to 1997, and by the time of the Asian market crash in 1997, the annual value of traded derivatives was more than ten times the value of global production" ("Cultures of Circulation: The Imaginations of Modernity," *Public Culture* 14, no. 1 (2002): 203–4).

6. What Marx called "fictitious capital formation" is in its classic definition the process by which money generates money. This could refer to any process of capital formation that follows the M–M^1 formula (as opposed to the M–C–M^1 formula in which money is routed through the commodity). It therefore can and often does take place outside the spaces of production. To say that finance operates in realms where value is removed from its proximity to labor is not by extension to endorse older, labor theories of value, nor to comment on alternative theories of value popular in mainstream economics today, but to draw particular attention to the ways finance tends to be culturally located in opposition to work.

Finance has been defined variously as the "forcing together of production and mutual indebtedness" (Martin); the "capitalization of income flows" (Hudson), or as any "claim on future productivity" (Haiven). Randy Martin, *An Empire of Indifference: American War and the Financial Logic of Risk Management* (Durham: Duke University Press, 2007), 3. Michael Hudson, "From Marx to Goldman Sachs: The Fictions of Fictitious Capital and the Financializations of Industry," *Critique* 38, no. 3 (2010): 424. Max Haiven, "Finance Depends on Resistance, Finance Is Resistance, and Anyway, Resistance Is Futile," *Mediations* 26, no. 1–2 (2012/13): 89.

Many critics define finance structurally in terms of the rise of circulation-based capitalism, the increased use of highly technical instruments of risk packaging, and the vast expansion of credit and debt. See circulation as argued by LiPuma and Lee, Marazzi, and Harvey; derivatives as argued by LiPuma and Lee; securitization by Martin; and debt by Dienst, Graeber, and Lazzarato. LiPuma and Lee, *Financial Derivatives*. Christian Marazzi, *The Violence of Financial Capitalism* (Los Angeles: Semiotexte, 2010). David Harvey, *The Limits to Capital* (New York: Verso, 2007), and *The Enigma of Capital: And the Crises of Capitalism* (Oxford: Oxford University Press, 2011). Randy Martin, *The Financialization of Daily Life* (Philadelphia: Temple University Press, 2002). Richard Dienst, *The Bonds of Debt* (New York:

Verso, 2011). David Graeber, *Debt: The First 5,000 Years* (Brooklyn: Melville House, 2011). Maurizio Lazzarato, *The Making of the Indebted Man: An Essay on the Neoliberal Condition*, trans. Joshua David Jordon (Los Angeles: Semiotexte, 2012).

7. Richard Godden, "Language, Labor, and Finance Capital," *PMLA* 126, no. 2 (2011): 414.

8. Greta R. Krippner, "The Financialization of the American Economy," *Socio-Economic Review* 3 (2005): 173–208.

9. Edward Chancellor's *Devil Take the Hindmost: A History of Financial Speculation* (New York: Plume, 2000) and Charles P. Kindleberger's *Manias, Panics, and Crashes: A History of Financial Crises* (New York: John Wiley & Sons, 2000) are the standard reference works on this history.

10. Arjun Appadurai, *Modernity at Large: Cultural Dimensions of Globalization* (Minneapolis: University of Minnesota Press, 1996); *Fear of Small Numbers: An Essay on the Geography of Anger* (Durham: Duke University Press, 2006), 30; *Banking on Worlds: The Failure of Language in the Age of Derivative Finance* (Chicago: University of Chicago Press, 2016), 125.

11. David Harvey, *A Brief History of Neoliberalism* (Oxford: Oxford University Press, 2005), 33. Krippner, in "Financialization," argues that financialization, neoliberalism, globalization, and postindustrialism are all intertwined. In contrast, Foster qualifies the view that these are synonyms: "This analysis of how financialization has heightened the disparities in income, wealth, and power helps us to put into perspective the view, now common on the left, that neoliberalism, or the advent of extreme free-market ideology, is the chief source of today's economic problems. Instead, neoliberalism is best seen as the political expression of capital's response to the stagnation-financialization trap." John Bellamy Foster, "The Financialization of Accumulation."

12. Many other historical accounts support the view that the processes of financialization since the early 1970s have resulted in an entirely new paradigm of capital accumulation. Global factors included, according to these accounts, the collapse of the post–World War II system of fixed exchange rates, the rise of the dollar standard, and the oil crisis. See Harvey, *Enigma of Capital*; Giovanni Arrighi, *The Long Twentieth Century* (London: Verso, 1994); Ernst Mandel, *Late Capitalism* (1975; New York: Verso, 1999); Jameson, "Culture and Finance Capital"; Michael Hardt and Antonio Negri, *Empire* (Cambridge, Mass.: Harvard University Press, 2001). In the United States, the 1970s saw the beginning of the breakdown of the long postwar détente between capital and labor. See Jefferson R. Cowie, *Stayin' Alive: The 1970s and the Last Days of the Working Class* (New York: New Press, 2010); Judith Stein, *Pivotal Decade: How the United States Traded Factories for Finance in the Seventies* (New Haven: Yale University Press, 2011). Monetarist fiscal policy rose as a primary tool of managing the economy under Reaganomics, as opposed to reducing unemployment. As deregulation and new technology allowed capital to travel farther faster, the post-Fordist crisis of overaccumulation produced

surpluses of liquidity seeking places for investment. Not finding them in production of goods and services, these capital "flows" sought speculative outlets or
tended to be cycled through an increasingly globalized economic system as loans,
particularly from banks of the global North to emerging economies of the global
South. Harvey has called the turn to financialization since 1973 "a way of dealing
with the surplus absorption problem" (*Enigma of Capital*, 30). Haiven attributes
globalization to labor's postwar successes in advanced economies, arguing that it
"emerged as a capitalist response to the Keynesian mediation" of labor struggles in
the global North ("Finance," 90).

    13. LiPuma and Lee, *Financial Derivatives*, 8.

    14. LiPuma and Lee, "Cultures of Circulation," 210.

    15. Joshua Clover, "Autumn of the System: Poetry and Financial Capital,"
Journal of Narrative Theory 41, no. 1 (2011): 34.

    16. Mathias Nilges, "Finance Capital and the Time of the Novel or, Money
without Narrative Qualities," *Topia* 30–31 (2013/14): 32.

    17. Joshua Clover, "Value/Theory/Crisis," *PMLA* 127, no. 1 (2012): 107–14.

    18. Two of the most prominent writers are *New York Times* columnist and
economics professor Paul Krugman and political commentator Kevin Phillips. Phillips refers to "plutocracy's *second* U.S. emergence" (emphasis in text) in *Wealth
and Democracy: A Political History of the American Rich* (New York: Broadway
Books, 2003), xvi.

    19. David Remnick, ed., *The New Gilded Age: The New Yorker Looks at the
Culture of Affluence* (New York: Modern Library, 2001), 1, xii. For criticism of
New Economy manifestos, see Thomas Frank, *One Market under God: Extreme
Capitalism, Market Populism, and the End of Economic Democracy* (New York:
Anchor, 2001); Doug Henwood, *After the New Economy* (New York: New Press,
2003), who I discuss at the beginning of chapter 4; and Kevin Phillips, *Bad Money:
Reckless Finance, Failed Politics, and the Global Crisis of American Capitalism*
(New York: Viking, 2008). A sampling from Phillips: "Newt Gingrich, the Speaker
of the U.S. House of Representatives, envisioned a politics in which major questions could be resolved by asking 'our major multinational corporations for
advice.' Technology guru George Gilder theologized that 'it is the entrepreneurs
who know the rules of the world and the laws of God.' Thomas Friedman, the
New York Times columnist, enthused, 'International finance has turned the world
into a parliamentary system' that allows initiates 'to vote every hour, every day
through their mutual funds, their pension funds, their brokers.' Even historian
Francis Fukuyama, normally sober, burbled that 'liberal democracy combine with
open market economics has become the only model a state could follow'" (180).

    20. Analyses of 1990s conspicuous consumption are offered by Paul Krugman,
"For Richer," *New York Times Magazine*, October 20, 2002; Robert H. Frank,
Luxury Fever: Why Money Fails to Satisfy in an Era of Excess (New York: Free
Press, 1999); and Dana Thomas, *Deluxe: How Luxury Lost Its Luster* (New York:
Penguin 2007).

21. Bruce Robbins, *Upward Mobility and the Common Good: Toward a Literary History of the Welfare State* (Princeton: Princeton University Press, 2007), xi.

22. Randy Martin argues that financialization cuts off the connection between social wealth and sites of capital accumulation in *An Empire of Indifference: American War and the Financial Logic of Risk Management* (Durham: Duke University Press, 2007), 6–7.

23. Christian Marazzi, in *The Violence of Financial Capitalism* (Los Angeles: Semiotexte, 2010), distinguishes the Google model from the Fordist model and the "Toyota" model (post-Fordist, flexible), by the way it makes finance completely "cosubstantial" with production (29), not a separate process. It is "not the nature of the product that determine[s] the productive organization . . . but rather the *relationship* between the production and circulation spheres" (57). See also LiPuma and Lee: "Production's most important product is rapidly becoming the production of connectivity itself—that is, the logistics, communication networks, global financial instruments, and technologies used to assist and amplify connectivity" (*Financial Derivatives*, 21–22).

24. LiPuma and Lee, *Financial Derivatives*, 2.

25. Richard Sennett, *The Corrosion of Character: The Personal Consequences of Work in the New Capitalism* (New York: Norton, 1998).

26. Martin, *Empire of Indifference*, 7, 8–9.

27. Fredric Jameson, *The Antinomies of Realism* (New York: Verso, 2013), 4–5.

28. LiPuma and Lee, *Financial Derivatives*, 2.

29. See, for instance, James Annesley, *Blank Fictions: Consumerism, Culture and the Contemporary Novel* (New York: St. Martin's Press, 1998).

30. Steve Fraser, *Every Man a Speculator: A History of Wall Street in American Life* (New York: Harper Perennial, 2006), 201. Fraser's history of Wall Street describes the changing sources of wealth in the closing years of the century that contributed to a new sense of abstraction: "While at the beginning of the 1890s the city's largest fortunes could be traced to a cluster of tangible trades like shipping, wholesale and retail trade, commission merchant, importing, food processing, and the like, ten years later the richest of the rich were described as 'capitalist,' 'corporate director,' and 'financier,' suggesting the influence of Wall Street in turning concrete forms of wealth production into abstract acts of moneymaking" (191).

31. In the Marxist analysis, rent is synonymous with returns on property ownership or property rights. Although the original rentier lived on income from inherited and/or invested wealth from land, the category of "property" is not limited to land and includes intellectual property (patents and copyrights), the holding of debts and charging of interest rates, and the selling of any goods and services for which a premium (monopoly) price can be charged. Harvey in "The Art of Rent" situates monopoly rent at the "nexus between capitalist globalization, local political-economic developments, and the evolution of cultural meanings and aesthetic values" (395). "All rent . . . is a return to the monopoly power of private ownership of any portion of the globe" (397). In this analysis, rentierism can

hardly be separated from economists' primary measure of economic value today: whatever price the market will bear. David Harvey, "The Art of Rent: Globalization and the Commodification of Culture," in *Spaces of Capital: Towards a Critical Geography* (New York: Routledge, 2001), 394–412. Lazzarato argues that it is "impossible to distinguish rent from profit" (*Making of the Indebted Man*, 21). See also Robert Pollin, "Resurrection of the Rentier," *New Left Review* 46 (2007): 140–53.

32. Joseph E. Stiglitz, *The Price of Inequality* (New York: Norton, 2013), 32.

33. Ibid., 38. Stiglitz argues that one of rent seeking's least subtle forms is when industries seek politically engineered market advantages by negotiating favorable tax breaks and government subsidies. But again, rent-seeking activities are not only practiced by big industry nor are its forms limited to direct political lobbying. Stiglitz includes as rent seeking any activity that resists transparency and regulation, since these discourage imbalances of information and/or monopolistic practices. Bruce Robbins includes shareholders in the category of rentiers since they receive unearned income and their primary interest is in keeping share prices high. Bruce Robbins, "On the Rentier," *PMLA* 127, no. 4 (2012): 905–11.

34. Through the socialization or even nationalization of certain types of investment, Keynes foresaw "the euthanasia of the cumulative oppressive power of the capitalist to exploit the scarcity-value of capital." John Maynard Keynes, "Concluding Notes on the Social Philosophy towards Which the General Theory Might Lead," chapter 24 in *The General Theory of Employment, Interest and Money* (1936), https://www.marxists.org/reference/subject/economics/keynes/general-theo ry/ch24.htm.

35. Thomas Piketty, *Capital in the Twenty-First Century*, trans. Arthur Goldhammer (Cambridge, Mass.: Harvard University Press, 2014), 25. I discuss Piketty further below. His conclusion includes the observation that "the entrepreneur inevitably tends to become a rentier" (571).

36. Robbins, "On the Rentier," 907. On the racial wealth gap in the United States that cannot be attributed to income, see Thomas M. Shapiro and Melvin L. Oliver, *Black Wealth/White Wealth: A New Perspective on Racial Inequality* (New York: Routledge, 1995).

37. Martin, *Empire*, 8.

38. Ibid, 15.

39. Jan Toporowski, "The Wisdom of Property and the Politics of the Middle Classes," *Monthly Review* 62, no. 4 (2010): 14. Toporowski also writes: "From the 1970s, the growing prosperity of the middle classes in the 'financially advanced' countries, such as the United States and Britain, was associated with a switch in their asset holdings, from modest holdings of residential property and direct ownership of stocks and shares, to residential property that was increasing in value, and indirect ownership of stocks and shares in the form of funded pension entitlements and insurance policies" (10). See also Phillips, *Bad Money*; and Hudson, "From Marx to Goldman Sachs." Phillips writes: "Over five years [2001–2006],

the housing sector seems to have provided some 40 percent of the growth in U.S. GDP and employment, representing stimulus on a grand, almost 1930s scale" (11). In turn, Hudson sees high finance as essentially made possible by "untaxed property revenue [that] is free to be capitalized into larger debts" (428).

40. Toporowski, "Wisdom of Property," 15.

41. Martin, *Empire*, 8.

42. Jan Toporowski, *The End of Finance: Pension Funds Derivatives and Capital Market Inflation* (London: Routledge, 1999), 1. Toporowski cites Charles P. Kindleberger's well-known account of financial panics, *Manias, Panics, and Crashes*, as demonstrating that "an era of finance commences with an increase of the amount of money coming into capital markets" and writes that "by 'era of finance' is meant a period of history in which finance prospers with such apparent brilliance that it takes over from the industrial entrepreneur the leading role in capitalist development" (1).

43. Blackburn, "Subprime Crisis," 67.

44. Jameson, "Culture and Finance Capital," 149.

45. Ibid., 153. Arrighi's *The Long Twentieth Century* theorizes a history of capitalism in which the twentieth century represents only the most recent of a series of long cycles from the Italian city-states of the late fourteenth and early fifteenth centuries, to Dutch financial power in the seventeenth and early eighteenth centuries, to the British empire of the long nineteenth century, to a long American cycle presumably reaching its late stages in the early twenty-first century. In a series of historical and geographically distinctive *belles epoques* finance capital becomes ascendant over other forms of return on capital, and profit increasingly comes from borrowing, lending, and speculating rather than material production or trade. The advantage of Arrighi's model is that it unites both sides of the account: it situates the contemporary period within a longer narrative of transformation in which the 1970s arguably marked, if not a clear break with the past, then certainly a distinct point of acceleration that made visible and consolidated shifts in the nature of capital that had been already well underway. At the same time the rise of finance, while not structurally "determined," nonetheless follows a fairly consistent internal logic of movement toward abstraction. This model thus powerfully combines structural and historical explanations for recurring eras of finance across different centuries and with different geographical centers.

46. Fernando Coronil, "Towards a Critique of Globalcentrism: Speculations on Capitalism's Nature," *Public Culture* 12, no. 2 (2000): 366.

47. Doug Henwood, *Wall Street: How It Works and for Whom* (New York: Verso, 1997), 138, 139, 40.

48. L. C. La Berge, "The Rules of Abstraction: Methods and Discourses of Finance," *Radical History Review* 118 (2014): 93, 96, 106. La Berge also offers a breakdown of different disciplinary usages: "In aesthetics, abstraction denominates an aesthetic mode of nonfigurative representation. In philosophy, it denotes something not realizable in time and space. In social theory, it indicates something

not fully realizable by a particular," and in Marxism it "serves as a conduit and hindrance to economic knowledge" (96). Within Marxism La Berge differentiates between "real abstraction," "lived abstraction," "second-order abstraction," and the "abstract dimension of value" (97).

49. Derek Sayer, *The Violence of Abstraction: The Analytic Foundations of Historical Materialism* (Oxford: Blackwell, 1987), 127.

50. Godden, "Language, Labor, and Finance Capital," 419.

51. Jameson, "Culture and Finance Capital," 260, qtd in Godden, "Language, Labor, and Finance Capital," 420.

52. La Berge, "Rules of Abstraction," 101.

53. Godden, "Language, Labor, and Finance Capital," 415.

54. Marazzi calls crisis the "over-production of self-referentiality" in which a financial instrument's ability to reflect underlying economic "realities" become suspect. Christian Marazzi, *Capital and Language: From the New Economy to the War Economy* (Los Angeles: Semiotexte, 2008), 35.

55. LiPuma and Lee, *Financial Derivatives*, 15.

56. LiPuma and Lee, "Cultures," 196.

57. Ibid., 209.

58. Leigh Clare La Berge, *Scandals and Abstraction: Financial Fiction of the Long 1980s* (New York: Oxford University Press, 2014).

59. Arrighi glosses the difference usefully as follows: "Marx's general formula of capital (M–C–M¹) can therefore be interpreted as depicting not just the logic of individual capitalist investments, but also a recurrent pattern of historical capitalism as world system. The central aspect of this pattern is the alternation of epochs of material expansion (M–C phases of accumulation) with phases of financial rebirth and expansion (C–M¹ phases). . . . Together the two epochs of phases constitute a full *systemic cycle of accumulation* (M–C–M¹)" (*Long Twentieth*, 6).

60. Piketty, *Capital*, 28.

61. In Piketty's historical framework, then, the late nineteenth and early twenty-first centuries are moments of a single tendency, which happened to be interrupted by the first and second world wars, in which rates of capital return have tended to exceed rates of growth based on output and wages (his formula $r>g$). The Great Depression and postwar period also saw political restrictions that compressed capital's growth. It was this long interregnum, Piketty argues, that allowed mainstream economics to develop theories about the ways primitive industrial capitalism had been restrained. He writes, "Broadly speaking, it was the wars of the twentieth century that wiped away the past to create the illusion that capitalism had been structurally transformed" (*Capital*, 118) and later that "it took two world wars to wipe away the past and significantly reduce the return on capital, thereby creating the illusion that the fundamental structural contradiction of capitalism ($r>g$) had been overcome" (572).

The controversy of Piketty's argument, I would argue, can be located in his statement that "the fundamental $r>g$ inequality, the main force of divergence in my theory, has nothing to do with any market imperfection. Quite the contrary: the more perfect the capital market (in the economist's sense), the more likely r is to be greater than g" (27). The idea that markets do not self-regulate, and in fact, tend to become more and more one-sided in favor of wealth is what places Piketty in opposition to mainstream economics and would seem to invite a Marxist interpretation of his data.

62. For instance, Gilligan and Vishmidt emphasize the neoliberal subject's imagining of itself as ultimately responsible for everything related to the self. Melanie Gilligan and Marina Vishmidt, "'The Property-Less Sensorium': Following the Subject in Crisis Times," *South Atlantic Quarterly* 114, no. 3 (2015): 612. Smith similarly characterizes a range of literary texts as "neoliberal" through an emphasis on self-management. Rachel Greenwald Smith, *Affect and American Literature in the Age of Neoliberalism* (New York: Cambridge University Press, 2015). See also Mathias Nilges, "The Anti-Anti Oedipus: Representing Post-Fordist Subjectivity," *Mediations* 23, no. 2 (2008): 27–70.

63. Anna Kornbluh, *Realizing Capital: Financial and Psychic Economies in Victorian Form* (New York: Fordham University Press, 2014), 4, 11. Kornbluh's emphasis on the performative aspect of fictionality disputes Mary Poovey's contention that the role of financial narrative was to induce belief, in which the realist novel was "deputized," as Kornbluh puts it, to lend its authority in securing representation to reality. She argues that the Victorians did not have to believe finance was real in order to act as if it was. Mary Poovey, *The Financial System in Nineteenth-Century Britain* (New York: Oxford University Press, 2002).

64. Timothy Bewes, "Capitalism and Reification: The Logic of the Instance," in *Reading Capitalist Realism,* ed. Alison Shonkwiler and Leigh Claire La Berge (Iowa City: University of Iowa Press, 2014), 213–41.

65. Kornbluh, *Realizing Capital*, 15.

66. Max Haiven and Jody Berland, "Introduction: The Financialized Imagination," *Topia* 30/31 (2013): 7–16.

67. Andreas Langenohl, "'In the Long Run We Are All Dead': Imaginary Time in Financial Market Narratives," *Cultural Critique* 70, no. 1 (2008): 9. In Langenohl's account, the financial "imaginative totality" appears to be different from other, pre–financial imaginaries because it emerges from financial circulation rather than from the commodification of labor.

68. The height of the "Gilded Age" was arguably 1873, the year that saw not only the publication of Twain and Warner's novel but the panic that ruined financial titan Jay Cooke (the most famous banker in America at the time) and the continued unfolding of the Credit Mobilier scandal, which threatened to envelop the Grant administration as it revealed gross corruption in the use of government subsidies to build the Union Pacific railroad. Many of the booms, crashes, and scandals of the period were related to railroads. In the national depression following the crash of 1873, half of all railroad bonds were in default. See Fraser, *Wall Street,* 123.

69. Fraser, *Wall Street*, 118.

70. "Between 1895 and 1904, eighteen hundred firms, centered especially in the capital-intensive, mass-production sector, were swallowed up in corporate mergers. . . . The 1900 Census recorded seventy-three industrial combinations valued at more than $10 million; ten years before there had been none. By 1909, a mere 1 percent of all industrial firms accounted for 44 percent of the value of all manufactured goods. . . . A thousand industrial companies were listed on the Exchange by 1901. . . . By 1903 the merger movement had revolutionized the economy." Fraser, *Wall Street*, 171.

71. Ibid., 111.

1. Virtue Unrewarded

1. Flory undertakes to survey the genre from 1792 to 1900. He classifies about 250 novels as belonging to it, divided into categories of literary merit, and argues the "economic protest in the general novel is probably the most pronounced phase of the new realism in American literature" (15). He writes: "In the period from 1860–1900 the strongest of our economic critics in fiction are also in many cases our ablest writers of the realistic novel. The relationship obviously is that both economic criticism—in the regular novel—and realism demand truth to life" (243). Claude Reherd Flory, *Economic Criticism in American Fiction: 1792 to 1900* (New York: Russell and Russell, 1937). Taylor takes Twain, Garland, Bellamy, Howells, and Norris as major authors. Walter Fuller Taylor, *The Economic Novel in America* (Chapel Hill: University of North Carolina Press, 1942). Neither critic considers Dreiser a major figure. Later criticism, still assuming a class basis, would view the economic novel as having disappeared when the novel turned to problems of consciousness rather than manners (see John Vernon, *Money and Fiction: Literary Realism in the Nineteenth and Early Twentieth Centuries* [Ithaca: Cornell University Press, 1984]).

2. A confusion addressed by, for instance, June Howard in *Form and History in American Literary Naturalism* (Chapel Hill: University of North Carolina Press, 1985).

3. Stories about financial speculation produced some of the earliest examples of American full-length fiction. See Karen Weyler, "A Speculating Spirit: Trade, Speculation, and Gambling in Early American Fiction." *Early American Literature* 31, no. 3 (1996): 207–42.

4. Walter Benn Michaels, *The Gold Standard and the Logic of Naturalism: American Literature at the Turn of the Century* (Berkeley: University of California Press, 1988), 46.

5. Alan Trachtenberg, *The Incorporation of America: Culture and Society in the Gilded Age* (1982; repr., New York: Hill and Wang, 2007), 54. By using the term *incorporation*, Trachtenberg focuses attention on how these historical developments seemed both pervasive and elusive at the same time.

6. Wilfred M. McClay, *The Masterless: Self and Society in Modern America* (Chapel Hill: University of North Carolina Press, 1994).

7. Jeffrey Sklansky, *The Soul's Economy: Market Society and Selfhood in American Thought, 1820–1920* (Chapel Hill: University of North Carolina Press, 2002).

8. Trachtenberg, *Incorporation*, ix, x.

9. Fraser, *Wall Street*, 201.

10. Wai Chee Dimock, "The Economy of Pain: The Case of Howells," *Raritan* 9, no. 4 (1990): n.p. See also Dimock, "Cognition as a Category of Literary Analysis," *American Literature* 67, no. 4 (1995): 825–31.

11. Fraser, *Wall Street*, 269.

12. Trachtenberg, *Incorporation of America*, 5.

13. Howard Horwitz, "To Find the Value of X: The Pit as a Renunciation of Romance," in *American Realism: New Essays*, ed. Eric Sundquist (Baltimore: Johns Hopkins University Press, 1982), 218, 217. Borrowing from historians Rogin and North, Horwitz describes a capital market as signaled by a transformation in the very definition of capital, such that the "distinction between credit and capital vanishes" (217) and capital becomes simply an index of the process of valuation and revaluation. Finance capitalism is distinct from industrial or productive capitalism, just as finance capital is distinct from capital more or less "directly" linked to its material origins.

14. William Dean Howells, *The Rise of Silas Lapham* (New York: Penguin, 1983), 298.

15. Patrick K. Dooley, "Ethical Exegesis in Howells's The Rise of Silas Lapham," *Papers on Language & Literature* 35, no. 4 (1999): 376. Lapham's resistance to recognizing the limits of his ethical obligations, and carrying his principles to what seems, from a business point of view, an extreme point, have puzzled some critics. Dooley, responding to essays by Dimock, Seelye, and O'Hara in *New Essays on "The Rise of Silas Lapham,"* ed. Donald Pease (New York: Cambridge University Press, 1991), describes recent criticism as "deconstruct[ing] the ethical claims" of Howells's novel and quotes John W. Crowley, from the introduction to the 1996 Oxford edition of *Lapham*, as wondering if the fact that the novel admits of such radically opposite readings does not "suggest its self-contradictory nature . . . [and perhaps ultimately its] fundamental incoherence" (363). Dooley concludes that Lapham's hesitance is a consequence of dealing with a large and unfamiliar entity: "First he is leery of basing moral judgments on the 'spreading out' of loss and pain over a larger number of persons and, second, he is suspicious of preying upon corporate entities" (374). Yet it is unclear what, specifically, about the "corporate entity" is a problem; the function of this vague entity in the text is simply to ensure that Lapham can't make a firm judgment about it; the text focuses less on the ethical status of the corporation per se than on the fact that Lapham cannot judge its "character." O'Hara questions whether we are meant to take Lapham's action as a self-sacrifice, asking, "Why is it right for the father to practice a form

of excessive moral heroism that it is wrong for his daughter to practice?" (Daniel T. O'Hara, "Smiling through the Pain: The Practice of Self in *The Rise of Silas Lapham*," *New Essays on "The Rise of Silas Lapham"*, ed. Donald Pease [New York: Cambridge University Press, 1991], 97). Since the novel rejects Penelope's logic in turning down Tom Corey's suit because she is afraid her sister's feelings will be hurt, it would seem inconsistent for it to advocate a superogatory self-sacrifice for the businessman, far above and beyond what conventional ethics seem to require.

16. Henry James, "The Jolly Corner," *The Novels and Tales of Henry James*, vol. 17 (New York: Charles Scribner's Sons, 1909), 435–86. All page citations are from this volume of the collected New York edition of James's works.

17. Deborah Esch, "A Jamesian About-Face: Notes on 'The Jolly Corner,'" *ELH* 50, no. 3 (1983): 587–605. See also Lee Clark Mitchell, "'Ghostlier Demarcations, Keener Sounds': Scare Quotes in 'The Jolly Corner,'" *Henry James Review* 28, no. 3 (2007): 223–31.

18. Mark McGurl, *The Novel Art: Elevations of American Fiction after Henry James* (Princeton: Princeton University Press, 2001), 50.

19. Ibid., 53.

20. Nicola Nixon, "Prismatic and Profitable: Commerce and the Corporate Person in James's 'The Jolly Corner,'" *American Literature* 76, no. 4 (2004): 809.

21. Ibid., 811.

22. Ibid., 820.

23. Ibid., 808, 809, 827.

24. Because the tableau is so exaggeratedly familiar, critics have tended to focus on whether Brydon's sentimental reunion with Alice should be interpreted as felicitous. Millicent Bell and Mark Fogel, for example, read the conclusion as an uncharacteristically happy one for James, a rewarding of Alice and Brydon with reciprocal love; Eric Savoy reads the conclusion as sinister, a revelation of Alice as vampiric and Brydon as coopted into compulsory heterosexuality (823, also 831n37). Millicent Bell, *Meaning in Henry James* (Cambridge, Mass.: Harvard University Press, 1991); Daniel Mark Fogel, "A New Reading of Henry James's 'The Jolly Corner,'" *Critical Essays on Henry James: The Late Novels*, ed. James W. Gargano (Boston: G. K. Hall, 1967); and Eric Savoy, "The Queer Subject of 'The Jolly Corner,'" *Henry James Review* 20, no. 1 (1999): 1–21.

25. Nixon, "Prismatic and Profitable," 824, 826. Nixon writes that "the constant correction and repetition of the pronouns—the referential slippage between 'I,' 'me,' 'he,' 'him,' and 'you' . . . create a yawning, insoluble gap between the signifiers and their ostensible referents" and the "dialogue destabilizes linguistically any assumption of coherent selfhood" (826).

26. Theodore Dreiser, *The Financier* (New York: Boni and Liveright, 1927; repr., New York: New American Library, 1995).

27. Other critics have attempted to account for the apparent contradictions in Dreiser's shifting views on determination and free will. Louis Zanine describes the

man of "reason" as an idealized figure in Dreiser's work. Genius, in this reading, might be seen to reveal a higher stage of development in which individuals consciously cease their long and ineffective struggle against the natural order of things. Louis Zanine, *Mechanism and Mysticism: The Influence of Science on the Thought and Work of Theodore Dreiser* (Philadelphia: University of Pennsylvania Press, 1993).

28. Michaels, *Gold Standard*. Michael Tratner, *Deficits and Desires: Economics and Sexuality in Twentieth-Century Literature* (Stanford, Calif.: Stanford University Press, 2002).

29. Gustavus Stadler, *Troubling Minds: The Cultural Politics of Genius in the United States, 1840–1890* (Minneapolis: University of Minnesota Press, 2006), xvii.

30. Bill Brown, *A Sense of Things: The Object Matter of American Literature* (Chicago: University of Chicago Press, 2003), 54–58.

31. *McTeague*, qtd. in Brown, *Sense of Things*, 55, 57.

32. Georg Lukács, "Narrate or Describe?" in *Writer and Critic: And Other Essays* (New York, Grosset and Dunlap, 1971), 110–48.

33. Jennifer Fleissner, *Women, Compulsion, Modernity: The Moment of American Naturalism* (Chicago: University of Chicago Press, 2004), 10.

34. On the novel's transcriptiveness, see Howard Horwitz, *By the Law of Nature: Form and Value in Nineteenth-Century America* (New York: Oxford University Press, 1991), 201. On its historical narrative, see Donald Pizer, *The Novels of Theodore Dreiser: A Critical Study* (Minneapolis: University of Minnesota Press, 1976), 7.

35. Larzer Ziff, afterword to *The Financier* by Theodore Dreiser (New York: New American Library, 1995), 457.

36. David A. Zimmerman, *Panic! Markets, Crises, and Crowds in American Fiction* (Chapel Hill: University of North Carolina Press, 2006), 200, 195, 196. Zimmerman argues that the text documents the limits of any system of accounting — financial, legal, moral, or narrative.

37. Leigh Claire La Berge, "Reading Finance Capital," in *Culture, Capital, and Representation,* ed. Robert J. Balfour (Houndmills: Palgrave Macmillan, 2010), 126.

38. June Howard, *Form and History in American Literary Naturalism* (Chapel Hill: University of North Carolina Press, 1985).

39. Michaels, *Gold Standard*.

40. Bruce Robbins, "Can There Be Loyalty in *The Financier?* Dreiser and Upward Mobility," in *The Cambridge Companion to Theodore Dreiser,* ed. Leonard Cassuto and Clare Virginia Eby (New York: Cambridge University Press, 2004), 112–26.

41. See Kevin W. Jett, "Vision and Revision: Another Look at the 1912 and 1927 Editions of Dreiser's *The Financier*." *Dreiser Studies* 29, no. 1/2 (1998): 51. I'm not convinced however that this rewriting was meant to lure the reader into identifying with a corrupt figure of capitalism and then expose the reader's identification as hypocritical.

42. In accommodating at the same time order and disorder, progression and disruption, Dreiser's account of history corresponds to the views of many scientific historians and economic writers of the period. One apparent feature of this tension in naturalistic historicism is an ability to represent discrete events as having no inherent meaning or moral significance, while at the same time generalizing about history in positive terms, as a teleological progression toward order or a "cosmic" equilibrium. The connections between *The Financier* and Dreiser's essay "Equation Inevitable" on the harmonies of the social-evolutionary process have been addressed elsewhere. I argue that the revised novel makes its scenes more generalizable according to naturalistic-scientific theories of history, but that "history" is more complex in the novel than many of the theories. Theodore Dreiser, "Equation Inevitable," in *Hey Rub-a-Dub-Dub: A Book of the Mystery and Wonder and Terror of Life* (New York: Boni and Liveright, 1920), 157–81.

2. Reaganomic Realisms

1. Michael M. Thomas, "The Greatest American Shambles," *New York Review of Books* 31, January 1991. If Thomas is right about the inadequacy of journalistic narratives to generate outrage over the S&L crisis, it is not for lack of trying. Pizzo calls the scandal an "inside job," a "hit-and-run," and an "orgy of greed and excess" (5, 4). Mayer, author of *The Greatest-Ever Bank Robbery*, calls it an "irruption of criminality," "outrageous and dishonest" accounting, and "atrocious theft" (3, 19). In comparison, Seidman, the FDIC chairman from 1985 to 1991, exhibits balanced restraint in calling the S&Ls an "industry born with a congenital defect" that met a "witches' brew . . . of misguided policy" concocted by a "long list of villains" (177, 178). (Seidman includes members of the Reagan administration in the long list.) Stephen Pizzo, *Inside Job: The Looting of America's Savings and Loans* (New York: HarperCollins, 1991). Martin Mayer, *The Greatest-Ever Bank Robbery: The Collapse of the Savings and Loan Industry* (New York: Scribners, 1990). Lewis William Seidman, *Full Faith and Credit: The Great S & L Debacle and Other Washington Sagas* (New York: Times Books, 1993).

2. Jane Smiley, *Good Faith* (New York: Knopf, 2003).

3. Michael Schaller, *Reckoning with Reagan: America and Its President in the 1980s* (New York: Oxford University Press, 1992), 110.

4. Kitty Calavita, Henry N. Pontell, and Robert H. Tillman, *Big Money Crime: Fraud and Politics in the Savings and Loan Crisis* (Berkeley: University of California Press, 1997), 10. Pizzo, *Inside Job*, 13. Schaller, *Reckoning with Reagan*.

5. After 1982 the "good faith" model of lending upon which the S&Ls had developed since the Depression—idealized in the figure of the benevolent bank president played by Jimmy Stewart in the 1946 Frank Capra film *It's a Wonderful Life*—entered into direct conflict of interest with the "full faith and credit" guarantee of the government. The guarantee of federal deposit insurance—created as part of New Deal regulation to avoid catastrophic bank failures of the type seen in

1929—protected individuals against loss of their life savings. In the new, post-1982 regulatory context, however, these also effectively protected the S&Ls against losses from bad investments. Although S&L investments were technically made with depositor "savings," the thrifts in reality now served as clearinghouses for finance capital seeking investment. Powerful incentives were created for what was essentially government-backed speculation. Investors flocked to the expanded investment possibilities that S&Ls offered: "the notion of 'risk,' that vexing side of market capitalism, had been eliminated" (Thomas).

6. "The Casino Society," *Business Week*, September 16, 1985, qtd. in Calavita, *Big Money Crime*, 15.

7. See George Sternlieb and James W. Hughes, *America's New Market Geography: Nation, Region, and Metropolis* (New Brunswick, N.J.: Center for Urban Policy Research, Rutgers University, 1988).

8. Schaller, *Reckoning with Reagan*, 69. See also John A. Kasarda, "People and Jobs on the Move: American's New Spatial Dynamics," in Sternlieb and Hughes, *America's New Market*, 217–42.

9. Schaller, *Reckoning with Reagan*, 111.

10. Jason Hackworth, *The Neoliberal City* (Ithaca: Cornell University Press, 2007), 78. Hackworth argues that real estate becomes a "quasi autonomous" form of capitalist development in the post-1970s economy, replacing the mid-twentieth-century "spatial fix" that "likely had petered out by the mid-1990s" (78). Hackworth characterizes three aspects to the neoliberal city: (1) inner city gentrification, (2) inner suburban devalorization, and (3) continued physical expansion of metropolitan areas (80–81).

11. Paul Zane Pilzer, *Other People's Money: The Inside Story of the S&L Mess* (New York: Simon and Schuster, 1989), 55.

12. Ibid., 54–55.

13. Catherine Jurca, *White Diaspora: The Suburb and the Twentieth-Century American Novel* (Princeton: Princeton University Press, 2001), 12. See also Keith Wilhite, "Contested Terrain," *American Literature* 84, no. 3 (2012): 617–44, which calls for a "more expansive treatment of suburban fiction as a discourse that operates within national and transnational geographies." While my argument is not in conflict with Wilhite's situating of the suburban novel within the discourses of U.S. isolationism and imperialism, particularly given the ways real estate speculation operates internationally in the 1980s, I see Smiley's novel as intentionally focused on the relationship between national and small-town local—skipping over the true postwar suburban.

14. James S. Duncan and Nancy G. Duncan, *Landscapes of Privilege: The Politics of the Aesthetic in an American Suburb* (New York: Routledge, 2004), 5.

15. David Harvey, *The Condition of Postmodernity* (Malden, Mass.: Blackwell, 1990), 305, qtd. in Duncan and Duncan, *Landscapes*, 26.

16. Stein writes: "The economy grew briskly after 1982. GDP rose from its –2.2 percent rate in 1982 to 4.5 in 1983 and 7.2 percent in 1984, and averaged

between 3 and 4 percent for the rest of the decade. What kind of a recovery was this? Reagan stated that the tax cuts would increase savings and thus investment to improve productivity and growth. But the recovery was led by consumption, not investment, and radically altered the composition of the economy, promoting non-tradable sectors like real estate, financial services, and defense and hobbling trad-able manufacturing and agriculture." Judith Stein, *Pivotal Decade: How the United States Traded Factories for Finance* (New Haven: Yale University Press, 2010), 267–68.

17. On yuppies also see Jay McInerney, "Yuppies in Eden," *New York Magazine*, September 28, 2008, 104–13.

18. Foster, "Financialization of Accumulation," 12.

19. Harvey, *Condition of Postmodernity*, 156.

20. Randy Martin has analyzed the financialization of "daily life" in detail. Max Haiven also notes that "personal debt became the means by which people claimed their share of social wealth" but argues that the working class's embrace of "financialization" is also a form of resistance to neoliberalism and capitalist culture. Haiven, "Finance Depends on Resistance," 95, 93.

21. Self argues: "California politics since 1945 have distilled to an essence what has been at stake in the nation: distribution of the assets and costs of post-war affluence; the triumph of growth liberalism and the vast inequalities it created and left unresolved; the possibilities of a progressive welfare state and the retrenchment of the tax revolt; the bonanza of Keynesian mass consumption and its social and environmental fallout." Robert O. Self, "Prelude to the Tax Revolt: The Politics of the 'Tax Dollar' in Postwar California," in *The New Suburban History*, ed. Kevin M. Kruse and Thomas J. Sugrue (Chicago: University of Chicago Press, 2006), 144.

22. Toporowski, "Wisdom of Property," 15.

23. Passed by an overwhelming two-to-one margin by voters, Proposition 13 (the Jarvis-Gann Initiative) took the drastic step of linking all assessments to 1975–76 property values and limiting any future tax increases to a small percentage. The effect on state revenues was dramatic, marking the beginning of a long stretch of budget cutting and, perhaps most visibly, decades of defunding of California public education. Prop 13 sources include Daniel A. Smith, *Tax Crusaders and the Politics of Direct Democracy* (New York: Routledge, 2013); David O. Sears and Jack Citrin, *Tax Revolt: Something for Nothing in California* (Cambridge, Mass.: Harvard University Press, 1982); Arthur O'Sullivan, Terri A. Sexton, and Steven M. Sheffrin, *Property Taxes and Tax Revolts: The Legacy of Prop 13* (New York: Cambridge University Press, 1995); and Stephanie Simon, "20 Years Later, Prop 13 Still Marks California Life," *Los Angeles Times*, May 26, 1998, A1.

24. Milton Friedman, "The Message from California," *Newsweek*, June 19, 1978, 26.

25. "Two years later, the former governor of California, Ronald Reagan, a proponent of Prop 13 and a long-time critic of the liberal state, won election to the presidency on a domestic platform of tax cuts, limited government spending, and

the assurance that less government would enhance both the personal freedom and personal finances of Americans." Becky Nicolaides and Andrew Wiese, eds., *The Suburb Reader* (New York: Routledge, 2006), 380. The Economic Recovery Tax Act of 1981, the largest income tax cut in American history—which set the stage for the supply-side agenda and was even taken as a model by future presidents (political scientists Jacob Hacker and Paul Pierson, for instance, call ERTA "'the guiding light' of George W. Bush's domestic agenda")—was enabled in part by tax resistance in California in the late 1970s. Jacob S. Hacker and Paul Pierson, *Off Center: The Republican Revolution and the Erosion of American Democracy* (New Haven: Yale University Press, 2005), 30.

26. Isaac W. Martin, *The Permanent Tax Revolt: How the Property Tax Transformed American Politics* (Stanford: Stanford University Press, 2008), 131. Martin chronicles Reagan's transformation from initial skeptic to full convert in a chapter called "Welcome to the Tax Cutting Party: How the Tax Revolt Transformed Republican Politics."

27. Stein writes that "in 1969, tax equity, not tax cuts, was the national goal. Often this meant shifting the burden to the wealthy and to business, not shrinking the government and cutting taxes, the mantra after 1980" (*Pivotal Decade*, 24–25).

28. Martin, *Permanent Tax Revolt*, 2, 24.

29. The leaders of Prop 13 portrayed it as a populist movement. Howard Jarvis called it "a victory against money, the politicians, the government" (qtd. in Smith, *Tax Crusaders*, xii). On election night he proclaimed, "Now we know how it felt when they dumped English tea in Boston Harbor! We have a new revolution. We are telling the government, 'Screw you!'" (qtd. in Smith, *Tax Crusaders*, 25). Critics argued that the movement exploited the politics of resentment, that it primarily benefited business and corporate interests, and that it did not, in fact, represent direct democracy or widespread citizen participation, even in evidence of high voter turnout. *Commonweal* declared that "what was sold to the voters as tax relief for the little-man homeowner was actually a boon to big-business property owners, many of whom live outside the state" (Nicolaides and Wiese, *Suburb Reader*, 384). Scholars in hindsight have further criticized the movement's claim to be grassroots driven. Smith argues that "while the tax crusaders swaddled their measure with populist rhetoric, their initiative campaigns . . . were more akin to '*faux* populist moments'—fleeting expressions of popular support for tax limitation initiatives crafted by entrepreneurial tax crusaders" (Smith, *Tax Crusaders*, 10). Contrast Smith to the argument of Jack Citrin that Prop 13's direct democracy "expresses a positive yearning for voice—for the chance to be heard and to participate" (qtd. in Smith, *Tax Crusaders*, xiii).

30. Nicolaides and Wiese, *Suburb Reader*, 388.

31. See Dolores E. Janiewski, "Towards a New Suburban History," *Social History* 33, no. 1 (2008): 60–67; Robert O. Self, *American Babylon: Race and the Struggle for Postwar Oakland* (Princeton: Princeton University Press, 2003); Kruse and Sugrue, *New Suburban History*.

32. Neil Smith, "Giuliani Time: The Revanchist 1990s," *Social Text* 57 (1998): 10.

33. Nicolaides and Wiese, *Suburb Reader,* 384.

34. Martin, *Permanent Tax Revolt,* 15, 9–10.

35. Constance Perin, *Everything in Its Place: Social Order and Land Use in America* (Princeton: Princeton University Press, 1989), x.

36. Ibid., 8.

37. Ibid., 129.

38. Jameson, "Culture and Finance Capital," 137.

39. Sara Ahmed, "Willful Parts: Problem Characters or the Problem of Character," *New Literary History* 42, no. 2 (2011): 231.

40. Leo Bersani, *A Future for Astyanax: Character and Desire in Literature* (Boston: Little, Brown, 1976), 52–53.

41. John Frow, "Spectacle Binding: On Character," *Poetics Today* 7, no. 2 (1986): 236.

42. Lenz calls the confidence man a "distinctly American version of the archetypal trickster" that arises and begins to have a literary life in the 1840s. Melville's confidence man inaugurates a new historical "type" that signals a problem of social legibility. He relies on the "fluid nature of society in the New World with its unique opportunities for self-government, self-promotion, self-posturing, and self-creation" (1) and becomes "a literary convention precisely at the point that we can distinguish his aesthetic moneymaking schemes from the exploding gimmicks of the traditional prankster" (74). Also important for Lenz, this figure belongs to the "imaginative territory" of the borderlands and the frontier. This "in-between" area that is not city or wilderness could also describe Smiley's small town. William Lenz, *Fast Talk and Flush Times: The Confidence Man as a Literary Convention* (Columbia: University of Missouri Press, 1985). In contrast, Balkun counters the argument about fluid society by arguing that the figure of the "American counterfeit" reveals the "*lack* of fluidity in the boundaries." Instead, the counterfeiter highlights a space of discrepancy and contradiction between ideology and practice. Mary McAleer Balkun, *The American Counterfeit: Authenticity and Identity in American Literature and Culture* (Tuscaloosa: University of Alabama Press, 2006), 14.

43. James Salazar, *Bodies of Reform: The Rhetoric of Character in Gilded Age America* (New York: New York University Press, 2010), 18. Balkun, *American Counterfeit.*

44. Ian Hunter, "Reading Character," *Southern Review* 16, no. 2 (1983): 232, qtd. in Frow, "Spectacle Binding," 235.

45. Deidre Shauna Lynch, *The Economy of Character: Novels, Market Culture, and the Business of Inner Meaning* (Chicago: University of Chicago Press, 1998), 9, 140.

46. Frow, "Spectacle Binding," 236.

47. In his examination of the relationship between major and minor characters in the realist novel, Woloch has described an allocation of textual attention

established by the degree to which different characters get more or less completely pulled into the narrative. Secondary and minor characters tend to become allegorized in relation to their organization around a primary character as "the discrete representation of any specific individual is intertwined with the narrative's continual apportioning of attention to different characters who jostle for limited space within the same fictive universe." Alex Woloch, *The One vs. the Many: Minor Characters and the Space of the Protagonist in the Novel* (Princeton: Princeton University Press, 2003), 13.

48. Perin, *Everything*, 116.

49. See Martin Mayer, *The Greatest-Ever Bank Robbery*.

50. Kitty Calavita, Henry N. Pontell, and Robert Tillman, *Big Money Crime: Fraud and Politics in the Savings and Loan Crisis* (Berkeley: University of California Press, 1999).

51. Salazar, *Bodies*, 3, 4–5.

3. Epic Compensations

1. Georg Lukács, *The Theory of the Novel* (Cambridge, Mass.: MIT Press, 1974), 32.

2. Richard Powers, *Gain* (1998; repr., New York: Picador, 1999), 347.

3. For Lukács, there was no overestimating the importance of the concept of totality. *History and Class Consciousness* placed the concept at the center of the Western Marxist tradition. The alienations of bourgeois life were the consequence of a failure to think the totality. To counteract the "second nature" of reification was one of the main purposes of the novel; to give shape to lived social contradictions its highest achievement. "The 'value' of a literary narrative," Fredric Jameson writes in his preface to Lukács's *The Historical Novel*, "is in this sense to be grasped in terms of its capacity to open a totalizing and mapping access to society as a whole" (7). Fredric Jameson, preface to Georg Lukács, *The Historical Novel*, trans. Hannah Mitchell (Lincoln: University of Nebraska Press, 1983).

4. Bruce Robbins, "Homework: Richard Powers, Walt Whitman, and the Poetry of the Commodity," *Ariel* 34, no. 1 (2005): 88.

5. Ursula K. Heise, "Toxins, Drugs, and Global Systems: Risk and Narrative in the Contemporary Novel," *American Literature* 74, no. 4 (2002): 771.

6. Franco Moretti, *Modern Epic: The World-System from Goethe to García Márquez* (New York: Verso, 1996), 209.

7. I do not intend to critique Lukács's conception of the epic; I assume, along with Martin Jay, that it is a romantic idealization that nonetheless offers a basis for Lukács to theorize his concept of totality. Martin Jay, *Marxism and Totality: The Adventures of a Concept from Lukács to Habermas* (Berkeley: University of California Press, 1984). For a defense that Lukács's idea of the epic is simply a "hermeneutical construct" meant to enable his theory of the novel, see J. M. Bernstein, *The Philosophy of the Novel: Lukács, Marxism, and the Dialectics of Form* (Minneapolis: University of Minnesota, 1984).

8. Fredric Jameson, "The End of Temporality," *Critical Inquiry* 29, no. 4 (2003): 702.

9. Jeffrey Williams, "The Issue of Corporations: Richard Powers' *Gain*," *Cultural Logic* 2, no. 2 (1999): http://clogic.eserver.org/2–2/williamsrev.html.

10. Jeremy Green, *Late Postmodernism: American Fiction at the Millennium* (New York: Palgrave Macmillan, 2005), 188, 189.

11. Heise, "Toxins, Drugs," 763, 769. I am not the first to use the term *epic* in the context of *Gain*. In this 2002 article, Heise mentions the term in her discussion of Powers's novel. However, in her book *Sense of Place and Sense of Planet: The Environmental Imagination of the Global* (New York: Oxford University Press, 2008), Heise refers to epic only in the introduction and nowhere in the revised discussion of *Gain*.

12. The widely cited phrase is from Powers's second novel, *The Prisoner's Dilemma*.

13. Joseph Dewey, *Understanding Richard Powers* (Columbia: University of South Carolina Press, 2002), 48. Charles Harris, "'The Stereo View': Politics and the Role of the Reader in *Gain*," *Review of Contemporary Fiction* 18, no. 3 (1998): 97–108. Tom LeClair, "Powers of Invention," review of *Gain*, *The Nation*, July 27–August 3, 1998, 33–35.

14. Heise, "Toxins," 769, 772.

15. Ibid., 765, 767.

16. Ibid., 773.

17. Fredric Jameson, *Postmodernism: Or, the Cultural Logic of Late Capitalism* (Durham: Duke University Press, 1991), 22.

18. Catherine Porter, "Reification and American Literature," in *Ideology and Classic American Literature*, ed. Sacvan Bercovitch and Myra Jehlen (New York: Cambridge University Press, 1986), 194.

19. Frank Norris, *The Octopus: The Epic of the Wheat; A Story of California*. (1901; repr., Harmondsworth: Penguin, 1986). Norris relied on journalistic accounts of an 1880 shootout at Mussel Slough, though his fictionalized version significantly departs from those accounts. See Adam H. Wood. "'The Signs and Symbols of the West': Frank Norris, *The Octopus,* and the Naturalization of Market Capitalism," in *Twisted from the Ordinary: Essays on American Literary Naturalism*, ed. Mary E. Papke (Knoxville: University of Tennessee Press, 2003), 107–27.

20. For a discussion of financial agency in *The Pit* see my dissertation, "The Financial Imaginary: Dreiser, DeLillo, and Abstract Capitalism in American Literature" (PhD diss., Rutgers University, 2007).

21. For in-depth studies of naturalist agency, see Walter Benn Michaels, Mark Seltzer, Howard Horwitz, and Jennifer Fleissner. For readings of naturalism as vexed by the contradictions of the "body" of production, see especially Michaels and Seltzer. Michaels describes *The Octopus* as attempting to resolve a problem of ontology posed by the disembodied status of the corporation. He finds a "corporate

moment" disseminated throughout the novel in which the natural body is dis-
posed, machine transformed into man, and material and immaterial repeatedly
fused, representing the new corporate personhood more fully than actual persons
can do. Michaels, *Gold Standard*. Mark Seltzer, *Bodies and Machines* (New York:
Routledge, 1992). Howard Horwitz, *By the Law of Nature: Form and Value in
Nineteenth-Century America* (New York: Oxford University Press, 1991). Fleissner, *Women, Compulsion, Modernity: The Moment of American Naturalism* (Chicago: University of Chicago Press, 2004).

22. Seltzer, *Bodies and Machines*, 28.

23. Formal attention to the epic structure of *The Octopus* has included its use
of epithets, battles, war councils, group feasting and its "jingoistic tone." Ronald
E. Martin, in *American Literature and the Universe of Force* (Durham: Duke University Press, 1983) notes the novel's "extremely plastic, undiscriminating narrative point of view" (175). Others defend the novel's narrative coherence by arguing
that it represents a "multi-perspective narrative structuring" (see Charles Duncan,
"'If Your View Be Large Enough': Narrative Growth in *The Octopus*," *American
Literary Realism* 25, no. 2 [1993]: 59); that it deliberately creates ironic distance
between Norris and Presley (Steven Frye, "Presley's Pretense: Irony and Epic Convention in Frank Norris' *The Octopus*," *American Literary Realism* 39, no. 3
[2007]: 213–21); and to argue that the novel "employs epic conventions with some
distance but is in fact a problem-play concerned with historical action and its representation in art" (Frye, "Presley's Pretense," 215). See also James L. Machor,
"Epic, Romance and Norris' Octopus," *American Literary Realism* 18, no. 1–2
(1985): 42–54.

Contemporary critics have returned to the classical allusions of the railroad,
not to discuss epic form but to emphasize the text's symbolic mode as dominating
over its realist one. According to Zena Meadowsong, Norris's Octopus is not
merely a "real" machine, but a "symbol of vast power," and the piling-up of
mythic associations drives the point home: the Octopus is also the Colossus, the
Leviathan, and, with its "single eye, cyclopean, red," the Homeric Cyclops. Meadowsong refers to "the failure of 'accuracy' in which the realism of the text gives
way, in Norris's view, to the superior truths of romance" ("Frank Norris's Weekly
Letter," 171, qtd. in Meadowsong). Zena Meadowsong, "Natural Monsters: The
Genesis and Deformation of the 'Experimental Novel,' *Studies in American Naturalism* 2, no. 1 (2007): 3–17. See also Frank Norris, "A Plea for Romantic Fiction," 1901.

24. Clare Virginia Eby, "The Octopus: Big Business as Art," *American Literary
Realism* 26, no. 3 (1994): 35.

25. Ibid., 38.

26. Colleen Lye, *America's Asia: Racial Form and American Literature, 1893–
1945* (Princeton: Princeton University Press, 2005). 83–84.

27. Russ Castronovo, "Geo-Aesthetics: Fascism, Globalism, and Frank Norris,"
boundary 2 30, no. 3 (2003): 181.

28. Andrew Hebard reads the railroad as a figure for the failure of rounded coherence. His focus on the machine as an agent of aesthetic disruption might be seen to complete a circle of critical attention from the title to the subtitle and back to the title. Hebard counters Castronovo's characterization of *The Octopus*'s quest for "aesthetic unity" by pointing to an aesthetic of ambiguity, incoherence, and spatial fracturing, and insists that the machine destroys any possibility of close-up aesthetic resolution. Hardly beautiful or coherent, the railroad is described as a monstrous agent of "hideous ruin" whose "grotesque corporeality interrupts Presley's aesthetic vision, '[driving] all thought of his poem from his mind'" (4). The railroad becomes a figure for the *failure* of rounded formal coherence. "This incoherence, this failed formalism," Hebard writes, is also "one of the aesthetic forms that American empire takes at the turn of the century" (4). Andrew Hebard, "The Naturalist Floorplan: Frank Norris and the Aesthetics of Imperial Administration," paper presented at the Futures of American Studies conference, Hanover, New Hampshire, June 2009.

Zena Meadowsong ("Natural Monsters") argues that the excessive monstrousness in descriptions of the engine (e.g., its "red, Cyclopean eye") mark the text's movement into a symbolic or mythic register ("Realism collapses—must collapse—under the symbolic pressure of the machine" [7]). Meadowsong asserts that in its recourse to myth the novel "draws attention to its own faultiness" and its "assertion of narrative incapacity" (4, 8).

29. Hebard, "Naturalist Floorplan," 4.

30. Castronovo, "Geo-Aesthetics," 180.

31. See Robbins, "Homework," for a reading of Laura's connection to Whitman's "aerial view."

32. Mikhail Bakhtin, *The Dialogic Imagination: Four Essays* (Austin: University of Texas Press, 1982), 34n3.

33. Bruno Latour. "Why Has Critique Run Out of Steam? From Matters of Fact to Matters of Concern," *Critical Inquiry* 30 (Winter 2004): 231. On the contemporary tendency toward conspiracy thinking, for example, Latour writes, "While we spent years trying to detect the real prejudices hidden behind the appearance of objective statements, do we now have to reveal the real objective and incontrovertible facts hidden behind the *illusion* of prejudices?" (227).

34. Ibid., 227.

35. Ibid., 242.

36. Lukács, *Theory of the Novel*, 49–50.

37. Wai Chee Dimock, "Genre as World System: Epic and Novel on Four Continents," *Narrative* 14, no. 1 (2006): 93, 92.

38. Dimock builds on the work of Mandelbrot and his use of fractal logic to answer the question, "How Long Is the Coast of Britain?" "Mandelbrot points out that there is no single answer to this question, since everything depends on the yardstick being used, the scale adopted to make the measurement. If an observer were to measure the coastline from the air, from a distance of twenty thousand feet,

that aerial vision would yield a clean line—and a shorter distance—since all the nooks and crannies would be passed over. If the observer were on the ground, measuring the coast at close range and on foot, in units of eight or nine inches, the coast of Britain would be much longer, thanks to the zigzags newly produced" (Dimock, "Genre as World System," 88). Benoît Mandelbrot, "How Long Is the Coast of Britain? Statistical Self-Similarity and Fractional Dimension," *Science* 156, no. 3775 (May 5, 1967).

39. Dimock, "Genre as World System," 88, 89.

40. Jay, *Marxism and Totality*, 512.

41. Axel Honneth, for instance, has elaborated a theory of reification as a failure of recognition. To be rooted in reified everyday culture in Honneth's view is to "remain entrapped within the subject/object opposition" (29) and the fetishization of the object as "other." Axel Honneth, *Reification: A New Look at an Old Idea* (Oxford: Oxford University Press, 2008). See also Timothy Bewes, *Reification: Or, The Anxiety of Late Capitalism* (London: Verso, 2002); and Kevin Floyd, *The Reification of Desire: Toward a Queer Marxism* (Minneapolis: University of Minnesota Press, 2009).

4. Financial Sublime

1. Doug Henwood, *Wall Street: How It Works and for Whom* (New York: Verso, 1997), 2. Henwood quotes from Jean Baudrillard, *The Transparency of Evil: Essays on Extreme Phenomena*, trans. James Benedict (New York: Verso, 1993), 10–11, 33.

2. Henwood, *After the New Economy: The Binge and the Hangover That Won't Go Away* (New York: New Press, 2003), 29, 28, 26.

3. Thomas Frank makes a similar case about business's search for legitimating grand discourses in the 1990s in *One Market under God: Extreme Capitalism, Market Populism, and the End of Economic Democracy* (New York: Doubleday, 2000).

4. Henwood, *Wall Street*, 2–3.

5. Don DeLillo, *Cosmopolis* (New York: Scribner, 2003).

6. See reviews by Michiko Kakutani, "Headed toward a Crash, of Sorts, in a Stretch Limo," review of *Cosmopolis, New York Times*, March 24, 2003; Walter Kirn, "Long Day's Journey into Haircut," review of *Cosmopolis, New York Times Book Review*, April 13, 2003; John Updike, "One-Way Street," review of *Cosmopolis, New Yorker*, March 31, 2003. For a defense, see Sven Philipp, "Words and Syllables," review of *Cosmopolis, Electronic Book Review* 29 (May 2003). A representative collection of reviews is compiled at *"Cosmopolis" Media Watch*, June 28, 2003.

7. James Wood, "Traffic," review of *Cosmopolis, New Republic*, April 14, 2003, 32.

8. Don DeLillo, *White Noise* (New York: Viking, 1985), 46.

9. Arjun Appadurai, *Modernity at Large: Cultural Dimensions of Globalization* (Minneapolis: University of Minnesota Press, 1996). Harvey, *Condition of Postmodernity*. Jameson, *Postmodernism*. Manuel Castells, "Information Technology and Global Capitalism," *Global Capitalism*, ed. Will Hutton and Anthony Giddens (New York: New Press, 2000), 52–73. Giovanni Arrighi, *The Long Twentieth Century: Money, Power, and the Origins of Our Times* (London: Verso, 1994). Immanuel Wallerstein, *World-Systems Analysis: An Introduction* (Durham: Duke University Press, 2004).

10. Emily Apter, "On Oneworldedness: Or Paranoia as a World System," *American Literary History* 18, no. 2 (2006): 366.

11. Joseph Tabbi, *Postmodern Sublime: Technology and American Writing from Mailer to Cyberpunk* (Ithaca: Cornell University Press, 1995).

12. Bruce Robbins, "The Sweatshop Sublime," *PMLA* 117, no. 1 (2002): 85.

13. Jerry A. Varsava, "The 'Saturated Self': Don DeLillo on the Problem of Rogue Capitalism," *Contemporary Literature* 46, no. 1 (2005): 80, 104.

14. David E. Nye, in *American Technological Sublime* (Cambridge, Mass.: MIT Press, 1994), traces the phrase *technological sublime* from Perry Miller's coining in *The Life of the Mind in America from the Revolution to the Civil War* (New York: Harcourt, Brace, and World, 1965) to Leo Marx's *The Machine in the Garden: Technology and the Pastoral Ideal in America* (New York: Oxford University Press, 1965) to John Kasson's *Civilizing the Machine: Technology and Republican Values in America, 1776–1900* (New York: Grossman, 1976). Nye's history of the American politics of the spectacular apparently invites us to adduce the latest modern and postmodern technologies to a chronology that includes the building of railroads, the electrification of cities, and the launch of the Apollo spacecraft. But I read the "mythmaking" of the digital sublime in the 1990s and 2000s as different: cybertechnology may offer an "objective spectacle," but it also represents our complex confrontation with a thoroughly and at times inescapably mediated reality, which raises further philosophical questions about our relations to language, discourse, and knowledge.

Amy Elias in *Sublime Desire: History and Post-1960s Fiction* (Baltimore: Johns Hopkins University Press, 2001) focuses on history, not technology, as testing the "sublime" limits of postmodern representation. I return to Elias's work in discussing historical representation in the final section of this essay.

15. Tabbi, *Postmodern Sublime*, 16.

16. Ibid., ix.

17. Vincent Mosco, *The Digital Sublime: Myth, Power, and Cyberspace* (Cambridge, Mass.: MIT Press, 2004), 20, 2–3.

18. Timothy Melley, *Empire of Conspiracy: The Culture of Paranoia in Postwar America* (Ithaca: Cornell University Press, 2000), vii.

19. Ibid., 7.

20. Frank Lentricchia, "Tales of the Electronic Tribe," *New Essays on "White Noise,"* ed. Frank Lentricchia (New York: Cambridge University Press, 1991), 87–113.

21. Updike, "One-Way Street."

22. See Gail Caldwell, "Bonfire of Inanities," review of *Cosmopolis, Boston Globe,* April 6 2003; and Mark Greif, "Bonfire of the Verities," review of *Cosmopolis, American Prospect* 14, no. 4 (2003): 54–55.

23. Don DeLillo, *Americana* (New York: Houghton Mifflin, 1971), 270.

24. Don DeLillo, *Underworld* (New York: Scribner, 1997), 825. As Sister Edgar, post-death, watches the H-bomb explode above the Arctic Ocean in 1961, "preserved in the computer that helped to build it," she glimpses a cross-section of historical relationships, the ordinarily invisible causes and effects radiating out from the technological event of the century: "Whole populations potentially skelly-boned in the massive flash—dem bones, dem bones, sing the washtub women. And Sister begins to sense the byshadows that stretch from the awe of a central event. How the intersecting systems help pull us apart, leaving us vague, drained, docile, soft in our inner discourse, willing to be shaped, to be overwhelmed—easy retreats, half beliefs" (826).

25. Ibid., 826.

26. For discussions of such systems, see Bruce Clarke's *Posthuman Metamorphosis: Narrative and Systems* (New York: Fordham University Press, 2008), in particular his discussion of informational systems theory; Lee and LiPuma on capitalist circulation: "Cultures of Circulation" and Joseph Tabbi's *Cognitive Fictions* (Minneapolis: University of Minnesota Press, 2002) on interactions between new media systems and technologies of consciousness.

27. Lee and LiPuma, "Cultures of Circulation," 198.

28. Wood, "Traffic," 32.

29. Vivian Gornick calls Wood a persistent "champion of the now painfully inadequate realist novel." The nineteenth-century references in Wood's *Cosmopolis* review suggest an Arnoldian point of view on the novel's developmental peak: Eric is Manhattan's "Malte Laurids Brigge"; an *Underworld* character's rapt tone is "bathetically close in impulse to Wordsworth on the Simplon Pass, or to Ruskin on Rouen Cathedral"; Packer's sexual encounter with his chief of finance is a "neural Waterloo." "Exchange: Vivian Gornick on James Wood," *Nation,* June 8, 2009, 2, 44.

30. Philipp, "Words and Syllables."

31. Jameson, *Postmodernism,* 37–38.

32. Jameson, "Culture and Finance Capital," 143. See also Wallerstein, Arrighi, and, for an analysis of contemporary neoliberalism, Amin. Wallerstein, *World-Systems Analysis.* Arrighi, *Long Twentieth Century.* Samir Amin, *Obsolescent Capitalism: Contemporary Politics and Global Disorder* (London: Zed, 2004).

33. William Greider, *One World, Ready or Not: The Manic Logic of Global Capitalism* (New York: Simon and Schuster, 1997), 227, 228, 15, 193.

34. Elias, *Sublime Desire.*

35. Kirn, "Long Day's Journey into Haircut."

36. David Cowart, *Don DeLillo: The Physics of Language,* rev. ed. (Athens: University of Georgia Press, 2003).

37. Economist Robert Schiller, whose briefings informed Greenspan's speech, describes the event this way: "When Alan Greenspan, chairman of the Federal Reserve Board in Washington, used the term *irrational exuberance* to describe the behavior of stock market investors in an otherwise staid speech on December 5, 1996, the world fixated on those words. Stock markets dropped precipitously. In Japan, the Nikkei index dropped 3.2%; in Hong Kong, the Hang Seng dropped 2.9%; and in Germany, the DAX dropped 4%. In London, the FT-SE 100 index was down 4% at one point during the day, and in the United States, the Dow Jones Industrial Average was down 2.3% near the beginning of trading. The words *irrational exuberance* quickly became Greenspan's most famous quote—a catch phrase for everyone who follows the market." Robert Schiller, *Irrational Exuberance* (Princeton: Princeton University Press, 2000), 3.

38. According to Timothy Noah on *Slate.com*, the quotation is from footnote 1,128 of the Kenneth Starr report. Noah writes, "The distinction between 'is' and 'was' was seized on by the commentariat when Clinton told Jim Lehrer of PBS right after the Lewinsky story broke, 'There is no improper relationship.' [I] confess[ ] that at the time he thought all these beltway domes were hyperanalyzing, and in need of a little fresh air. But it turns out they were right: Bill Clinton really is a guy who's willing to think carefully about 'what the meaning of the word "is" is.'" "Bill Clinton and the Meaning of 'Is,'" *Slate.com*, September 13, 1998.

39. See "Debunked: Clinton's Haircut at LAX Delayed Flights," *Politus* 28 (April 2004); and "*NY Times* Rehashed Pres. Clinton Haircut Myth," *Media Matters for America*, February 9, 2007.

40. Don DeLillo, "In the Ruins of the Future," *Harper's,* December 2001, 33–34.

41. Don DeLillo, *Falling Man* (New York: Scribner, 2007).

42. The photograph in question, taken by AP photographer Richard Drew on the morning of September 11, 2001, provoked controversy first for having been printed and second for having been withdrawn. In an article in *Esquire* magazine on the censorship of the photograph, Tom Junod describes it as an image that "many regarded as irredeemable." DeLillo has said he did not know the photograph was titled *Falling Man* when he titled his book. Tom Junod, "The Man Who Invented 9/11," *Esquire,* June 2007, 38.

43. John Leonard, "The Dread Zone," review of *Falling Man, Nation,* May 28, 2007, 21.

44. Andrew O'Hagan similarly claims, "After the 'nonfiction novel,' after the New Journalism, after several decades in which some of American's most vivid writing about real events was seen to be in thrall to the techniques of novelists, September 11 offered a few hours when American novelists could only sit at home while journalism taught them fierce lessons in multivocality, point of view, the structure of plot, interior monologue, the pressure of history, the force of silence, and the uncanny." Sam Anderson asks, rhetorically, "What can art possibly add to an event we've already experienced and re-experienced so often?" And Frank Rich

redeploys DeLillo's words from his *Harper's* essay: "An event like 9/11 cannot be bent to 'the mercies of analogy or simile.'" Many have also criticized the novel as too static, lacking plot or movement, too much in limbo, or without a "living, pulsing" center. See also reviews by Jennifer Szalai, James Ledbetter, Malcolm Jones, and, finally, James Wood, who identifies DeLillo as one of the postmodern writers whose style the events of 9/11 have rendered obsolete. Andrew O'Hagan, "Racing against Reality," review of *Falling Man*, *New York Review of Books*, June 28, 2007. Sam Anderson, "Code Red," review of *Falling Man*, *New York*, May 14, 2007, 75–79. Frank Rich, "The Clear Blue Sky," review of *Falling Man*, *New York Times Book Review*, May 27, 2007, 1. Jennifer Szalai, "After the Fall," review of *Falling Man*, *Harper's*, July 2007, 91–98. James Ledbetter, "An Airborne Literary Event?" review of *Falling Man*, *Village Voice*, May 8, 2007: 53. Malcolm Jones, "Up from the Ashes," review of *Falling Man*, *Newsweek*, May 14, 2007, 72. James Wood, "Black Noise," review of *Falling Man*, *The New Republic*, July 2, 2007, 47–50.

45. Timothy Bewes, "The Novel as an Absence: Lukács and the Event of Postmodern Fiction," *Novel* 38, no. 1 (2004): 6.

46. Ibid., 7, 5. To revise this claim, and break out of the determinism that realism or its impossibility as the only options, Bewes adapts Lyotard's version of postmodernism (a "dynamic, creative mode") to argue for postmodern literature as the *occasion* of the event. In this view, aesthetic forms are animated precisely to deliver a sense of the novel's absence—the disappearance of the possibility of a kind of Lukácsian sensuous wholeness—within the recognizable form of a novel. The difference from the failure model of postmodernism lies in the foregrounded relationship between possibility and impossibility, presence and absence, the perpetuation of a quest for totality, all of which constitute their own new sensory ("essential") experience.

47. Ibid., 5, emphasis in original.

5. Liquid Realisms

1. Leerom Medovoi, "'Terminal Crisis?' From the Worlding of American Literature to World-System Literature." *American Literary History* 23, no. 3 (2011): 657, 658n7.

2. Mohsin Hamid, *How to Get Filthy Rich in Rising Asia: A Novel* (New York: Riverhead, 2013). Teddy Wayne, *Kapitoil: A Novel* (New York: Harper Perennial, 2010).

3. Medovoi, "'Terminal Crisis,'" 657.

4. Brian Richardson, "The Poetics and Politics of Second Person Narrative," *Genre* 24 (1991): 312. See also Brian Richardson, *Unnatural Voices: Extreme Narration in Modern and Postmodern Fiction* (Columbus: Ohio State University Press, 2006).

5. For example, see Aijaz Ahmad's well-known critique in *In Theory: Classes, Nations, Literatures* (New York: Verso, 1994) of Jameson's essay "Third-World

Literature in the Era of Multinational Capitalism," *Social Text* 15 (1986): 65–88. See further discussions of this debate in Caren Irr, "Postmodernism in Reverse: American National Allegories and the 21st-Century Political Novel," *Twentieth Century Literature* 57, no. 3/4 (2011): 516–38; and in Betty Joseph, "Neoliberalism and Allegory," *Cultural Critique* 82 (2012): 68–94.

6. Peter Mountford, *A Young Man's Guide to Capitalism* (New York: Houghton Mifflin, 2011). James Scudmore, *Heliopolis* (New York: Europa Editions, 2010). Mohsin Hamid, *The Reluctant Fundamentalist* (New York: Harcourt, 2007).

7. Ryan Poll, "Aesthetic Borders and Invisible Pipelines," paper presented at the American Studies Association Annual Meeting, San Antonio, Tex., November 2010. Imre Szeman in his work on end-of-oil narratives describes "petrorealism" as thinking strategically rather than systemically about peak oil. Such narratives focus on countries or political entities pursuing their strategic interests rather than acknowledging scarcity as a collective global problem. Szeman describes the petrorealist narrative as leaving no room for imagining any kind of systemic change, only the short-term jockeying of interests. Imre Szeman, "System Failure: Oil, Futurity, and the Anticipation of Disaster," *South Atlantic Quarterly* 106, no. 4 (2007): 805–23. See also Ross Barrett and Daniel Worden, "Oil Culture: Guest Editors' Introduction," *Journal of American Studies* 46, no. 2 (2012): 269–72; and Stephanie LeMenager, *Living Oil: Petroleum Culture in the American Century* (New York: Oxford University Press, 2014).

8. Arrighi, *Long Twentieth Century*, 227.

9. Caren Irr, "Toward the World Novel: Genre Shifts in Twenty-First-Century Expatriate Fiction," *American Literary History* 23, no. 3 (2011): 663, 668. See also Irr, *Toward the Geopolitical Novel: U.S. Fiction in the Twenty-First Century* (New York: Columbia University Press, 2013).

10. Besides *Kapitoil*, Irr names Joseph O'Neill's *Netherland* (2008), Claire Messud's *The Emperor's Children* (2006), Colum McCann's *Let the Great World Spin* (2009), and Susan Choi's *A Person of Interest* (2009).

11. Irr, "Toward the World Novel," 671.

12. Ibid.

13. Daniel Worden, "Oil Abstractions," *American Book Review* 33, no. 3 (2012): 16.

14. On cosmopolitanism, the novel, market circulation, and the development of an "American-global" sensibility see Rita Barnard, "Fictions of the Global," *Novel* 42, no. 2 (2009): 207–15; Timothy Brennan, "Cosmo-Theory," *South Atlantic Quarterly* 100, no. 3 (2002): 659–91; Sarah Brouillette, "World Literature and Market Dynamics," in *Institutions of World Literature: Writing, Translation, Markets*, ed. Stefan Helgesson and Pieter Vermeulen (New York: Routledge, 2015), 93–107; Pheng Cheah, *What Is a World? On Postcolonial Literature as World Literature* (Durham: Duke University Press, 2016); Neil Lazarus, *The Postcolonial Unconscious* (Cambridge: Cambridge University Press, 2011); Franco Moretti,

"Conjectures on World Literature," *New Left Review* 1 (January/February 2000): 54–68; Rebecca L. Walkowitz, "Comparison Literature," *New Literary History* 40, no. 3 (2009): 567–82; and "The Location of Literature: The Transnational Book and the Migrant Writer," *Contemporary Literature* 47, no. 4 (2006): 527–45.

15. See Ruby Cutolo, "Mohsin Hamid: The Meeting of East and West," *Publishers Weekly*, November 26, 2012, 22.

16. Zygmunt Bauman, *Liquid Modernity* (Cambridge: Polity, 2000).

17. Haiven, "Finance," 99. In Haiven's formulation, liquidity refers to the measure of resistance that capitalism encounters as part of its daily rounds of accumulation. His example of a particularly liquid space is a shopping mall. Any aspect of the mall's design that removes impediments to consumption—easy parking, easy payment—lowers the "coefficient of resistance" in the system. Haiven offers no apparent escape from the "pervasive indifference" of capital's logic since by definition any potential resistance has been preemptively factored into the price. But perhaps more problematic is that this model of the system cannot anticipate running out of resources, unless we actually believe the system is capable of rationally pricing severe shortages. The greater the degree of capitalist viscosity, in other words, the sooner scarcity will have to be confronted politically.

18. Ibid., 99.

19. LiPuma and Lee, *Financial Derivatives*, 135, qtd. in Richard Godden, "Labor, Language, and Finance Capital," *PMLA* 126, no. 2 (2011): 415–16. Reminding us that liquidity is part of Marx's definition of the threefold function of money (a measure of value, or price, a medium of circulation, or liquidity, and a form of general equivalence, or precious or hoardable "treasure"), Godden argues that "neither money nor labor power seems particularly pertinent to the new monies of neoliberal finance. Risk and volatility, as subsets of liquidity, might seem to stand where gold and production once stood."

20. Ibid., 416.

21. Bauman, *Liquid Modernity*, 34. For further discussion of the "new individualism" that Bauman describes as the "fading of human bonds and the wilting of solidarity" that are "the other side of the globalization coin," see Jiri Pribán, ed., *Liquid Society and Its Law* (Abingdon: Ashgate, 2007), 35.

22. Pribán, *Liquid Society*, 7.

23. Brian McHale, *Postmodernist Fiction* (New York: Routledge, 1987), 223.

24. Mieke Bal, *Narratology: Introduction to the Theory of Narrative*, 2nd ed. (Toronto: University of Toronto Press, 1997), 31.

25. Sarah Brouillette, *Literature and the Creative Economy* (Stanford: Stanford University Press, 2014), 85, 90. Brouillette emphasizes the "psychological harm" involved in conceiving of the self as an ideal economic actor and the social pathology that results from a constant process of the "individualization of . . . suffering" (92). See also Gilligan and Vishmidt, who call the entrepreneurial self the "individualized 'meta-subject' of the contemporary capitalist order." Melanie Gilligan and Marina Vishmidt, "'The Property-Less Sensorium': Following the

Subject in Crisis Times," *South Atlantic Quarterly* 114, no. 3 (2015): 612. On the neoliberal subject see also Mathias Nilges, "The Anti-Anti Oedipus: Representing Post-Fordist Subjectivity," *Mediations* 23, no. 2 (2008): 27–70; and Rachel Greenwald Smith, *Affect and American Literature in the Age of Neoliberalism* (New York: Cambridge University Press, 2015).

    26. Appadurai, *Fear of Small Numbers*, 50–53. Appadurai theorizes a tendency of majorities to develop a "predatory identity" in relation to proximate minorities.

    27. On the television program *Asia Rising* and the reinforcement of the "rising" trope by Western journalism, see Weihsin Gui, "Creative Destruction and Narrative Renovation: Neoliberalism and the Aesthetic Dimension in the Fiction of Aravind Adiga and Mohsin Hamid," *Global South* 7, no. 2 (2014): 173–90. My reading of the novel differs from that of Gui, who proposes that "the ruthless entrepreneurial subject of Rising Asia becomes first suffused and then sublimated into collaborative—rather than conquering or calculating—selves" (186) and suggests that the novel "redistributes the optimism and exuberance associated with innovation and creative destruction onto a romantic and intersubjective register" (185).

    28. My argument here takes a different path from that of narrative theorists who have analyzed models of "social mind." See for example the 2015 special issue of *Narrative* with introduction by Maximilian Alders. Certainly, the variety of models of relationship between individual and multiple voices make clear that it cannot simply be assumed, for instance, that the plural "we" dominates the singular "I" (or vice versa) or, conversely, that any one can exist independently of the authority of the other. Maximilian Alders, "Introduction: Social Minds in Factual and Fictional Narration," *Narrative* 23, no. 2 (2015): 113–22.

    29. Pheng Cheah, *What Is a World? On Postcolonial Literature as World Literature* (Durham: Duke University Press), 2, 8.

    30. Ibid., 10.

    31. Monika Fludernik, "Second-Person Narrative as a Test Case for Narratology: The Limits of Realism." *Style* 28, no. 3 (1994): 20.

    32. See Jed Esty and Colleen Lye, "Peripheral Realisms Now," *Modern Language Quarterly* 73, no. 3 (2012): 269–88.

Epilogue

    1. Toral Gajarawala, "The Fictions of Finance," *Dissent* (Summer 2015): n.p. See also Rebecca Colesworthy, "Introduction: Capital's Abstractions," *Textual Practice* 28, no. 7 (2014): 1169–79; "Fictions of Finance," special issue, *Journal of Cultural Economy* 6, no. 1 (2013); A. Carico, and D. Orenstein, "Editors' Introduction: The Fictions of Finance," *Radical History Review* 2014, no. 118 (2014): 3–13.

    2. Moretti, "Conjectures on World Literature."

    3. Eric Cazdyn and Imre Szeman, *After Globalization* (Malden, Mass.: Wiley-Blackwell, 2011), 7.

4. For discussion of U.S. fiction of middle-class economic decline, see Samuel Cohen, "Generation Gone Down: Contemporary Plots of Decline," paper given at the Modern Language Association convention, Austin, Tex., January 2016.

5. Sennett, *Corrosion of Character*, 99.

6. Lauren Berlant, *Cruel Optimism* (Durham: Duke University Press, 2011), 6, 11, 52.

7. David Denby, in his memoir of losing money on 1990s tech stocks, *American Sucker* (Boston: Little, Brown, 2004) turns to Dreiser's *The Financier* to understand the "moral" definition of character.

Smiley, Jane: *Good Faith,* xx, xxxii, 29, 31–36, 38–44, 46, 48–51, 124
Smith, Neil, 43
Stadler, Gustavus, 22
Stein, Judith, 42, 143–44n16, 145n27
Stiglitz, Joseph, 134n33
subject: demands of selfhood, xv; economic selfhood, xvii; neoliberal, xxvii, 115
Szeman, Imre, 125, 156n7

Tabbi, Joseph, 78–79, 80, 91, 153n26
taxation, xviii, xix, 39, 41, 42. *See also* Proposition 13
Taylor, Walter Fuller, 1, 5, 138n1
Toporowski, Jan, xix–xx, 41, 134n39, 135n42
Trachtenberg, Alan, 2–3, 5, 138n5

Updike, John, 83

Varsava, Jerry, 79

Wallerstein, Immanuel, 78
Wall Street, xxii, xxxi, 4, 28. *See also* Fraser, Steve
Wayne, Teddy: *Kapitoil,* xviii, xx, xxxii, 99–108, 109, 121, 124
Wilhite, Keith, 143n13
Wolfe, Tom, 83–84
Woloch, Alex, xx, 48, 146–47n47
Wood, James, 76, 90, 92, 153n29
Worden, Daniel, 107
world novel, 109, 124, 156–57n14
world-systems literature, 99

yuppies, 40

zero-sum, 103–5
Zanine, Louis, 141
Zimmerman, David A., 26

ALISON SHONKWILER is associate professor of English at Rhode Island College. She is coeditor of *Reading Capitalist Realism*.